Four Seasons Cookbook

A collection of over 700 Amish recipes from the parents of West Lykens Valley School District students.

Amish Cooking

Our Standard Abbreviations

tsp.	-teaspoon	**sm.**	-	small
T.	-tablespoon	**med.**	-	medium
c.	-cup	**lg.**	-	large
oz.	-ounce or ounces	**pt.**	-	pint
lb.	-pound or pounds	**qt.**	-	quart
sq.	-square	**doz.**	-	dozen
ctn.	-carton or container	**bu.**	-	bushel
pkg.	-package	**env.**	-	envelope
btl.	-bottle	**pkt.**	-	packet
gal.	-gallon	**mg.**	-	milligram
gm.	-gram	**temp.**	-	temperature
approx.	-approximately			

ISBN 1-890050-23-7

1st Printing 1998
2nd Printing 1998
3rd Printing 1999
4th Printing 1999

Printed By
Brookside Bookstore & Printing
420 Weaver Rd.
Millersburg, Pa. 17061

Equivalent Weights and Measure

pinch	as much as can be taken between tip of finger and thumb	7/8 c.	3/4 c. + 2 Tbsp.
		1 c.	1/2 pt. or 8 fl. oz.
		2 c.	1 pt. or 16 fl. oz.
dash	less than 1/8 tsp.	2 pts.	1 qt.
60 drops	1 tsp.	4 c.	1 qt. or 32 oz.
1 tsp.	1/3 Tbsp.	4 qts.	1 gal.
1 1/2 tsp.	1/2 Tbsp.	8 qts.	1 peck
1 Tbsp.	3 tsp.	4 pecks	1 bushel
2 Tbsp.	1/8 c. or 1 fl. oz.	1 lb.	16 oz.
4 Tbsp.	1/4 c.	1 gram	0.035 oz.
5 1/3 Tbsp.	1/3 c.	1 kilogram	2.21 lbs.
8 Tbsp.	1/2 c. or 4 oz.	1 oz.	28.35 grams
10 2/3 Tbsp.	2/3 c.	1 lb.	453.59 grams
12 Tbsp.	3/4 c.	1 tsp.	4.9 milliliters
16 Tbsp.	1 c. or 8 oz.	1 Tbsp.	14.8 milliliters
3/8 c.	1/4 c. + 2 Tbsp.	1 c.	235.6 milliliters
5/8 c.	1/2 c. + 2 Tbsp.	1 liter	1.05 qts. or 1000

Contents of Cans

Of the different sizes of cans used by commercial canners, the most common are:

Size	Average Contents
8 oz. can or jar	1 cup
picnic	1 1/4 cups
10 oz. can	1 1/4 cups
12 oz. can vacuum	1 1/2 cups
14 – 16 oz. or #300 can	1 3/4 cups
16 – 17 oz. or #303 can	2 cups
#1 tall can	2 cups
1 lb. 4 oz. or 1 pt. 2 fl. oz. or #2 can or jar	2 1/2 cups
1 lb. 13 oz. can or jar or #2 1/2 can	3 1/2 cups
#3 can or 32 oz.	4 cups
1 qt. 14 fl. oz. or 3 lb. 3 oz. or 46 oz. can	5 3/4 cups

Oven Temperatures

Slow	250°- 300°
Slow-Moderate	325°
Moderate	350°
Quick-Moderate	375°
Moderately Hot	400°
Hot	425° - 450°
Very Hot	475° - 500°

Introduction

When this idea for a new cookbook surfaced to help pay for expenses, upgrading some math books, extensive remodeling, etc., I wondered if people really would want another cookbook. Our school board consists of 5 members and is responsible for 3 one-room schools with about 26-30 pupils each.

We are known as "horse and buggy Amish". We believe in the best education that can be obtained through grade 8. We finance our own schools without public monies, except for fund-raisers like this one.

After we decided to do this cookbook, and as time went on, this project became very interesting. We decided to add some one-line sayings, some poems, writings, hints and tips, some substitutions, measures, and of course a little humor.

We hope you will be pleased by what you find. It has been a pleasure putting this together for you! Enjoy!

The West Lykens Valley School Board

Table of Contents

Notes

Snacks

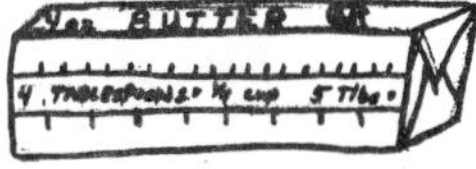

This day is mine
God gave this glorious day to me
To do with as I choose
Each precious moment it contains
Is mine, but once to use

I'll carefully and wisely try
To plan my day once more
So I'll not make the same mistakes
That I have made before

Nacho Dip

1 1/2 lb. ground beef, browned
1/2 lb. mozzarella cheese, grated
1/2 lb. cheddar cheese, grated
1 lb. Velveeta cheese, grated
1 med. onion, chopped
1 med. pepper, chopped
28 oz. or 1 qt. tomatoes, drained and chopped
4 oz. chili peppers, chopped

Add all ingredients together in crock pot, add garlic powder, chili powder, and Tabasco to taste. Simmer until hot and cheese is melted. Serve with nacho chips.

Linda Stoltzfus

Sharp Cheese Dip

1 1/2 lb. sharp cheese, grated
1-16 oz. container sour cream
1/4 c. sour cream & onion powder
1 tsp. salt
milk, enough to make runny

Combine all ingredients and refrigerate a couple of hours, until it stiffens.

Elizabeth Petersheim

Cheese Dip

2 eggs, beaten
2 T. sugar
2 T. vinegar
pinch of salt
1 T. butter
8 oz. cream cheese
1 sm. onion
1 green pepper
or
1 T. parsley

Combine first 5 ingredients and thicken over low heat. When cool add remaining ingredients.

Lena Riehl
Annie Lapp
Linda Stoltzfus

Cracker Dip

16 oz. sour cream
16 oz. cream cheese
3/4 c. sugar
1 tsp. vinegar
pinch of salt
3/4 c. sour cream and onion powder mix

Mix well.

Elizabeth Stoltzfus

Cracker Dip

2 eggs
2 T. sugar
2 T. vinegar
2 T. butter
1/2 tsp. salt
1 8 oz. pack cream cheese

Beat the eggs. Add sugar, vinegar, salt and butter. Thicken on low heat (not too thick). When partly cool add softened cream cheese, season with diced onion and pepper to taste. Sour cream can also be added to this if desired.

Linda Stoltzfus

Fruit Dip

1 8 oz. pkg. cream cheese, softened
1 cool whip
1 T. orange juice
a little marshmallow cream

Combine all ingredients. Mix thoroughly. Chill. Serve with apple slices or other fruit.

A Friend

Fruit Dip

1 stick butter
1 8 oz. cream cheese
1 8 oz. cool whip
1 8 oz. marshmallow cream
strawberry jello or jelly if desired

Combine all ingredients together.

Anna Mae Fisher

Fruit Dip

7 oz. marshmallow creme
1 c. sour cream
1 8 oz. cream cheese
1 8 oz. cool whip
1 c. 10x sugar
2 tsp. strawberry jam

Mix all ingredients well.

Linda King

Fruit Dip

8 oz. cream cheese
1/2 c. marshmallow cream
8 oz. whipped topping
1/4 c. orange jello

Mix well and dip any fresh fruit in this mixture.

Naomi Lapp

Creamy Caramel Dip

8 oz. cream cheese
3/4 c. brown sugar, packed
1 c. sour cream
2 tsp. vanilla
1 c. cold milk
1 box instant vanilla pudding
assorted fresh fruit

In a mixing bowl beat cream cheese and brown sugar until smooth. Add sour cream, vanilla, milk and pudding mix, beating well. cover and chill for at least 1 hour. Serve as a dip for fruit.

Anna Mae Stoltzfus

Caramel Apple Dip

1 can sweetened condensed milk
8 milk caramels
1/2 stick butter

Put in saucepan or double boiler and cook on medium heat until caramels are melted stirring all the time. Serve with apples, bananas, pineapples etc.

Annie King

High Fiber Snack

3 c. oatmeal
1 c. honey
1 c. coconut
1 c. peanut butter
1 c. nuts or raisins
1/2 c. bran
1/4 tsp. salt

Place the oatmeal, coconut, nuts, bran and salt in a bowl, mix well. Mix the honey and peanut butter separate. Combine the 2 mixtures. Form small bars or press into a pan.

Lena Riehl

Holiday Party Mix

1 lg. box cheerios
1 lg. box kix
1 lg. box corn chex
1 bag sm. pretzels
1 can mixed nuts
1 1/2 c. margarine
1 1/2 c. butter
season salt
garlic salt
2 T. accent, optional

Mix the first 7 ingredients. Sprinkle with season salt and garlic salt. Bake at 250° for 2 hours. Stir every 30 minutes.

Kate Stoltzfus (Steve)

Pizza Flavor Crispix Snack Mix

1/4 c. parmesan cheese
3 T. Mrs. Wages spaghetti sauce mix
2 tsp. basil
2 tsp. oregano
2 tsp. garlic powder
8 c. crispix cereal
4 c. pretzel nuggets
3 T. vegetable oil

Combine cheese, sauce mix and spices. Set aside. In a 2 gallon bag combine crispix cereal and pretzel nuggets. Pour oil over cereal mixture, tossing gently to coat. Add cheese/ sauce mixture to bag, tossing gently until cereal mixture is thoroughly coated. Store in airtight container.

Mattie Beiler

Honey Nutty Snack Mix

1 c. brown sugar, packed
1/2 c. margarine, softened
1/4 c. light corn syrup
1/2 tsp. salt
1/2 tsp. baking soda
6 c. cheerios
1 c. nuts
1 c. raisins

Heat oven to 250°. Heat brown sugar, margarine, corn syrup and salt, stirring constantly until bubbly around edges. Remove from heat, stir in soda. Pour over cereal, nuts and raisins. Stir until all is well coated. Pour into a well greased cake pan. Bake 15 minutes. Stir a few times. After cooling, break into pieces.

Anna Mae Stoltzfus

Harvest Popcorn

2 qt. fresh popped popcorn, unsalted
2 1 3/4 oz. cans shoestring potatoes
1 c. mixed nuts, salted
1/4 c. butter, melted
1 tsp. dill weed, dried
1 tsp. Worcestershire sauce
1/2 tsp. lemon pepper seasoning
1/4 tsp. garlic powder
1/4 tsp. onion powder

In a large roasting pan mix first 3 ingredients together, set aside. Mix remaining ingredients together. Pour over popcorn mixture stirring until evenly coated. Bake at 325° for 10 minutes, stirring mixture once. Cool. Store in tight containers. Yield 2 1/2 qt.

Naomi B. Beiler

When you stop to think, don't forget to start again.

Caramel Popcorn

2 c. brown sugar
1/2 c. karo
1 c. margarine
1 tsp. vanilla
1/2 tsp. baking soda

Stir to boil first 3 ingredients and when boiling continue to boil 5 minutes without stirring, then add remaining ingredients. Hold over popcorn before you add soda as it really sizzles. Bake popcorn 1 hour at 250°, stirring every 15 minutes.

Ada King

Caramel Popcorn

7 qt. popcorn
2 c. brown sugar
1/2 c. corn syrup
1 tsp. vanilla
1 c. peanuts
1 c. butter
1 tsp. salt
1/2 tsp. soda

Boil sugar, butter, corn syrup and salt for 5 minutes. Remove from heat and add soda and vanilla. Pour over popcorn and bake at 250° for 1 hour. Stir occasionally.

Barbara Stoltzfus

Grandmother's Spiced Nuts

1 egg white
1 tsp. cold water
1/2 c. sugar
1/4 tsp. cloves
1/4 tsp. cinnamon
3/4 tsp. salt
4 c. nuts

Beat egg white slightly, add water and beat till frothy. Fold in nuts. Combine sugar, salt and spices. Stir through nuts. Bake on a greased cookie sheets 30 to 40 minutes at 300°. Stir every 15 minutes.

Sarah Esh

Seasoned Pretzels

2 12 oz. bags pretzels
1/4 tsp. garlic salt
1/2 tsp. dill weed
1/2 tsp. lemon pepper
1 envelope ranch salad dressing mix
1 c. salad oil

Put in texas pail. Turn a few times. Let season overnight. Bake at 300° for 20 minutes. This is a great way to freshen up stale pretzels or to put zest to fresh ones.

Elizabeth Petersheim

Sour Cream & Onion Pretzels

1 lb. pretzels
1 c. butter
3 T. sour cream & onion powder

Bake at 150° for 1-1 1/2 hours.

Sadie Lapp

Pretzel Treat

1 18 oz bag broken pretzels
1 pkg. original ranch dressing mix dry
1 T. lemon pepper seasoning
3/4 c. oil

Place pretzels in cake pan. Mix ingredients and pour over pretzels. Place in 200° oven for 1 hour. Stirring every 15 minutes.

Anna Mae Stoltzfus

We often take for granted the very things that most deserve our gratitude.

Vegetable Crackers

pastry flour
salt
baking powder
lard, to make a rich pastry
cheese, melted or grated
tomato juice, instead of water to complete the dough
celery salt
chicken soup base
parsley flakes
grated carrot
grated onion

Roll thinly, cut and bake. Delicious! Vary the ingredients according to taste and supply. Use whole wheat, rye, barley or rice flour. Substitute oil for lard.

Katie Ruth Esch

Cheese Ball

2-3 lb. cheese, any mixture of cream cheese, sharp, yellow, longhorn and muenster
1 1/2 stick celery, ground
1 onion, ground & juice drained

Mix all together with celery & onion. Roll balls in ground walnuts or bacon bits.

Martha Smucker

Cheese Ball

2 8 oz. cream cheese
2 c. sharp cheese, shredded
1 T. pimento, chopped
1 T. onion, chopped
1 T. red pepper, chopped
1 T. lemon juice
2 T. Worcestershire sauce
1/2 tsp. lemon pepper

Combine softened cream cheese & cheddar cheese, mixing until well blended. Add remaining ingredients. Mix well. Chill. Shape into ball or log and roll in finely chopped pecans.

Lena King

Cheese Whiz

1 lb. cheese, processed or cheddar
2 c. evaporated milk
1 1/2 tsp. salt
2 eggs, beaten
1 1/2 tsp. dry mustard

Cube cheese and melt in double broiler. Add milk, salt and mustard. Remove from heat. Stir in eggs. Return to heat till eggs thicken slightly. Pour into dish and cool, slowly stirring occasionally. Store in refrigerator

Katie Ruth Esch

A Morning Prayer

Lord in the quiet of this morning hour
I come to thee for peace, for wisdom, power
To view the world today through love filled eyes
Be patient, understanding, gentle, wise
To see beyond what seems to be and know
Thy children as thou knowest them and so
Naught but good in anyone behold
Make deaf my ears to slander that is told
Silence my tongue to aught that is unkind
Let only thoughts that bless dwell in my mind
Let me so kindly be so full of cheer
That all I meet may feel thy presence near
Clothe me in thy beauty this I pray
Let me reveal thee through all the day

The Business Of The Day

**It's just the way we carry through
The business of the day
That makes and molds the character
The things we do and say
The way we act when we are
The attitudes we take
The sort of pleasures we enjoy
The kind of friends we make
It's not the big events alone
That makes us what we are
And not the dizzy moments when
We're swinging on a star
It's just the things that happen as
Along the road we plod
The little things determine what
We're really worth to God.**

Drinks

My Kitchen

The kitchen is the nicest spot
In all the home to me
It's here that neighbors, dropping by
Pull up a chair for tea
And as we sit and smile and talk
Our hearts are filled with cheer
The bonds of friendship, tried and true
Grow stronger year by year.

Truly this is the heart of home
And all who pass this way
Can tell what we've been doing here,
Our working and our play
It is a warm and cozy spot
Where hearts can rest
And although other folks may smile,
I like my kitchen the best!

Tea Concentrate

5 c. tea
5 1/2 c. water
2 c. sugar

Mix together tea, water and sugar. Let set overnight. Next morning drain and freeze.

Anna Mae Fisher

Tea Concentrate

4 c. water
2 c. tightly packed fresh tea leaves
2 c. sugar

Boil water and sugar together for 5 minutes. Add tea leaves, cover and let stand 6 to 7 hours or overnight. Strain. Can be frozen. Use about 1 cup concentrate to 2 quarts water or to suit taste.

Rebecca Lynn Fisher

Meadow Tea To Freeze

4 qt. water
4 c. sugar
4 c. fresh tea leaves

Bring water to boil. Remove from heat and add tea leaves. Let sit for 15 minutes. Remove leaves. Add sugar and cool. Put in quart boxes and freeze. To serve combine 1 part concentrate with 3 parts water.

Kate Glick
Linda Stoltzfus

Russian Tea

2 c. tang
1 1/4 c. instant tea, no sugar or lemon
1 12 oz. can wylers lemonade mix
1 1/3 c. sugar
1 tsp. cinnamon
1/2 tsp. cloves
1/2 tsp. ginger

Mix everything together and store in tight container. Put 1 or 2 teaspoons in a mug of hot water. Very good to sip on those cold winter days!

Naomi B. Beiler

Chocolate Syrup

1 c. cocoa powder
3 c. sugar
1/4 tsp. salt
2 c. hot water
1 T. vanilla

Mix dry ingredients in saucepan with a small amount of water, stirring until smooth. Add remaining water and boil 3 to 5 minutes. Remove from heat. Add the vanilla. Pour in jar, cover tightly when cool and store in refrigerator. To serve, use approximately 2 T. syrup per cup of milk or as desired. Serve hot or cold. This is similar to Hershey's canned syrup.

Arie Blank
Naomi King

Hot Chocolate Mix

10 c. carnation dry milk
1 lb. nestle quick
11 oz. coffee cream
1 c. 10x sugar

Mix all ingredients together. Add 1/4 cup mixture to 1 cup of hot water.

Sylvia King (Mervin)

A day of worry is more exhausting than a week of work

Hot Cocoa

1/4 c. plus 1 T. Hershey's cocoa
1/2 c. sugar
1/3 c. hot water
4 c. milk
3/4 tsp. vanilla
dash of salt

Combine cocoa, sugar and salt in medium saucepan, blend in water. Bring to boil over medium heat, stirring constantly, boil and stir 2 minutes. Add milk, stir and heat. Do not boil. Remove from heat. Add vanilla. Beat till foamy. Makes about 1 quart.

Katie Ruth Esch

Quick Root Beer

2 c. sugar
1 tsp. dry yeast
4 tsp. root beer extract
enough water to fill gallon jug

Put sugar into a gallon jug. Add yeast and root beer extract. Fill jug with lukewarm water. Stir or shake until dissolved. Put in sun or a warm place for 3 or 4 hours, then refrigerate.

Sarah Ann Lapp
Linda King

Grape Juice

4 c. grapes
4 c. water
3/4 c. sugar

Bring the grapes and water to a boil and put through sieve. Then mix 4 cups juice with the sugar. Boil 10 minutes. Jar and seal. To use, mix 1 part juice and 1 part water. Chill and serve.

Marie Hoover
Mrs. Elmer Stoltzfus

Rhubarb Juice Punch

2 c. rhubarb, diced
1 1/4 c. sugar
4 c. water
1/2 c. orange juice, frozen concentrate
2 c. ginger ale

Combine rhubarb, sugar and water. Boil 5 minutes. Strain and cool. Add orange juice and ginger ale.

Linda King
Esther Fisher

Refresher Appetizer

2 c. sugar
4 c. water
2 c. orange juice
1/4 c. lemon juice
grated rind of 2 oranges

Dissolve sugar in water & boil for 20 min. Remove from heat. Add orange & lemon juice & orange rind. Cool. Pour into ice cube trays & freeze. Put 2-3 cubes in glass. Fill glass with ginger ale.

Anna Mae Fisher

Lemonade

1 gal. water
1 c. sugar
3 lemons

Mix ingredients. Better if it sets an hour or more before drinking. Add more sugar depending on your taste.

Annie Lapp

Best Ever Lemonade

2 c. sugar
6 lemons
2 gal. water

Slice lemons and mix well with sugar. Let set for 2 hours and mash occasionally. Add water. Do not leave lemon rinds in the water for more than 4 hours or the drink will become bitter.

Lena King
Sylvia Lantz
Katie Mae Stoltzfus

Punch

1 pkg. strawberry kool aid, unsweetened
1 pkg. cherry kool aid, unsweetened
1 6 oz. frozen lemonade, concentrate
1 6 oz. frozen orange, concentrate
3 c. sugar
6 qt. water

Combine all ingredients. Stir. Chill and serve.

Rebecca Lynn Fisher

Orange Pineapple Drink

3 cans frozen orange juice
1 lg. can pineapple juice
2 1/2 qt. water
ginger ale

Mix all ingredients together. Using more or less water to suit your taste. Chill and serve.

Elizabeth Stoltzfus

Orange Milk Nog

1 1/2 c. orange juice
1 c. milk
2 eggs

Combine orange juice, milk and eggs. Beat well.

Sarah Esh

Orange Slush

1 6 oz. jello, orange
1 - 2 c. sugar
1 qt. water, boiling
1 46 oz. pineapple juice
1 12 oz. frozen orange juice
1 qt. water, cold

Dissolve jello and sugar in boiling water. Add pineapple and orange juices and cold water. Freeze, stirring occasionally, should be in the freezer until slushy. To serve fill a glass 3/4 full with slush and pour ginger ale over slush to fill the glass.

Ada King

Citrus Slush

2 1/2 c. sugar
3 c. water
12 oz. frozen orange juice concentrate
12 oz. Frozen lemonade
1 46 oz. can pineapple juice
3 c. cold water
4 qt. lemon-lime soda or ginger ale, chilled
lemon slices

In 6 quart pan bring sugar and 3 cups water to a boil, stirring until sugar dissolves, remove from heat. Stir in frozen orange juice and lemonade concentrates until melted. Stir in pineapple juice and 3 cups cold water until well blended. Pour into 2-13x9x2" baking pans. Cover and freeze until mixture is firm. Cut each pan full of frozen juice into squares. Place into a 2 gallon punch bowl or thermos jug. Slowly pour chilled soda over squares. Stir until punch is slushy. Makes about 2 gallons or 32 1 cup servings.

Anna Zook

Slushed Punch

1 lg. box strawberry jello
2 c. boiling water
1 c. sugar
1 sm. can frozen orange juice
1 lg. can unsweetened pineapple juice
6 c. water

Mix together and freeze. Remove from freezer two hours before serving. Add 2 quarts ginger ale or 2 quarts grapefruit soda.

Amos and Naomi Beiler

Evergreen Punch

3 pkg. lime cool aid
2 c. sugar
2 qt. water
1 lg. can pineapple juice
1 bottle ginger ale

Mix all ingredients together.

Martha Smucker

Frozen Golden Punch

5 bananas, mashed
16 oz. frozen orange juice
1 can pineapple juice
1/4 c. lemon juice
4 c. sugar
2 qt. water

Combine sugar and water. Bring to boil. Cool. Combine all ingredients and pour into containers to freeze. Makes about 1 gallon concentrate. To serve, combine equal parts of frozen concentrate and ginger ale.

Annie King

Springtime Punch

2 c. sugar
2 1/2 c. water
1 c. fresh orange juice
1 c. fresh lemon juice
1 6 oz. can frozen pineapple juice concentrate, thawed
2 qt. ginger ale, chilled

In a saucepan bring sugar and water to a boil. Boil for 10 minutes. Remove from heat. Stir in lemon, orange and pineapple juices. Refrigerate. Just before serving, combine with ginger ale in large punch bowl. Makes around 3 quarts.

Sarah Fisher

Punch

1 qt. ginger ale
1 can punch
1 qt. orange sherbet

Mix all ingredients together. Add ice cubes.

Rachel Stoltzfus

Sunshine Fruit Punch

1 can apricot juice
1 can orange juice
1 can white grape juice
1 can pineapple juice
1 box lemon sherbet
ginger ale to taste

Mix all together for a delicious beverage!

Mattie Beiler

Golden Punch

1 8 qt. pkg. lemonade mix, make 6 qt. juice
1 can unsweetened pineapple juice
2 12 oz. cans frozen orange juice, as directed
1 16 oz. bottle sprite or 7-up
orange or pineapple sherbet

Mix all ingredients together.

Arie Speicher

Orange Sherbet Drink

2 gal. water
2 cans frozen orange juice
3 qt. orange sherbet
2 3 liter orange soda
1 1/2 gal. vanilla and sherbet
3 biggest size ginger ale

Mix ingredients together.

Anna Mae Stoltzfus
Mrs. Elmer Stoltzfus

Delicious Orange Drink

1 lg. frozen orange juice
1 lg. frozen lemon juice
1 qt. orange sherbet
2 lg. bottles ginger ale

Mix frozen juice and sherbet together till slightly thawed. Beat until foamy. Last of all, add ginger ale. A refreshing drink for weddings.

Lena King

Cream Sherbet Punch

1 qt. orange sherbet
1 qt. vanilla ice cream
1 qt. ginger ale or 7-up
2 lg. cans pineapple juice

Frozen orange juice can be used instead of pineapple juice. Combine sherbet and ice cream with juice. Blend until smooth. Add ginger ale or 7-up before serving. Serves 8-12.

Elizabeth Kauffman

Wedding Punch

2 1/2 c. pineapple juice, chilled
1 pt. lime, lemon or raspberry sherbet
1 pt. vanilla ice cream
12 oz. ginger ale or 7-up

Combine pineapple juice, sherbet and 1 cup ice cream. Beat until smooth. Add ginger ale or 7-up. Spoon remaining ice cream into punch. Serve immediately.

Country Dairy Punch

4 c. vanilla ice cream, slightly softened
4 c. lime sherbet, slightly softened
4 c. milk
2 c. water
4 c. ginger ale
1 6 oz. can frozen lemonade concentrate
1 6 oz. can frozen limeade concentrate

In large punch bowl, stir together ice cream, sherbet and milk. In 1 quart pitcher, stir together lemonade concentrate, limeade concentrate and water. Pour over ice cream mixture. Add ginger ale. Stir until slightly mixed. Yield 32 1/2 cup servings.

Rachel Stoltzfus

No one can pick a peck of pickled peppers.
They have to be picked before they can be pickled.

Have you ever thought how much your wife
so fair and young today-
will do the common work day tasks
till her silver wedding day?

Twenty-five years, let's figure it out.....
wash thirteen hundred times
and a laundry isn't a beauty shop,
nor tuneful a washtubs' rhyme.

Nine thousand and one hundred and twenty-five
mornings she'll make the beds-
sweep the floor and tidy the room
and see that the family is fed.

Three times a day – that's' twenty seven thousand
three hundred and seventy five meals
and for years and years from 5 to 9
children tagging around her heels.

And then the ironing every week
that's thirteen hundred again
and the buttons that have to be sewn on
and the rips and tears to mend.

Housecleaning time each spring and fall
and the canning, why no one knows
what a woman does in twenty five years
just for her board and clothes.

Salads

Kind hearts are the garden
Kind thoughts are the roots
Kind words are the blossoms
Kind deeds are the fruits.

Dressing For Salads

3 c. miracle whip or mayonnaise
1 c. white sugar
1 T. mustard
1 tsp. vinegar
dash of salt

Mix together. Serve on salads.

Kate Stoltzfus

French Salad Dressing

1 c. mayonnaise
1/2 c. catsup
2 T. mustard
1/3 c. sugar
2 T. or more salad oil

Mix well.

Annie King

House Salad Dressing

16 eggs
8 c. mayonnaise
3 c. vinegar/water, mixed half/half
8 c. white sugar
6 tsp. salt
3 c. mustard

Cook together, stirring constantly. Will scorch easily.

Esther Fisher

Lydia's Salad Dressing

1 c. sugar
4 eggs
1/4 c. vinegar
1/2 tsp. salt
1/2 tsp. mustard
3 T. butter
1/4 c. water

Bring to boil, stirring constantly. Cool. When cool add 2 cups mayonnaise.

Naomi King (Jake)

Salad Dressing

1 c. catsup
3/4 c. sugar
1 c. salad oil
1/2 tsp. salt
3 tsp. vinegar
onion powder
pepper

Blend all together. Use on lettuce salads.

Marie Hoover

Toss Salad Dressing

4 eggs, beaten
2 c. sugar
1-2 tsp. mustard
3 T. butter
1/2 c. vinegar
1 1/2 tsp. salt
1 pt. mayonnaise
spices as desired

Cook the first 6 ingredients together. Cool. Add the mayonnaise and spices as desired, like season all, paprika, garlic salt and spike. Use for macaroni, potato, tossed salad, coleslaw or whatever you wish.

Linda King
Martha Smucker
Ada King
Anna Mary Smucker

Potato Salad Dressing

3 c. water
3/4 c. vinegar
2 c. sugar
1/4 tsp. pepper
3 tsp. salt

Bring to a boil. Stir a 2 1/2 heaping tsp. flour and beat 1 egg to it and then paste with water.

Arie Speicher

What we do for others we do for God.

Broccoli Salad

1 lg. head broccoli, uncooked
1 med. onion, chopped
10 slices bacon
1 c. mayonnaise
1/2 c. sugar
2 T. vinegar
4 oz. cheese, optional

Cut bacon in bits and fry. Mix with mayonnaise, sugar and vinegar. Pour over rest of ingredients and let stand for 1 hour or more before serving.

Amos and Naomi Beiler
Annie Lapp

Broccoli Salad

1/2 c. sugar
1/2 c. mayonnaise
1/2 c. sour cream
1 c. broccoli
1/2 c. cauliflower

Mix the first 3 ingredients together. Then add to the remaining ingredients.

Linda Stoltzfus

Carrot Salad

3 tsp. salt
1 1/2 c. sugar or honey
1 1/2 lemon, juiced
1 1/2 c. salad dressing
12 eggs, hard boiled
6 c. carrots, grated
celery and onion to suit taste
3 T. gelatin
1 1/2 c. water

Dissolve gelatin in water to soften, stir till dissolved or hot. Do not boil. Mix together all ingredients.

Sylvia Stoltzfus (Amy)

Every family needs at least three books in their home. A cookbook, a checkbook and The Good Book.

Chicken Salad

8 c. chicken, diced
4 c. celery, diced
8 eggs, hard boiled, cut fine
3/4 c. olives, chopped
2 c. salad dressing
1 tsp. salt

Toss ingredients together. Add salad dressing. Chill and serve on lettuce leaf.

Arie King

Ham Salad

2 c. cooked ham, ground
3 stalks celery
1 lg. dill pickle
1/4 tsp. dry mustard
1/4 tsp. onion juice
1/2 c. mayonnaise
1/2 tsp. salt
1 T. lemon juice

Put ham, celery and pickle through coarse blade of food chopper. Add remaining ingredients and mix. May also add grated cheese and hard boiled eggs if desired. Delicious to eat on bread as sandwiches hot or cold.

Arie King
Sadie Lapp

Egg Basket Salad

hard boiled eggs
mayonnaise
sugar
green pepper
lettuce leaves
french dressing

Cut hard boiled eggs in half crosswise. Remove the yolks and mash them till smooth. Add mayonnaise and a little sugar. Form into tiny balls and put several in the cavity of each egg white. Cut a tiny slice off the bottom of the egg white to make them stand upright. Insert handles cut from a green pepper. Place on lettuce leaf and serve with french dressing.

Katie Ruth Esch

Pa. Dutch Cucumber Salad

3-4 sm. cucumbers
1 tsp. salt
1 med. onion, thinly sliced into rings
1/2 c. sour cream
1 T. fresh chives, chopped or 1 tsp. dried chives
2 T. vinegar
1/2 tsp. dried dill seed
1/4 tsp. pepper
pinch sugar
lettuce leaves, optional
tomatoes, sliced, optional

Peel cucumbers, slice paper thin into a bowl. Sprinkle with salt. Cover and refrigerate 3 to 4 hours. Rinse and drain cucumbers. Pat gently to press out excess liquid. Combine cucumbers and onion in a large bowl, set aside. In a small bowl combine sour cream, vinegar, chives, dill seed, pepper and sugar. Just before serving add dressing to cucumbers and toss. If desired, arrange lettuce and tomatoes in a serving bowl and spoon cucumbers into middle.

Mattie Beiler

Dandelion Salad

1 qt. dandelion leaves
4 slices bacon
3/4 c. sour cream
2 tsp. sugar
2 tsp. vinegar
4 tsp. flour
salt and pepper to taste
2 eggs, hard boiled

Gather the dandelion leaves in the early spring while they're still tender. Wash and drain. Fry bacon till crisp and crumble. Drain off fat except 2 T. Add the combined flour, sugar and vinegar. Stir over low heat till thickened. Add sour cream, salt and pepper. Pour over greens while still warm. Add chopped eggs. Good for what ails you!

Katie Ruth

51% of being smart is knowing what you're dumb at.

Potato Salad

1 c. sugar
1/4 c. vinegar
2 T. mustard
2 c. mayonnaise
1 can condensed milk
eggs, hard cooked
carrots, chopped
onion, chopped
celery, chopped

Mix first 5 ingredients and add to cooked and chopped potatoes and remaining ingredients.

Sara Ann Lapp

Potato or Macaroni Salad

8 potatoes, or 1 lb. macaroni
1 c. celery, diced
1 c. onion, diced
1 doz. eggs, hard boiled, diced
2 c. sugar
1/2 c. vinegar or lemon juice
5 eggs
1 T. mustard
1 T. butter
1/2 to 1 tsp. salt
2 c. mayonnaise

Cook potatoes in skins till soft. Peel and dice or cook macaroni. Add celery, onion and hard boiled eggs. Mix remaining ingredients together, except the mayonnaise. Cook on medium heat till thickened or just below boiling point, stirring constantly. Remove from heat and cool 5 minutes then add mayonnaise. Add to first mixture. Makes 3 quarts.

Anna Mae Fisher
Elizabeth Petersheim

24 Hour Macaroni Salad

12 c. macaroni
12 eggs, hard boiled
1/2 c. onions, chopped
2 c. celery
3 c. salad dressing
6 tsp. prepared mustard
2 tsp. salt
2 1/2 c. white sugar
1/4 c. vinegar

Mix together and chill 24 hours before serving.

Anna Mary Smucker
Ada King

Spinach Salad

1 egg
1/2 c. sugar
2 T. water
2 T. vinegar
4 T. mayonnaise
1 bag spinach, washed and cut
1 med. onion, chopped
4 eggs, hard boiled
bacon, cooked and crumbled

Heat first 4 ingredients till thick, about 5 minutes. Let cool then add remaining ingredients.

Katie Ruth

Bountiful Vegetable Salad

1 c. cauliflower, chopped
1 c. broccoli, chopped
1 c. celery, chopped
1 c. carrot, sliced 1/4"
1 c. green pepper, chopped
1 c. cucumber, peeled, seeded and chopped
1/2 c. mayonnaise
1/2 c. sour cream
1/4 c. French dressing
2 T. sugar
2 T. green onion, sliced
1 T. tarragon vinegar
1 tsp. salt

In a large bowl toss together all ingredients. Cover and refrigerate 6 hours or overnight. Yield; 6 3/4 cup servings.

Rachel Stoltzfus

Delicious Vegetable Salad

1 head cabbage, coarsely shredded or chopped
3 tomatoes, peeled and diced
2 carrots, grated
1 onion, chopped
1 pepper, chopped
1/2 lb. longhorn cheese, diced
2/3 c. sugar
2/3 c. vinegar
1 1/4 tsp. salt
1/4 tsp. pepper
2 tsp. celery seed
2/3 c. oil

Put the first 6 ingredients in a bowl. Mix the next ingredients except the oil and bring to a boil. Cool and add the oil. Pour over the vegetables.

Lena King
Linda Rhiel

Layered Salad

1 head lettuce, chopped
1 c. celery, diced
4 eggs, hard boiled, diced
1 pkg. frozen peas
1 med. onion, chopped
8 slices bacon, fried and crumbled
2 c. mayonnaise
1 T. sugar
4 T. cheese, grated

Place all ingredients in a large bowl in order given. Do not stir. Make at least 8 hours before serving.

Rebecca Lynn Fisher

Pasta Salad

1 lb. pasta, twists
1 lg. green pepper, diced
2 tomatoes, cut into chunks
1/2 lb. provolone cheese, cubed
1/2 lb. ham, cubed
1 sm. onion, chopped
Italian salad dressing to suit taste

Cook pasta according to package directions. Rinse with cold water and drain well. Combine with remaining ingredients. Mix gently and thoroughly. Cover. Chill at least 4 hours.

Naomi B. Beiler

Taco Salad

1 lb. hamburger
1 pkg. taco seasoning
tortilla chips
kidney beans
sour cream
lettuce, chopped
tomatoes, chopped
peppers, chopped
onion, chopped
1/2 stick butter
1/2 lb. Velveeta cheese
3/4 c. sour cream

Brown the hamburger. Add taco seasoning. Mix and simmer according to package instruction. Layer bottom of dish with plain tortilla chips. Add hamburger, kidney beans and layer of sour cream. Add chopped lettuce, tomatoes, peppers and onion. Make cheese sauce with butter, Velveeta and sour cream. Pour over top.

Ruth Ann Esch

Enjoying Sprouts

1/3 c. alfalfa seeds, or any other kind of seeds
1 glass gal. jar

Fresh sprouts are a good substitute for lettuce. Never use treated seeds. Put approximately 1/3 cup alfalfa seeds, or any other kind, in a glass gallon jar. Cover seeds with water and soak overnight. In the morning drain off the water. A thin piece of cloth such as organdy tied over the mouth of the jar works well for a strainer. Rinse seeds morning and evening, using cool water. Drain well each time. If weather is warm, rinse 3 times a day. Keep growing sprouts in a dark cabinet or covered with a towel till they are about 2" long and leaves start to grow. Now place the jar in a sunny window for a day so the sprouts become green. On cloudy days it takes longer to turn green, but it might be a good idea to refrigerate them nights. They can be eaten without being green. It takes 5-7 days for the whole process. When sprouts are ready, rinse and drain well. Wash away the hulls of the seeds and unsprouted seeds as you rinse them. Store in a cold place. If properly done they keep well for about a week. Unsprouted seeds or too much moisture may cause them to turn sour.

Katie Ruth Esch

Apple Salad

2 c. water
3/4 c. brown sugar
2 T. clear jell
1 tsp. vanilla
1 T. butter, golden brown

Cook together until thickened.

Anna Mae Stoltzfus

Smile, it makes people wonder what you're up to!

Apple Salad

1/2 c. water
1 T. flour
1/2 c. sugar
1 egg
1 tsp. vinegar
1 T. butter
1 can pineapple, drained
1 12 oz. cool whip
apples
bananas

Heat the pineapple juice and water. Mix the egg, flour, sugar vinegar and butter together, add to the juice and cook till thickened. Cool. Mix with the cool whip then add apples and bananas.

Elsie Fisher

Apple and Banana Salad

1 lg. lemon jello
3 3/4 c. hot water
3 T. sugar, if desired
pinch of salt
3 apples, diced
3 bananas, diced
1 can pineapples, drained
1/2 c. water
1/2 c. pineapple juice
1/2 c. sugar
2 T. flour
1 egg

Mix together the first 7 ingredients. Chill till firm. Cook the water, pineapple juice, sugar, flour and egg until thickened. When cool, add cool whip or dream whip. Pour on jello mixture. Top with chopped walnuts, if desired.

Lena King

Carrot Salad

1 box orange jello
2 T. sugar
1/2 c. carrots, finely grated
1 c. pineapples, crushed

Mix jello as directed on box using slightly more water and 2 T. sugar. When jello starts to thicken, add carrots and pineapples. Stir and let set.

Arie King

Cottage Cheese Salad

1 can pineapples, crushed
1 med. ctn. cottage cheese
1 med. ctn. cool whip
1 3 oz. lime jello

Mix all together and serve.

Katie Glick

Cranberry Salad

1/2 lb. cranberries, crushed
3 apples, shredded
1/2 c. pineapples, crushed
1 1/2 c. sugar
1 6 oz. strawberry jello
1 c. hot water
1 c. cold water

Dissolve jello in hot water, add cold water. Let jell partially then add other ingredients. Chill and serve.

Marie Hoover

Indiana Salad

2 pkg. lime jello
4 c. hot water
1 can pineapples, crushed
2 env. dream whip
1 8 oz. cream cheese
1 c. sugar
3 egg yolks
3 T. flour
1 1/2 c. liquid, pineapple juice and water

Mix the first 5 ingredients together and chill. Cook the remaining ingredients together. Cool before putting on top of jello.

Rachel Stoltzfus

Jello Salad

1 c. jello, any flavor
5 c. water
2 8 oz. cream cheese
3/4 of a sm. ctn. cool whip
1 1/2 pt. peaches, sm. pieces

Make some of the water hot and dissolve jello, add remaining water. Let jello thicken a little before you add the remaining ingredients. Pour into molds.

Annie Lapp

Jello Salad

1 6 oz. cherry jello
2 c. boiling water
2 c. cold water
1 3 oz. lemon jello
1/2 c. sugar
1 c. boiling water
1 8 oz. cream cheese
1 can carnation milk

Mix cherry jello and 2 cups boiling water till jello dissolves, add 2 cups cold water. Let set until firm. Mix lemon jello, water and sugar together. Pour over cream cheese and add carnation milk. Beat real well and pour on top of cherry jello.

Mrs. Elmer Stoltzfus

Small Orange Mold

1 lg. box orange gelatin
1 8 oz. cream cheese
1 box cool whip
1 11 oz. can mandarin oranges, or about 5 fresh oranges, peeled

Mix dry gelatin and cream cheese. Add 1 1/2c. boiling water and 3/4 c. cold water. Stir till dissolved. Refrigerate until slightly thickened then beat with fork till mushy. Add cool whip, fruit and a little orange juice. Put in mold and chill 1 1/2 hours.

Linda King

Orange Cream Fruit Salad

1 20 oz. can pineapple tidbits, drained
1 16 oz. can peaches, drained
1 can mandarin oranges, drained
2 bananas, sliced
1 med. apple, chopped
1 3.4 oz. pkg. vanilla pudding mix, instant
1 1/2 c. milk
1/3 c. frozen orange juice concentrate
3/4 c. sour cream

In a large bowl, combine fruits. Set aside. Beat instant pudding mix, milk and orange juice for 2 minutes. Add sour cream, mix well. Spoon over fruit. Cover and refrigerate for 2 hours.

Sarah Fisher

Orange Sherbet Salad

1 6 oz. pkg. orange jello
3 3/4 c. hot water
1 pt. orange sherbet
1 med. box cool whip
sm. marshmallow, as desired

Mix the jello and hot water. Let cool then add the remaining ingredients. Pour into molds.

Linda Stoltzfus

Pineapple Salad

1 can pineapples, crushed
1/2 c. sugar
2 eggs
2 T. flour
1 pkg. sm. marshmallows, approx. 24
2-3 bananas, sliced
1-2 c. whipping cream

Drain the juice from the pineapples. Heat the juice then add the flour, eggs and sugar. Cook till thick. Before serving add the marshmallows, bananas, pineapples and cream.

Rebecca Speicher
Ada King

Pistachio Salad

9 oz. frozen whipped topping
1 box 3 3/4 oz pistachio pudding, instant
1 20 oz can pineapples, crushed
1/2 c. nuts, optional
1 c. sm. marshmallow
maraschino cherries, optional

Mix the pistachio pudding and pineapples with juice. Add the frozen whipped topping, mix till well blended. Add nuts and marshmallow. Chill and serve.

Rebecca Lynn Fisher
Anna Zook

Cleaning house while children are growing is like shoveling snow when it's still snowing.

Pretty Pink Salad

1 1 lb. 4 oz. can pineapples crushed, not drained
1 3 oz. strawberry or raspberry jello
16 lg. marshmallows
1 8 oz. cream cheese, softened
1/4 c. milk
2 c. whipped topping or cool whip

Heat first 3 ingredients till marshmallows are melted. Cool. Beat cream cheese and milk till smooth then fold in whipped topping. Mix with gelatin mixture. Pour into molds.

Annie Lapp

Sweetheart Salad

2 c. pineapples, crushed
1/2 c. sugar
1 1/2 T. plain gelatin
1/4 c. water
6 oz. Philadelphia cream cheese
2 T. lemon juice
2 T. cherry juice
1 c. whipping cream
12 maraschino cherries

Dissolve gelatin in cold water. Add pineapples to sugar. Bring to boiling point and add gelatin, stir till gelatin is dissolved. Add lemon and cherry juice. Cool. Mash cream cheese and add chopped cherries. Combine with pineapple mixture, adding a small amount at a time. Chill until slightly thicken. Whip cream and blend with salad mixture. Mold and chill.

Elizabeth Kauffman

Yum Yum Salad

1 20 oz. can pineapples, crushed
1 pineapple can of water
1/2 c. sugar
1 6 oz. box strawberry jello
2 pkg. whipped topping mix
8 oz. pkg. cream cheese

Boil crushed pineapples, water and 1/2 c. sugar for 5 minutes. Turn burner off and add jello. Cool. Mix whipped topping mix with milk and add cream cheese, beat well. Stir into jello mixture.

Sadie Lapp

Christmas Salad

1 6 oz. pkg. cherry jello
1/3 c. lemon jello
1 c. boiling water
1 8 oz. pkg. cream cheese, softened
8 oz. cool whip
6 oz. lime jello
3 1/2 c. hot water

Red part: Make cherry jello according to directions on box, pour in molds and let set firmly. Middle part: Mix lemon jello and 1 cup boiling water then add cream cheese, mix well, and add cool whip. Pour on top of first mixture and let set firmly. Green part: Mix lime jello and 3 1/2 cups hot water, cool well before putting on top of second mixture.

Linda Stoltzfus

Ginger Ale Salad

2 T. unflavored gelatin, 1 1/2 pkg.
2 1/2 T. cold water
1 c. boiling water
3/4 c. sugar
2 T. lemon juice
2 c. ginger ale
1 c. crushed pineapples, drained
1 c. apples, diced or 1 c. seeded grapes or pears
2 T. flour
1/2 c. sugar
2 eggs, beaten
1 1/2 T. butter
1 c. pineapple juice
1 8 oz. cool whip

Dissolve gelatin in cold water. Add hot water and sugar. Stir until dissolved. Add lemon juice and ginger ale. Chill till partly set. Stir in fruit. Pour into pan or mold. Chill until set. Topping: Mix flour and sugar. Add beaten eggs, butter and pineapple juice. Cook till thickened. Cool. Add cool whip. Spoon on top of salad. Sprinkle with nuts if desired.

Annie King
Anna Mae Stoltzfus

One of the ingredients for success is patience.

7-up Salad

1 6 oz. pkg. lemon gelatin
2 c. boiling water
2 c. 7-up beverage
2 bananas, sliced
1 lg. can crushed pineapples, drained, save juice
1 c. pineapple juice and water to make 1 c.
1/2 c. sugar
2 T. butter
2 T. flour
1 egg, well beaten
1 c. coconut, flaked
1/2 c. nuts, chopped
1 c. whipped topping

Mix boiling water and lemon gelatin until dissolved. Add 7-up, crushed pineapples and bananas. Pour into a 9x13" pan and let cool until firm. Topping: Cook pineapple juice, sugar, butter, flour and egg till thickened. Cool. Fold in coconut, nuts and whipped topping. Spread over firm gelatin and refrigerate.

Katie Mae Stoltzfus

A Christian Garden

First plant four rows of peas;
Presence
Preparedness
Perseverance
Promptness
Next, plant three rows of squash;
Squash gossip
Squash criticism
Squash Indifference
Now put in row of lettuce;
Let us be faithful
Let us obey rules and regulations
Let us love one another
No garden is complete without turnips;
Turn up for meetings
Turn up with a smile
Turn up with new ideas
Turn up with determination to make everything count for something good and worthwhile

Breads & Rolls

Homemade Bread

Of all the housewife's duties,
I think it must be said
There's nothing I like better
Than baking homemade bread.

I picture now my loved ones
As we all sit down to eat
Ah! Warm homemade bread
Is always such a treat.

I knead the flour in
And turn it round and round
We'd so much rather bake our bread
Than buying it in town.

The store-bought bread can substitute
And might not taste so bad
But it doesn't contain the loving pats
I put into our bread.

And when I punch my hands, Into a risen dough
It feels as soft as baby's cheek, I kissed a moment ago.

And soon the house was filled
From one end to the other-
The delicious smell of homemade bread
Freshly baked by my Mother!

Buttered Rolls

1 sm. T. yeast
1 c. warm water
2 eggs, beaten
1/4 c. sugar
1/4 c. oil
1 tsp. salt
3 1/2 c. flour

Dissolve the yeast in the warm water. Add the remaining ingredients. For raisin rolls add, 1 c. raisins and 1 tsp. cinnamon. Let rise 1 1/2 to 2 hours. Shape about the size of an egg. Makes 2 large bread pans. Bake at 325° to 350° for 25 minutes.

Sarah Esh

Home Made Rolls

7 T. sugar
1 T. salt
2 T. butter
1 pt. warm water
1 pt. warm milk
1 yeast cake

Mix ingredients together. Add flour to make a soft dough. Let set for 45 minutes. Knead. Let rise until double size. Knead again. Let rise and put in pans. Let rise and bake.

Arie King

Honey Whole Wheat Rolls

2 pkg. or 2 T. yeast
1 c. warm water
1/4 c. butter or margarine, melted
1/4 c. honey
1 egg
3/4 c. whole wheat flour
1/2 c. old fashioned oats
1 tsp. salt
2 1/4 to 2 3/4 c. all purpose flour

Dissolve yeast in water. Stir in the butter, honey, egg, wheat flour, oats, salt and 1 cup flour, beat until smooth. Add enough remaining flour to form a soft dough. Knead dough until smooth and elastic. Place in a greased bowl turning to grease top. Cover, let rise until doubled, about 1 hour. Shape into 15 rolls. Place in a greased 13"x9"x2" baking pan. Cover and let rise until doubled. Bake at 375° for 20 minutes or until golden brown. Brush with butter.

Mrs. Elmer Stoltzfus

Potato Buns

2 c. sugar
1 c. Wesson oil
2 c. water
5 eggs
2 T. salt
2 T. yeast, dissolved in a little water
12 c. flour or till right consistency
2 c. mashed potatoes

Work well and refrigerate overnight. In the morning roll out with rolling pin till about 1/2" thick and cut with donut cutter or desired size. Place on cookie sheets and let rise to right size. It takes long to rise. Bake at 350° about 10 to 15 minutes or until a golden brown.

Lena King

Sweet Buns

1 c. warm water
1/2 c. sugar
1/4 cake yeast or 1/2 tsp. dry yeast
lard, size of walnut
1/4 tsp. salt
flour, to make a soft dough

Let rise until double in size. Form rolls. Let rise again and bake.

Arie King

Church Buns

1 c. milk, boiled
1 c. lukewarm water
1/3 tsp. vanilla
1/2 c. sugar
1/3 T. salt
1 1/3 T. yeast dissolved in 1/3 c. warm water
1/2 c. oil
5 1/3 c. bread flour, (occident)
2 eggs

Makes approximately 50 buns. This recipe is also very good to use for sticky buns.

Rebecca Lynn Fisher

A brook would lose it's song if it had no rocks.

Cinnamon Buns

2 cakes yeast
1 c. lukewarm water
1 tsp. sugar
1 c. milk, scalded and cooled
1/2 c. shortening
3/4 c. sugar
1 1/2 tsp. salt
2 eggs
7 c. flour

Pour yeast into cup of lukewarm water. Add the tsp. sugar and let stand 5 minutes. Scald milk and let cool to lukewarm. Cream together shortening and the 3/4 cup sugar and salt, add beaten eggs. Add the yeast mixture and milk. Gradually add the flour. Let rise until double the size or a couple hours. Then roll out and brush with butter and a coat of brown sugar and sprinkle cinnamon. Roll together like a jelly roll. Let rise again. Bake at 350°.

Rebecca Speicher

Sticky Buns

1 c. milk, scalded
1/4 c. lard
1 tsp. salt
1/4 c. granulated sugar
1 T. yeast
2 eggs, beaten
1/4 c. lukewarm water
3 1/2 c, flour
4 T. butter
1 c. brown sugar
1/4 c. warm water
2 T. molasses

Add milk, lard, sugar and salt, stir together well then add beaten eggs and the yeast dissolved in water. Stir in flour and beat well. Let rise 2 hours. Knead. Let rise 10 minutes. Roll out and spread with melted butter, brown sugar and cinnamon. Let rise 1 hour. Bake at 350° to 400° for 25 minutes.

Sylvia King

The only people that never fail are those who never try.

Potato Sticky Buns

2 1/2 T. dry yeast
2 c. warm water
1/2 c. sugar
2 tsp. salt
1 egg
1/4 c. shortening
6 to 7 c. flour
1 stick margarine
2 c. brown sugar
1/3 c. water
2 tsp. honey

Add some mashed potatoes which makes them good n' soft! Dissolve yeast in warm water, add sugar, salt, egg, shortening and flour, work till elastic. Let rise in refrigerator overnight. Syrup; combine margarine, brown sugar, water and honey, boil for 2 min. Roll out the dough and spread with 2 T. melted butter, sprinkle with brown sugar and cinnamon. Nuts and raisins if desired. Roll up as jelly roll. Cut in 1" pieces and place in pans on top of syrup. Let rise about 1 1/2 hours. Bake 20 min. at 375°. Makes about 3 dozen. Delicious!

Ada King

Quickie Stickie Buns

1 1/2 c. flour
2 pkg. yeast
3/4 c. milk
1/4 c. oil
1/2 c. water
1/4 c. sugar
1 tsp. salt
1 3/4 c. flour
1 egg
1 1/2 c. raw apple, chopped
3/4 c. butter
1 c. brown sugar
1 tsp. cinnamon
1 T. light corn syrup
1 T. water
3/4 c. nuts

In a lg. bowl mix 1 1/2 cup flour and yeast. Heat milk, water, oil, sugar and salt until warm. Pour into yeast mixture, add egg, beat well. Stir in 1 3/4 c. flour. Add apple. Dough is very sticky. Cover and let rise for 30 min. While dough is rising mix topping. Heat the butter, brown sugar, cinnamon, corn syrup, water and nuts until melted. Pour in a 13"x9"x2" pan. Stir down batter and drop by T. onto topping. Bake 20 min. at 350°. Cool 1 min. then dump upside down on cookie sheet. Makes 24. Quick and easy to make.

Naomi B. Beiler

Monkey Bread

2 cans Pillsbury biscuits
1/2 c. sugar
1 tsp. cinnamon
1/2 stick butter
3/4 c. brown sugar

Make biscuits into balls and roll in a sugar and cinnamon mixture. Boil the butter and brown sugar, pour over the balls. Add nuts if desired. Bake at 300° for 20 minutes.

Elsie Fisher

Long Johns

1 c. milk, scalded and cooled
2 pkg. yeast, dissolved in 1 c. warm water
1/2 c. shortening
2/3 c. sugar
2 eggs, beaten
6 c. bread flour
1 pt. milk
1 egg
1 c. sugar
1 T. cornstarch
little butter

Mix the first 6 ingredients together. Let rise till doubled or 2 hours. Roll and cut in strips. Let rise 1/2 to 1 hour. Fry in deep lard. Filling; mix remaining ingredients. Cook until thick. Put icing on top.

Rachel Stoltzfus

Thank God for dirty dishes
They have a tale to tell
While others may go hungry
We're eating very well
With home and health and happiness
We shouldn't want to fuss
For by this stack of evidence
God's been very good to us.

Cream Cheese Danish

1/2 c. warm water
2 pkg. dry yeast
1 tsp. sugar
1 c. sour cream
1/2 c. butter
1/2 c. sugar
1 tsp. salt
2 eggs, beaten
4 c. flour

2 8 oz. pkg. cream cheese
3/4 c. sugar
1 egg, beaten
1/8 tsp. salt
2 tsp. vanilla
2 c. 10x sugar
4 T. milk
2 tsp. vanilla

Combine warm water, yeast and sugar till dissolved, set aside. Heat sour cream on low till barely bubbly, add butter, sugar and salt till dissolved, cool till lukewarm, add 2 eggs and combine with yeast mixture, add flour, mixing well, cover and refrigerate overnight. Make filling next morning. Beat the cream cheese and 3/4 c. sugar together well, add 1 egg, salt and vanilla mixing well. Divide dough into 4 portions. Roll out each portion on floured surface into a 12"x8" rectangle. Spread 1/4 of cream cheese mixture in the center of each rectangle. Fold over dough and pinch edges together. Place rolls on a greased baking sheet with seam side down. Slit each roll on top halfway through dough at 2" intervals resembling a braid. Cover and let rise till double. Bake at 350° for 12 to 15 minutes. Do not over bake. Glaze; mix until smooth, 10x sugar, milk and vanilla. Spread over loaves while they are still warm. Makes 4 loaves.

Arie Blank

Bread

3/4 c. warm water
2 T. yeast
1 qt. warm water

1 stick butter
3/4 c. sugar
1 T. salt
approx. 10 c. bread flour

Mix 3/4 warm water and yeast let set for 5 minutes. Mix in remaining ingredients.

Barbiann Esch

Homemade Bread

6 c. lukewarm water
4 T. yeast
1 c. sugar
3 T. salt
1 c. oil
5 lb. bread flour

Mix the water, yeast and sugar till yeast is dissolved then add remaining ingredients. Use enough flour to clean bowl. Moisten pan with oil. Knead again in 1 hour. Let rise again and put in pans. Makes 7-1 1/4 loaves.

Elizabeth Petersheim

Bread

1/2 c. lukewarm water
1/2 T. sugar
1 1/2 T. yeast
3 c. lukewarm water
4 T. Wesson oil
1/2 c. sugar
1/2 T. salt
4 c. flour

Mix together the first 3 ingredients. Add the remaining ingredients. Add more flour till right consistency. Let rise 1 hour then punch down. Let rise 1 hour and put in pans. Bake 350° for 1/2 hour.

Linda King

White Bread

3 c. warm water
2 T. yeast, scant
1/3 c. granulated sugar
2 tsp. salt
1 T. Crisco, heaping
1/4 c. mashed potatoes
occident flour (bread flour)

Mix very well, then let rise for 5 minutes. Work dough again and do this 3 times. Let rise till double in size before putting in pans. Bake at 350° for 30 minutes. Yields 3-4 loaves.

Sylvia King

People have a way of becoming what you encourage them to be. Not what you nag them to be.

Bread

3 c. warm water
1/2 c. sugar
1 tsp. salt
1/4 c. vegetable oil or lard
1 1/2 T. lecithin, optional
2 tsp. vinegar, optional
8-9 c. flour
1 1/2 T. yeast

To make brown bread use 2 T. blackstrap and 2 cups whole wheat flour and less white flour.

Lena Reihl
Ada King

Oatmeal Bread

3 1/2 c. boiling water
2 c. oatmeal
1 c. honey or 1/2 of it sugar
2 T. salt
2 T. yeast
1 c. lukewarm water
4 eggs, beaten
2 c. whole wheat flour
1/3 c. lard, melted
bread flour

Pour boiling water over oatmeal. Add the honey and salt. Let set 1/2 hour. Dissolve the yeast in lukewarm water. Add eggs. Mix all together and add whole wheat flour. Finish with bread flour. Pour melted lard over bread dough when finished mixing and work it in for 1 minute.

Sylvia Stoltzfus
Katie Glick

Give us this day our daily bread
Man shall not live by bread alone
Our Lord and Master said
But by the Living Word of God
Our souls need to be fed.

Wheat n' Bran Bread

1 c. sugar or honey
4 tsp. salt
2 T. shortening
3 c. milk, scalded
2 c. warm water
1 egg
2 c. wheat bran
1 c. wheat germ
2 c. whole wheat flour
2-3 T. instant yeast
7 c. white bread flour

Put in large bowl the following, sugar, salt and shortening. Add milk, water and egg, beat till shortening is dissolved. Then add wheat bran, wheat germ and wheat flour mix well. Add yeast and mix well. Then add white bread flour. Dough should be somewhat sticky. Knead. Cover and let rise in warm place till double. Divide into 4-5 small loaves. Heat oven to approx. 100° then turn off. Place loaves in oven to rise. Keeping the dough very warm enhances rising. Bake 1/2 hour at 350° or until side of loaf is slightly brown. Butter top to keep crust moist. To keep bread moist put in plastic bags while still hot. Freeze what won't be used in a day or so to keep fresh. 100% whole wheat flour can be used in place of dry ingredients listed.

Marie Hoover

Whole Wheat Bread

2 pkg. dry yeast
4 c. warm water
1/2 c. margarine or butter,
1/4 c. molasses
1/2 c. honey
2 tsp. salt
6 c. whole wheat flour
4 c. white flour

Dissolve yeast in warm water. Combine margarine, molasses, honey and salt, mix well. Add yeast mixture. Gradually add flour. Turn onto floured surface and knead until smooth. Place in greased bowl and let rise until double. Punch down. Let dough rest a few minutes. Shape into 4 loaves. place in greased bread pans. Let rise about 1 hour. Bake at 375° for 35-40 minutes.

Rachel Z. Stoltzfus

100% Whole Wheat Bread

6 c. warm water
3/4 c. Canola oil
3/4 c. honey
2 T. lecithin
2 T. gluten
2 vitamin c, crushed
3 T. instant yeast
15-16 c. wheat
5 c. flour
2 eggs, beaten
2 T. salt

Mix the first 6 ingredients and let set while you grind the wheat. Add flour. Mixing well add eggs and salt. Use only enough flour to bring to proper consistency. Not to thick, not to thin. Knead 3 times at 15 minute intervals. Put into 6 pans and let rise again. Bake at 350° for 30 minutes.

Elizabeth Stoltzfus

100% Whole Wheat Bread

12 c. whole wheat flour, approx.
5 1/4 c. hot water
1/2 c. Canola oil
1/2 honey
1 1/2 tsp. salt
4 T. dough enhancer
3 T. instant yeast

Mix together, water, oil and honey. Add salt and dough enhancer, mix well. Add 4 1/2 cups flour, mix well. Add yeast, then rest of the flour, approx. 8 cups, only till right consistency or until dough is barely sticky. Grease hands with oil. Knead for 20 minutes by hand or 10 minutes with mixer. Form loaves. Place in 150° oven, do not preheat, for 35 minutes, then turn up heat to 350° and bake about 20 minutes.

Linda Stoltzfus

A refrigerator is where you put dabs of food on dishes you don't want to wash.

Banana Bread

2/3 c. sugar
1/3 c. shortening
2 c. all purpose flour
2 tsp. baking powder
1/4 tsp. baking soda
1/4 tsp. salt
1 c. ripe bananas, mashed

In a large bowl, cream sugar and shortening, mixture does not get smooth. Combine flour, baking powder, soda and salt. Add to creamed mixture alternately with bananas beating after each addition, the batter will be thick. Spoon into greased 9"x5"x3" loaf pan. Bake at 350° for 40-45 minutes or until bread tests done with a toothpick. Cool in pan for 10 minutes before removing to a wire rack.

Mattie Beiler

Peanut Butter Bread

2 c. flour
4 tsp. baking powder
1 tsp. salt
1 c. milk
1/2 c. sugar
2/3 c. peanut butter

Sift dry ingredients, add sugar, milk and peanut butter. Bake in loaf pan in a 420° oven.

Arie King

Pumpkin Bread

1 tsp. nutmeg
1 tsp. cinnamon
3 c. sugar
1 c. oil
4 eggs, beaten
1 1/2 tsp. salt
1 c. pumpkin
2/3 c. water
2 tsp. soda
3 c. flour

combine the first 6 ingredients together and beat well. Add remaining ingredients. Bake at 350°. Let pans set for 15 minutes after taking out of the oven.

Elizabeth Kauffman

Compliment three people each day.

Pumpkin Bread

8 T. butter, softened
2 1/2 c. white sugar
4 eggs
1/2 c. raisins
1/2 c. nuts, chopped
1/2 c. water
2 c. pumpkin, cooked
2 tsp. baking soda
1/2 tsp. baking powder
1 tsp. cinnamon
1 tsp. cloves
1 tsp. salt
3 c. flour

Blend butter and sugar. Add eggs, raisins, nuts, water and pumpkin, Blend well. Add remaining ingredients. Pour into 2 large greased bread pans. Bake at 350° for 50-60 minutes. Use toothpick to check if finished. Delicious topped with cool whip or cream cheese frosting.

JR Lapp

Nut Bread

3 c. flour
1 c. milk
3/4 c. nut meats, any kind, ground
1 c. sugar
2 tsp. baking powder
1/2 tsp. salt

Mix all ingredients. Let stand in cake pan 30 minutes. Bake 45 minutes at 375°. Use any desired icing.

Arie King

Raisin Bread

1/2 c. lard
1/2 c. sugar
1 T. cinnamon
2 T. salt
2 eggs, beaten
2 T. yeast in 1 c. warm water
1 1/2 c. warm milk
15 oz. raisins, covered with water and simmered until soft
7-8 c. flour

Mix altogether. Let rise 1/2 hour. Knead real good. Let it rise double in size. Put in pan and bake at 350°. Makes 4 loaves.

Naomi Esh

Rhubarb Nut Bread

1 1/2 c. brown sugar
2/3 c. liquid shortening
1 egg
1 c. sour milk
1 tsp. salt
1 tsp. soda
1 tsp. vanilla
2 1/2 c. flour
1 1/2 c. fresh rhubarb, diced
1/2 c. nuts, chopped
1/2 c. brown sugar
1/2 tsp. cinnamon
1 T. butter, melted

Stir the first 10 ingredients together in order listed. Pour into 2 well greased & floured loaf pans. Mix the last 3 ingredients for the topping. Place evenly over the top of each loaf. Bake 40 min. at 325°. Do not over bake. Cool 10 min. then remove from pans.

Amos and Naomi Beiler

Pineapple Zucchini

3 eggs
2 c. sugar
2 tsp. vanilla
1 c. oil
2 c. zucchini, peeled & grated
3 1/2 c. flour
1 c. crushed pineapple, well drained
1 1/2 tsp. salt
1 1/2 tsp. baking soda
3/4 tsp. baking powder

Mix eggs, sugar, vanilla and oil, blend until light. Add zucchini and dry ingredients alternating with pineapple. Bake in well greased & floured bread pans. Bake 1 hour or until done at 325°. Makes 2 loaves.

Susie Blank

Always remember to forget
The troubles that pass away
But never forget to remember
The blessings that come each day.

Zucchini Bread

1 tsp. salt
1 tsp. soda
1/2 tsp. baking powder
3 tsp. cinnamon
3 c. flour
2 c. sugar
1 c. oil
3 eggs
3 T. vanilla
2 1/2 c. zucchini, chopped
1/2 c. nuts, chopped

Mix all ingredients together. Pour into greased & floured bread pans. Bake at 275° for 60 minutes.

Linda King
Sarah Fisher
Esther Fisher
Rebecca Lynn Fisher

Pizza Dough

1 T. dry yeast
1 c. warm water
3 c. flour
1 tsp. sugar
1 1/2 tsp. salt
1/4 c. salad oil

Dissolve yeast in warm water with the sugar, salt and oil. Add the flour then let rise. Roll on your pan as any other pizza dough.

Marie Hoover
Barbara Stoltzfus

Best Ever Pizza Dough

2 c. warm water
1 pkg. yeast
1 tsp. salt
1/2 T. vegetable oil
5 1/2 c. flour

Dissolve yeast in warm water. Add salt and oil, stir well. Add 5 cups of flour, mix well. Slowly add more flour until still stretchable, not dry. Put on cookie sheet or pizza pan. Add your favorite toppings.

Elizabeth Stoltzfus

Jiffy Pizza Dough

2 c. flour
1 T. baking powder
1 tsp. salt
2/3 c. milk
1/3 c. oil

Mix all ingredients. Bake at 350° for 15 minutes. Makes one large pizza.

Anna Zook

Wedding Waffers

4 qt. flour
butter size of an egg
1 tsp. baking powder
lard
milk
egg

mix the first 4 ingredients together make like a rich pie dough, using lard. Put milk and beaten egg to it. Roll out on cookie sheets. Sprinkle with salt and seasoned salt. Bake in 400° oven.

Rachel Stoltzfus

Homemade Noodles

1 doz. egg yolks
3 whole eggs
1/2 c. water
3 T. salt
flour

Mix first 4 ingredients together and beat well. Add enough flour to make a stiff dough.

Elizabeth Stoltzfus

Those who make bread don't loaf.

Garlic Bread Sticks

1/2 c. margarine, softened
1/2 tsp. garlic powder
1/2 tsp. parsley
8 slices white bread

Trim crusts from bread, if desired. Spread both sides of bread with margarine. Sprinkle with garlic powder and parsley. Cut each slice into 4 sticks. Bake at 350° for 10-15 minutes.

Sylvia Esch

Whole Wheat Soft Pretzels

2 T. instant yeast
1 1/2 c. lukewarm water
1/2 tsp. salt
4 c. freshly ground whole wheat flour
1/2 c. hot water
2 T. baking soda

Mix water and salt, add half of the flour, then add instant yeast and rest of flour until it handles nice and is not too sticky. Knead for 5-10 minutes. Let rise 15 minutes. Grease hands with oil and shape pretzels. Mix hot water and baking soda. Dip pretzels into soda solution, sprinkle with salt. Place on greased cookie sheets and bake at 500° for 10 minutes. Brush with butter. Good and good for you!

Linda Stoltzfus

Soft Pretzels

3 c. water
1 T. yeast
1/2 tsp. salt
1/2 c. brown sugar
3 1/4 c. bread flour
4 c. regular flour
1 c. water
2 tsp. soda

Mix first 6 ingredients. Let set awhile. Mix the water and soda. Dip pretzels in soda solution before baking. Put pretzel salt on them before baking. Melt 1 stick butter and brush on after baked.

Anna Zook

Soft Pretzels

1 1/2 T. yeast
1 3/4 c. warm water
1/4 tsp. salt
1/2 c. brown sugar
4-5 c. flour
1 c. hot water
4 tsp. baking soda
pretzel salt

Mix first 5 ingredients together. Let rise 1/2 to 1 hour. Mix and knead. Do not punch down. Cut into strips and roll or twist them. Mix the hot water and baking soda. Dip the pretzels in soda mixture. sprinkle with pretzel salt. bake at 500° till brown about 10-15 minutes.

Sylvia King

Honey Mustard Sauce

1/2 c. honey
1/2 c. mustard

Combine ingredients together. Good for dipping sauce, sandwich spread, marinade and soft pretzels.

Annie King

Donuts

2 T. yeast
1 c. lukewarm water
1 tsp. sugar
1 c. milk, scalded and cooled
1/2 c. shortening, part butter for flavor
2/3 c. sugar
1 T. salt
2 whole eggs or 4 yolks, beaten
7 c. or more sifted flour
1 c. mashed potatoes

Mix all ingredients. Knead like bread and let rise to double its size. Roll out 1" thick and cut with donut cutter. Let donuts rise to right size and fry.

Lena King
Katie Glick

Our love for God is best seen in our love for others.

Funnel Cake

2 c. milk
2 eggs
4 c. flour
1 tsp. baking powder
1/2 tsp. salt
3 tsp. vanilla

Beat egg with vanilla and milk. Add the dry ingredients. Drop batter into deep fat heated to 375°. Fry till puffy and golden brown, turning once. Remove and drain on paper towel.

Sylvia Esch

Recipe for Life

1 c. good thoughts
1 c. kind deeds
1 c. consideration
3 c. forgiveness
2 c. well beaten faults
3 c. sacrifice
6 c. prayer

Mix thoroughly with tears of joy, sorrow and plenty of sympathy. Flavor with love and kindness. Blend in thoroughly, 6 cups prayer. Bake well with the heat of human kindness and serve with a smile.

Sandwiches

Day By Day

I'm disenchanted now that Summer
Has returned to Fall,
Then I realize that it's beauty
Is the best of all.

Then when Autumn disappears
To Winter's silver haze,
I miss the paintbrush of God's hand
That made these rainbow days.

Then suddenly it's Spring again
A different kind of hue,
When colors burst out from the ground
In moods of joy and blue.

When Summer once again appears
I'm so thankful, and so gay
That God has shared His all with me
His beauty, day by day.

The Seasons, Oh how wonderful!
They give each soul a lift,
How much God must love me
To give me such a gift.

James Joseph Huesgen

Calico Eggs Sandwich

4 eggs, hard boiled and coarsely chopped
3/4 c. ham, diced
1/2 c. shredded cheese
1/4 c. mayonnaise
2 T onions, finely chopped
1/2 tsp. dry mustard

Mix ingredients together.

Naomi King (Jake)

Egg Salad Sandwiches

1 doz. eggs, hard boiled
1 sm. onion, chopped
2 tsp. salt
1 c. mayonnaise
1 T. sugar
dash of pepper
chopped celery
season-all or other spices

Mash eggs with potato masher and add all other ingredients. Serve on bread.

Katie Ruth Esch

Ham Salad Sandwiches

2 c. ham, cooked
3 stalks celery
1 lg. dill pickle
1/4 tsp. dry mustard
1/4 tsp. onion powder
1/2 c. mayonnaise
1/2 tsp. salt
1 T. lemon juice

Put ham, celery and pickle through coarse blade of food chopper. Add remaining ingredients.

Rebecca Spiecher

Tuna Salad Sandwiches

3 eggs, hard boiled
1 can tuna
2 T. peppers, chopped
2 T. onions, chopped
1/4 lb. Velveeta cheese
2 T. sweet pickle, chopped or pickle relish
2 T. olives, chopped
1/2 c. mayonnaise

Spread in hamburger buns and wrap in foil. Put in oven till they are warm.

Arie Spiecher

Tuna Burgers

1 7 oz. can tuna, flaked
1 c. celery, chopped
1/2 c. olives
1 sm. onion, minced
1/2 c. mayonnaise
1/2 c. American cheese
salt and pepper to taste

Mix all ingredients together. Split and butter 6 hamburger buns. Fill buns with tuna mixture. Wrap in aluminum foil. Place in oven for 15-20 minutes at 350°.

Lena King

Tuna Burgers

1 can 6 1/2 oz. tuna
1 c. grated cheese
1 med. onion, chopped
3 eggs, hard boiled, chopped
salt
pepper
mayonnaise
olives, optional

Mix ingredients together. Put on hamburger rolls and wrap in aluminum foil and bake for 20 minutes at 350°.

Sylvia King
Linda Ruth Esh
Annie King
Sylvia Lantz
Rachel Stoltzfus

Cheese Burgers

2 lb. hamburger
3/4 c. oatmeal
1 tsp. salt
1/2 c. tomato juice
pepper, to taste
brown sugar, to taste
onions, if preferred

Mix ingredients together. Bake at 350° for 20 minutes. Put cheese on top and serve.

Sylvia Lantz

When facing a difficult task, act as though it is impossible to fail.

Spam Burgers

1 can Spam
2 tsp. onion, minced
1/2 lb. sharp cheddar cheese or Velveeta or white American
3 tsp. milk
2 tsp. mayonnaise
2 tsp. pickle relish or 4 T. sweet pickle, chopped

Mix all ingredients together. Put on top of buns. Wrap in foil and bake at 350° for 20 minutes or till done.

Kate Stoltzfus (Steve)
Amanda Stoltzfus

Hot Dog Surprise

2 c. hotdogs, ground
2 c. ham, chopped
1/2 c. cheese, grated
2 eggs, hard cooked
2 T. pickle relish
1 tsp. onion, chopped
3 T. catsup
1 tsp. mustard'
3 T. mayonnaise, optional

Put in buns. Wrap in tin foil and bake at 350° for 10-12 minutes.

Linda King
Elizabeth Kauffman
Sadie Lapp
Elsie Fisher

Hot Dog Sandwiches

8 hot dogs, ground
6 pickles, ground
5 eggs, hard cooked, chopped
1 onion, chopped
2 T. mayonnaise
2 tsp. mustard
1/4 lb. grated cheese
little ketchup, optional

Mix together and divide onto hot dog rolls. Bake 15-20 minutes at 350°.

Annie Lapp
Sarah Fisher

A gentle word scatters sunshine on our way.

Hamburger Hot Dog Bake

12 slices bread
butter or margarine
1 lb. lean ground beef
1/4 c. ketchup
1 tsp. salt
6 hot dogs
2 med. onions, sliced
6 slices white American cheese
2 eggs, beaten
1 c. milk

Spread 6 slices of bread with butter, put in greased 13"x9"x2" pan. Toast lightly in 350* oven. Prepare beef like you would for beef barbecue. Spread evenly over toast. Cut hot dogs in half and lengthwise. Put on top of toast and beef.

Followed by onion and cheese slices. Put remaining bread slices on top. Combine eggs and milk. Pour over all. Bake in 350° oven for 45 minutes. Makes 6 servings.

Naomi B. Beiler

Shredded Pork Sandwiches

1 3-4 lb. boneless pork shoulder roast
1 1/4 c. ketchup
1/2 c. water
1/2 c. celery, chopped
1/4 c. onion, chopped
1/4 c. lemon juice
3 T. vinegar
2 T. Worcestershire sauce
2 T. brown sugar
1 1/2 tsp. ground mustard
1 tsp. salt
1/2 tsp. pepper

Place roast in large kettle. Combine the rest of the ingredients and pour over roast. Cook until meat is tender and pulls apart easily. Shred meat with fork. Serve on buns.

Mrs. Elmer Stoltzfus

Life is like an onion, you peel off one layer at a time and sometimes you cry.

Sloppy Joe Sandwiches

2 T. fat
1 lb. hamburger
2 med. onions, chopped
1 tsp. salt
1/8 tsp. pepper
1 T. flour
1 c. water
1/2 tsp. Worcestershire sauce
3/4 c. catsup
10 sandwich buns

Melt fat in skillet. Add hamburger, onions, salt and pepper. Cook until meat is lightly browned, stirring occasionally. Blend flour and water, pour into meat, mixing well. Add Worcestershire sauce and catsup, simmer, stirring occasionally for 15 to 20 minutes, until desired consistency is obtained. Serve on warmed sandwich buns.

Stromboli

1 1/3 c. warm water
2 T. oil
1 T. yeast
1/2 tsp. salt
4-5 c. bread flour

Mix, let rise. Divide into 3 parts. Roll 1/4" thick, put your favorite meats & cheese on, fold edges and press together. Brush butter on top, sprinkle season salt on top. Bake at 350° for 25 minutes. Let set 10-15 minutes. Cut and serve.

Naomi Lapp
Sylvia Lantz

Vegetable Pizza

1 8 oz. can crescent rolls dough
8 oz. cream cheese
1/2 c. mayonnaise or 8 oz. sour cream
1 4 oz. env. ranch dressing mix
1 c. cauliflower, finely chopped
1 c. broccoli, finely chopped
1/2 c. shredded cheese

Press roll dough in a 9"x13" pan. Bake at 375° for 13 min. or until browned. Cool. Combine softened cream cheese, mayonnaise and ranch dressing mix until smooth. spread on crust. Top with cauliflower, broccoli and cheese.

Linda Stoltzfus
Sarah Fisher

Angel Cake

I hope there's a kitchen in Heaven
For my mother when she gets there
Most of her life she spent baking
Cookies and rolls made with care.

There must be a heavenly oven
A place where angels can bake
Where my mother will wear a gold apron
And make up rich angel cake.

And tables will be solid marble
With dishes of silver and pearl
And the baker's in there shiny halos
Will roll out a pie in a whirl.

There must be a kitchen in Heaven
Waiting for mother's like mine
They will never stop cooking and baking
As long as there's angels to dine.

Soups

Remembering

I used to dream of paradise
A kitchen small and cozy
A copper kettle singing and
A table with a posy.
Perhaps a hearth (my wildest wish!)
With smell of maple burning
An oval rug, a rocking chair
And shelves with books for learning.
I used to dream of cookie sprees,
And brown wheat bread- a-baking
Roasting chicken, chili soup
And pickles in the making.
I'd dream of little hands to hold
A fat and smiling dimple,
A hug at night and story time
Homey things and simple
I'd dream of firm and sturdy steps
A lifting of the latch string
A nuzzle and a "Howdy, Hon!"
(I'd be busy patching)
My one and only home again
When work outside was through.
Life couldn't have been kinder
My dreams have all come true.

Potato Soup

4 slices bacon, diced
1 c. celery, finely chopped
1/2 c. onions, chopped
1 lg. potato, peeled and finely chopped to make 1 1/2c.
1 c. shredded carrot
2 whole allspice
1 bay leaf
1 tsp. salt
1/4 tsp. pepper
1/2 c. sour cream
2 c. water
2 T. flour
1 1/2 c. half & half or light cream
1 lb. potatoes, peeled, cooked and mashed to make 1 1/2 c.

Fry bacon till crisp, drain and reserve drippings. Cook onions and celery in drippings. Add potatoes, carrots, allspice, bay leaf, salt, pepper and water, cook till soft. Remove bay leaf and allspice. Combine sour cream and flour, stir in half & half, stir into potato mixture. Cook and stir till thick and bubbly. Stir in mashed potatoes and bacon.

Anna Mae Fisher

Cheesy Broccoli Soup

1/4 c. chopped onion
1 T. margarine
1 1/2 c. milk
3/4 lb. Velveeta cheese, cubed
1 10 oz. pkg. frozen broccoli
dash of pepper

In a 2 quart sauce pan cook onion in margarine until tender. Add remaining ingredients. Stir over low heat until cheese spread is melted and mixture is hot.

Kate Stoltzfus

Broccoli Soup

1/4 c. onions
2 T. butter
1/2 tsp. Salt
1/2 pkg. Wide noodles
1 head broccoli, cooked
1 lb. yellow processed cheese
6 c. water
6 c. milk
6 chicken bouillon cubes

Cook onion in butter for 3 min. Add water, cubes and noodles, boil for 3 min. Add milk, broccoli and cut up cheese. Simmer till cheese is melted. Serves 20 people.

Barbiann Esch

Cheese Broccoli Chowder

2 c. water
1 c. celery
1 c. carrots
1/2 c. onion
1 lb. broccoli
1/2 c. butter
1/2 c. flour
2 tsp. salt
1/4 tsp. pepper
1/4 lb. or 4 c. cheese
2 c. ham
4 c. milk

Combine ingredients. Heat and serve.

Martha Smucker

Cauliflower Soup

1 med. head cauliflower
1/4 c. butter
3 c. chicken broth
1 tsp. Worcestershire sauce
1 tsp. salt
1/4 c. onion, chopped
1/4 c. flour
2 c. milk
1 c. or 4 oz. sharp cheese, grated

Cook cauliflower in salt water, drain and chop. Cook onion in butter, blend in flour. Add broth, milk etc. Stir until thickened. Add cauliflower bring to boil. Add cheese.

Amanda Stoltzfus

Cauliflower Soup

1 head cauliflower
2 c. milk
1/2 c. butter
1/4 tsp. salt
1 c. Velveeta cheese, cubed
1/2 c. water
1/3 c. flour

Cook cauliflower and cut into small pieces. Heat milk, butter, salt and cheese. Thicken with water and flour mixture.

Arie Speicher

Our Father, Thou hast given us so much. Give us one thing – A grateful heart.

Spinach Soup

1 tsp. butter
1 1/2 c. onion, chopped
1 qt. spinach, pureed
1/2 tsp. garlic powder
1 tsp. salt
1/2 tsp. celery salt
dash pepper
1 c. evaporated milk
1 pt. milk

In sauce pan melt butter, sauté onion. Combine rest of ingredients, add onions. Bring to boiling point. Serves 12-14.

Corn Chowder

6 slices bacon
1/2 c. onions, chopped
2 c. potatoes, diced
1 1/2 c. water
2 T. butter
2 T. flour
2 tsp. salt
1/2 tsp. pepper
2 c. cream corn
3 c. milk

Cut up bacon and fry until crisp. Remove bacon from pan and fry onions in bacon fat until transparent, but not brown. Cook potatoes in water with salt, onion and bacon until potatoes are soft. Add pepper and corn. Melt butter in small pan. Add flour and blend. Add milk, stirring constantly and cook until smooth and thickened. Add to corn mixture. Serve.

Lena King

Old Fashioned Corn Soup

beef broth, with beef cut fine
1/2 c. celery
1 qt. corn
1 c. potatoes, diced

Boil broth, celery and potatoes until soft. Add salt, pepper and parsley to taste. Add rivals.

Rachel Stoltzfus

Harvest Corn Chowder

1 med. onion, chopped
1 T. butter
3 c. creamed style corn
3 c. whole kernel corn
4 c. potatoes, diced
1 can cream of mushroom soup
3 c. milk
1 med. green pepper, chopped
salt and pepper to taste
1/2 lb. bacon, fried and crumbled

In a Dutch oven sauté onion and pepper until tender. Add corn potatoes, soup, milk, salt and pepper. Simmer until vegetables are tender. Garnish with bacon.

Naomi B. Beiler

Spaghetti Soup To Can

10 qt. canned tomato juice
3 lb. spaghetti
4 lb. hamburger
3 stalks celery
1 qt. carrots, shredded
4 onions
1 lb. butter
3 lb. dried great northern beans
salt to taste
brown sugar to taste

Cook spaghetti. Melt butter and fry onion. Add hamburger. Chop celery fine and cook. Cook the carrots. Soak beans overnight and cook until soft. Mix this all together. Put into jars and cold pack for 2 hours. Makes approx. 35 quarts.

Lena Riehl
Linda King
Anna Zook
Katie Glick

A wise old owl sat in an oak;
The more he saw the less he spoke;
The less he spoke the more he heard;
Let's try to imitate that bird.

Vegetable Soup

1 qt. potatoes
1 qt. carrots
1 qt. corn
1 qt. green beans
1 qt. onions, chopped
1 lb. navy beans, soak overnight
12 beef cubes
1 box beef broth, George Washington
1 qt. celery, cooked
1 qt. spaghetti or alphabets
6-7 qt. tomato juice
1/2 c. brown sugar
3 lb. hamburger
1/4 lb. butter
2 T. chili powder

Cook vegetables in salt till not quite soft. Mix all ingredients together. Cold pack for 2 hours. Don't make your jars more than 3/4 full.

Elizabeth Kauffman
Rebecca Speicher

Tomato Soup To Can

6 onions, chopped
1 bunch celery, chopped
8 qt. tomatoes, quartered
1 c. sugar
1/4 c. salt
1 c. butter
1 c. flour

Cook onions in a little water. Wash and add chopped celery and tomatoes, cook until tender. Put through a sieve. Return juice to kettle. Add sugar and salt. Cream butter and flour, add to juice. Blend well and simmer till slightly thickened. Cook as long as you would for gravy. Put soup into jars and seal. I cold pack for 30 minutes. When serving, put into sauce pan and add 2 pinches baking soda. Heat slightly, stirring in an equal amount of milk.

Linda Stoltzfus
Ada King
Linda King

How come some lemonade is flavored with artificial lemon while furniture polish and dish soap are made with real lemon?

Tomato Soup

14 qt. tomatoes, un-peeled
14 sprigs parsley or parsley flakes
14 T. flour or 1 c.
14 T. butter
1 c. sugar
1 1/2 qt. water
salt and pepper to taste

Cook tomatoes, parsley and butter until soft. Put through strainer then return to stove. make a paste with flour and water, add to juice. Add sugar, salt and pepper. Boil for 20 minutes. Put in jars and cold pack for 30 minutes.

Mrs. Elmer Stoltzfus

Oyster Stew

9 oysters
2 T. butter
2 T. oyster juice
4 c. milk
1/2 tsp. salt
1/8 tsp. pepper

Fry oysters in the butter for 5 minutes. Add the juice and cook 15 minutes more. Add milk and seasonings and heat.

Sylvia Esch

New England Clam Chowder

1 can Gorton's chopped clams
3 c. water
6 c. milk or light cream
3/4 c. butter
3 lg. onions, chopped
8 lg. potatoes, peeled and diced
salt and pepper to taste

Drain clams, reserve liquid. Sauté onion in butter, add potatoes and clam liquid, cover and simmer about 15 minutes until potatoes are soft. Add clams cook 3 minutes. Add water and milk. Heat, but do not boil. Thicken with flour if desired. Makes 24 servings.

Anna Mae Fisher

Seeing ourselves as others see us wouldn't do much good. We wouldn't believe it anyway.

Ham and Bean Soup

1 gal. ham broth
1 qt. celery, finely chopped
2 qt. ham, cubed
1 gal. northern beans, rinse and drained
1/2 gal. kidney beans, rinse and drained
2 lg. cans Campbell's tomato soup
1/2-1 c. brown sugar

Cook ham broth until boiling. Add celery and ham. Bring to a boil again. Add remaining ingredients. This is good to can. Can also add hard boiled eggs if desired, but not to can.

Sylvia King

Easy Ham and Bean Soup

2 c. ham broth
3 c. leftover ham, cubed
1/4 c. onion, chopped
1/4 c. celery, chopped
dash of parsley
dash of pepper
2 c. canned great northern beans
1 T. brown sugar

Cook onion and celery in broth for 15 min. Add rest ingredients, cook together. Add 4 T. brown butter and as much milk as desired. Thicken with flour, if desired.

Naomi Lapp

Ham and Bean Soup

5 lb. great northern beans
4 1/2 - 5 lb. ham or bacon
1 qt. onions, chopped
1 qt. carrots and potatoes, finely diced
2 qt. tomato juice
2 tsp. salt
2 tsp. season salt
1 tsp. pepper

Mix all ingredients. Cold pack for 2 hours.

Sadie Fisher

Food for thought –
Only people who do things make mistakes.

Hamburger Soup

1 c. onions, chopped
1/2 c. green peppers, chopped
1 lb. ground beef
2 c. tomato sauce or juice
1 tsp. salt
1/8 tsp. pepper
2 c. carrots, sliced
2 c. potatoes, diced
1 tsp. seasoned salt
1/3 c. flour
1 qt. milk

Brown ground beef, onion and pepper. Drain off fat. In large kettle, cook vegetables, tomato juice and seasonings until vegetables are tender. Make a paste with 1/3 c. flour and 1 cup milk. Add to hot soup, stirring well. Add remaining milk. Heat thoroughly.

Mrs. Elmer Stoltzfus
Arie Blank

Chunky Beef Soup

3 qt. water
2 lg. cans beef broth
4 qt. tomato juice
2 onions, chopped and cooked
4 qt. potatoes, cooked
4 qt. carrots, cooked
3 qt. peas, cooked
2 qt. green beans, cooked
10 lb. hamburger or 3 lg. roasts, cooked and cubed

If you use the roasts you will have your own beef broth. Bring to a boil and add other ingredients, which have been cooked. Mix together. Add some beef soup base to taste. Can be thickened a little with clear jell if desired. Put in jars and cold pack 2 hours.

Linda Stoltzfus

It is when we forget ourselves that we do things that are most likely to be remembered.

Speck Soup

2 c. ham, cubed
2 med. onions, chopped
5 c. potatoes, cubed
1 1/2 c. water
1 qt. milk
1 qt. corn
2 T. butter
2 T. flour
2 tsp. soda
3 6 oz. cans tomato paste
salt and pepper to suit taste

Combine first 4 ingredients, cook till soft. Add milk. In separate pan melt butter, add flour, soda and tomato paste, stirring till smooth. Heat and add to ham mixture. Add cooked corn.

Naomi B. Beiler

Turkey Chowder

4 c. broth and meat pieces
1 med. onion
1 c. carrots
1 c. celery
1 c. potatoes
salt to taste
2 c. milk
6 T. flour
1 c. Velveeta cheese
1/4 c. butter

Cook the first 6 ingredients together until soft. Add the remaining ingredients and cook until thick. A delicious one dish meal.

Elizabeth Stoltzfus

Chili

1 lb. hamburger
1/2 c. brown sugar
2 T. mustard
1 med. onion, chopped
2 14 oz. kidney beans
1 pt. tomato juice
1/2 tsp. salt
1/4 tsp. pepper
1 tsp. chili powder or to suit taste

Brown first 4 ingredients together. Then add rest of ingredients and simmer 1 hour.

Naomi Lapp

The time to make friends is before you need them.

Chili

1 lb. ground beef
1/2 c. onion, chopped
1/2 c. celery, chopped
3 T. flour
1/4 c. brown sugar
1/4 c. catsup
4 c. tomato juice
2-3 T. chili powder
1 lb. can kidney beans
salt and pepper

Fry together the meat, onion and celery. Add flour and stir. Add the rest of the ingredients and simmer 30 minutes.

Rebecca Lynn Fisher

Chili Soup To Can

6-9 lb. hamburger
3/4-1 c. onion
14 qt. tomato juice
3 qt. kidney beans, cooked
2 tsp. chili powder
1 tsp. red pepper
1-5 c. brown sugar
3/4-1 c. salt
3 c. corn starch
3 qt. water

Cook together 5 minutes. Cold pack for 2 to 3 hours. Makes 25 qt.

Lena Riehl

New Hampshire Cheese Soup

1 1/2 c. potato, chopped
1 c. onion, chopped
1/4 c. carrot, chopped
1/4 c. celery, thinly sliced
1 c. water
1 c. sharp cheddar cheese, shredded
2 c. chicken broth
1/2 c. milk

Cook vegetables until tender. Add remaining ingredients.

Sylvia Stoltzfus (Gid)

**Have you heard of the new garlic diet?
You don't lose weight, but you look thinner from a distance!**

Chile Con Carne

1 T. shortening
1 onion
1 lb. ground beef
1 tsp. salt
1/8 tsp. pepper
1 T. chili powder
2 c. V8 juice
1 can chili beans

Sauté onion in shortening. Add meat and simmer until redness disappears. Add all remaining ingredients and simmer 30 minutes.

Amos and Naomi Beiler

Cream of Mushroom Soup

1/4 c. margarine or butter
1 lb. fresh mushrooms, chopped
4 1/2 c. milk
4 beef bouillon cubes
1 c. boiling water
1/4 c. flour
1 tsp. salt
1 tsp. dried parsley

Melt margarine and sauté mushrooms over medium heat for about 8 minutes, stirring often. Stir in 4 cups milk. Reduce heat to low. Dissolve bouillon cubes in boiling water and add to soup. Combine flour, salt, parsley and 1/2 c. milk, blending till smooth. Add to soup and cook till soup thickens. Makes 6-8 servings.

Katie Ruth Esch

Cream of Chicken Soup

1/4 c. margarine or butter
5 T. flour
3 chicken bouillon cubes
3 c. boiling water
1/2 c. chicken, finely chopped
1 c. rich milk

Melt the margarine or butter in sauce pan over low heat. Blend in the flour. Dissolve the bouillon cubes in the boiling water and gradually add to the margarine and flour mixture, stir until smooth. Add chicken and bring to a boil over medium heat. Stir in the milk. Add additional seasonings if desired.

Katie Ruth Esch

The Stew of Life

We all know that whatever goes into the stew pot determines how the stew will turn out. Will it taste good or bad. Will the seasoning be just right. Let us consider ourselves as the stew pot. The stew will be made over our entire lifetime. How much effort will we use to get our stew perfect. We will list here some ingredients that will help to determine the character of our stew.

Honesty	**Pleasant**
Kindness	**Thankful**
Loving	**Sharing**
Helpful	**Pure & Clean Thought**
Trustworthy	**Honorable**
Pleasant	**Joyful**
Forgiving	**Politeness**
Cheating	**Lying**
Stealing	**Coveting**
Drunkenness	**Disrespectful**
Lewdness	**Shameful**
Gluttony	**Filthiness**
Slandering	**Hateful**
Spiteful	**Cursing**

If we have done bad things and we can't get them out of the pot we must dilute it with lots of good. Live your life the best you can, then trust in grace for what you can't.

Be cheerful!

Breakfast Foods

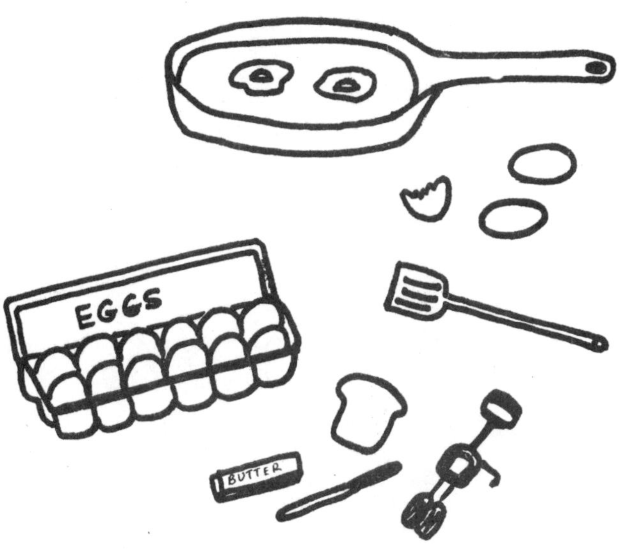

Good Morning God

You are ushering in another day untouched and freshly new, so here I come to ask you God if you'll renew me too? Forgive the many errors that I made yesterday and let me try again, Dear God, to walk closer in thy way, but Father I am well aware I can't make it on my own. So take my hand and hold it tight for I can't walk alone.

Breakfast For 40-50 People

12 lb. potatoes
1 lb. fully cooked ham, diced
1 lg. onion, chopped
1 c. green pepper, chopped
1/2 c. butter, divided
4 tsp. salt
1/2 tsp. pepper
1 tsp. paprika
1 lb. cheese, shredded
1 c. butter, melted
50 eggs, beaten
4 tsp. salt
5 c. milk

Potatoes; Peel and cook potatoes until tender. Chill overnight. Grate into large bowl. Sauté ham, onion and pepper in 1/4 cup butter until tender. Cool and add to potatoes. Add 4 tsp. salt, pepper and paprika and mix well. On griddle fry potato mixture in remaining 1/4 cup butter until browned. Place hot potatoes on platters with layers of cheese in between. Oven Scrambled Eggs; Divide 1 cup melted butter into 2-13"x9"x2" baking pans. Combine eggs and salt, mix well. Gradually stir in milk. Pour evenly into the 2 baking pans. Bake uncovered at 350° for 10 minutes, stir and bake 10-15 minutes more until eggs are set.

Naomi B. Beiler

Baked Oatmeal

1/2 c. brown sugar
1/4 c. white sugar
1/2 c. oil
2 eggs
3 c. oatmeal
2 tsp. baking powder
1/2 tsp. salt
1 c. milk

Bake in 2 quart casserole at 350° for 30-40 minutes.

Sylvia Lantz

Hot Whole Wheat Cereal

3 c. milk
3 T. whole wheat flour
1 T. butter

Heat milk and add whole wheat flour that has been added to 1 cup milk and make like a gravy. Add melted butter.

Sylvia Esch

Corn Meal Mush

2 1/2 pt. water
2 T. salt
2 c. corn meal
1 pt. cold water

Bring 2 1/2 pints water to a boil with salt. Add the corn meal mixed with a pint of cold water, but do not allow liquid to boil while adding. Cook slowly 30 minutes or longer, stirring frequently to keep smooth. Put in pan for cooling. Slice to desired thickness and fry until brown.

Rebecca Speicher

Corn Meal Mush

1 c. corn meal
3 c. water
1 tsp. salt
1 T. butter
brewer's yeast

Mix the first 3 ingredients together and cook slowly 10 minutes. You can add more cornmeal if it isn't thick enough.
Thicken to the right consistency to drop in patties and fry. After it is done cooking add the butter and a generous shaking of yeast, stir in the mush until butter is melted. Serve with eggs or syrup.

Rebecca Speicher

Pink Salmon & Stewed Crackers

7 oz. salmon
1 T. butter
2 c. milk, scant
1 pkg. crackers

Lightly fry salmon in butter. Pour in milk and heat. Pour over crackers and cover to steam a few minutes.

Sylvia Esch

A little faith
A little prayer
A little knowing God is there

Cheese Omelet

2 T. melted butter
3 T. flour
1/2 tsp. soda
1/4 c. cheese, cut fine
3 eggs, beaten
1/2 c. milk, scalded

Mix the above ingredients and bake at 350° for 50-55 minutes.

Potato Omelet

2 c. raw potatoes, grated
1/4 c. green peppers, chopped
1/4 c. onion, chopped
2 T. margarine
4 eggs, beaten
1/2 tsp. salt
1/2 c. grated cheese
4 strips bacon, browned

Heat the first 4 ingredients in a skillet till tender. Combine the eggs and salt, pour over mixture in skillet. Cover and cook on low heat till set. Sprinkle the cheese and crumble the bacon over top.

Arie Blank

Omelet Soufflé

12 eggs, beaten well
1 tsp. salt
1 tsp. dry mustard
3 c. milk
1 1/2 lb. smoked sausage or ham, fried and cut up
6 slices bread, cubed
1 c. shredded cheese

Mix all ingredients together and pour into 9"x13" pan. Put in refrigerator overnight. Bake at 350° for 45 minutes or till done. Turn it over when halfway done and sprinkle another cup of cheese on top.

Esther Fisher

A smile is a light in the window of the face showing the heart is at home.

Bacon and Egg Bake

6 slices bacon, or more
1 med. onion, sliced
1 can cream of mushroom soup
1/4 c. milk
5 eggs, hard cooked, sliced
2 c. shredded cheddar cheese
salt and pepper
English muffins or toast

Fry bacon till crisp, drain fat, using 2 T. to sauté onion. Stir in the remaining ingredients. Pour into a 10"x6" baking dish and top with crumbled bacon. Bake at 350° for 20 minutes. Serve over toast or toasted muffin halves.

Katie Ruth Esch

Crustless Bacon & Egg Quiche

8 bacon strips, fried, diced or bacon bits
1 1/2 c. milk
1/2 c. Bisquick
3 eggs
1/4 c. butter, melted
dash pepper
1 c. shredded cheddar cheese

Beat together the milk, Bisquick, eggs, butter and pepper. Pour into greased 9" pie pan. Sprinkle bacon and cheese on top. Gently press below surface with a fork. Bake at 350° for 30 minutes or until knife inserted near center comes out clean. Let stand 10 minutes before cutting.

Mattie Beiler
Lena Riehl

Breakfast Casserole

2 c. bread, dried, cubed
1 c. shredded cheese
4 eggs, beaten
2 c. milk
1/2 tsp. salt
1/2 tsp. dry mustard
1/8 tsp. onion powder
dash pepper
4 slices bacon, fried, drained, crumbled

Place bread and cheese in the bottom of a greased 10"x6" pan. Combine eggs, milk and seasonings. Pour into baking dish. Sprinkle with bacon. Bake at 325° for 1 hour. For variety top with buttered corn flakes, hot peppers or ham.

Anna Mary Smucker

Sunday Brunch

8 slices bread
1/4 c. melted butter
6 eggs
1 tsp. salt
1 lb. grated cheese
1 pt. milk
onion flakes or onion salt
Dash of pepper

Cut bread into 1" squares. Place in a greased casserole. Beat eggs, milk and seasonings. put the melted butter on top and spread the grated cheese over all. Refrigerate overnight. Bake at 325° for 45 minutes.

Ruth Ann Esch

Sausage Egg Casserole

9 slices bread, buttered, cubed
1/2 lb. Velveeta cheese or any other kind cheese
1 lb. sausage or ham
8 lg. eggs
2 c. milk
1 tsp. paprika
1 tsp. dry mustard
1/2 tsp. salt
1/4 tsp. oregano

Use 8"x12" pan. Put bread cubes in first, top with sausage or ham then the cheese on top. Beat eggs, add milk and seasonings. Pour over everything. Bake uncovered at 350° for 30-45 minutes. Serves 8.

Sylvia King
Susie Blank

Sausage Soufflé

1 lb. sausage
10 slices bread
6 eggs, beaten
1 c. grated cheese
3 c. milk
1 tsp. dry mustard
1/4 tsp. oregano, optional

Fry sausage and drain. Tear bread into cubes and place in 9"x13" pan. Combine eggs, milk cheese seasonings and sausage. Pour over bread. Sprinkle parsley on top. Bake 350°-400° for 1 hour. May be refrigerated overnight.

Annie King
Sarah Fisher

Country Breakfast

14 slices bread
1 1/2 c. cubed ham
16 oz. cheddar cheese, grated
16 oz. mozzarella cheese, grated
6 eggs
3 c. milk
1/2 tsp. dry mustard
1/8-1/4 tsp. onion powder
3 c. corn flakes, uncrushed
1/2 c. butter, melted

Grease a 13"x9"x2" baking pan. Layer as follows: 1 layer bread, 1 layer ham, 1 layer cheese and continue until all is used. Combine eggs, milk and seasonings. Pour over layers and refrigerate overnight. Remove from refrigerator 30 minutes before baking. Combine the corn flakes and butter. Sprinkle over casserole. Cover loosely with foil. Bake at 375° for 45 minutes.

Linda King
Katie Mae Stoltzfus

Brunch Strudel

12 slices bread, cubed
8 eggs
1 c. onion, chopped, optional
4 c. shredded cheese
2 c. ham, cubed
1 tsp. salt
1/2 tsp. pepper
1 c. milk

Place bread cubes in pan. Put layers of onion, ham and cheese. Beat eggs, milk and seasonings together and pour over layered cubes. Bake at 350° for 45-50 minutes. If bread cubes are not dried use one less egg and only 3/4 cup milk.

Mrs. Elmer Stoltzfus
Rachel Stoltzfus

Salute the day with peaceful thoughts, and peace will fill your heart; Begin the day with joyful soul, and joy will be your part.

Breakfast Dish

1 lb. bacon
3 c. dried beef or ham
1 4 oz. can sliced mushrooms
1/2 c. flour
1/8 tsp. pepper
4 c. milk
16 eggs
1 c. evaporated milk
1/4 tsp. salt
1/4 c. butter

In a large skillet, cook bacon till crisp, remove bacon onto a paper towel to drain. Discard all but 1/4 cup bacon drippings. Add beef, mushrooms, flour and pepper to the drippings. Stir until thoroughly combined. Gradually add milk. Cook and stir until thickened. Stir in bacon. Set aside. In large bowl, beat eggs, milk and salt. Melt butter in another greased skillet. Add eggs till scrambled. Place 1/2 of the eggs in a 13"x9" greased baking dish, pour 1/2 of the sauce over the eggs, spoon on remaining eggs, then rest of sauce. Cover and bake at 300° for 50 minutes.

Ada King

Ham and Eggs Brunch Bake

1/2 c. onion, chopped
1 T. butter
1/2 lb. ham, chopped
2 c. Bisquick baking mix
1/2 c. cold water
1 c. shredded cheese
1/4 c. milk
2 eggs
1/4 tsp. salt
1/4 tsp. pepper
2 T. chives

Mix ingredients together. Heat oven to 350° and bake for 25-30 minutes.

Arie Speicher

If you have given up trying to open something, tell a four year old not to touch it.

Bacon n' Egg Pizza

1 8 oz. refrigerated biscuits or make your own dough
3 eggs, beaten
1 T. milk
5 slices crisp bacon, crumpled
1 tsp. chives or onions, chopped
1 c. shredded cheese
dash of salt

Flatten biscuits on pizza pan. Combine eggs, milk and salt. Pour onto biscuit shell. Sprinkle with bacon, chives and cheese. Bake at 350° for 20 minutes. Top with crisp bacon slices if desired.

Anna Zook

Cinnamon French Toast

1 lg. egg
2 egg whites
1/4 c. milk
1/2 tsp. vanilla
1/2 tsp. cinnamon
1/8 tsp. nutmeg
8 slices bread

In a shallow bowl, using a wire whisk or fork, beat egg and egg white till foamy. Add milk and seasonings. Beat well. Dip bread slices into mixture, turning to coat. Place bread slices on prepared skillet. Cook until golden brown, turning once. Top with maple syrup to serve.

Linda Stoltzfus

French Toast Bake

1 loaf French bread
8 eggs
1 c. milk
1 c. half & half
2 tsp. vanilla
1/2 tsp. nutmeg
1/2 tsp. cinnamon
1/2 tsp. mace
3/4 c. butter, softened
1 1/2 c. brown sugar
1 1/3 c. pecans or walnuts, chopped
3 T. dark corn syrup

Heavily butter a 13"x9" pan. Fill pan with bread slices to within 1/2" of top. Mix together next 7 ingredients and pour over bread slices. refrigerate, covered overnight. Make topping with remaining ingredients and pour over bread slices just before baking. Bake at 350° for 50 minutes.

Barbiann Esch

French Toast Bake

8 slices bread, toasted, buttered
4 eggs
2 c. milk
2/3 c. maple syrup
dash of salt
dash of cinnamon

Lay the toast in a baking dish. Mix remaining ingredients and pour over toast. Set baking dish in another pan of hot water to bake. Bake at 375° for 35 minutes.

Mrs. Elmer Stoltzfus

Pancake Mix

10 c. flour
5 tsp. baking powder, rounded
1 T. baking soda
1/4 c. sugar
3 tsp. salt, optional
3 c. corn flake crumbs
2 c. old fashioned rolled oats
3 c. whole wheat flour

Combine all ingredients. Cover & store. When ready to use mix 1 1/2 cups pancake mix with 1 egg & 1 1/2 cups milk.

Sylvia Lantz

Lizzie's Pancakes

2 c. flour
1-1 1/2 c. milk
2 eggs
2 tsp. baking powder
1 tsp. salt
3 T. sugar
2 T. butter

Sift flour, baking powder, salt and sugar. Add beaten eggs and milk, beat well and add butter.

Katie Glick

Begin your day with friendliness, keep friendly all day long; keep in your soul a friendly thought, your heart a friendly song

Pancakes

3 egg yolks
1 c. milk
1 c. flour
pinch of salt
3 egg whites, beaten stiff
1 T. sugar
2 tsp. baking powder, heaping
2 T. butter, melted

Beat egg yolks and milk together. Sift dry ingredients together and add to mix. Add melted butter. Fold in egg whites just before baking. Have the griddle hot.

Arie King

Lightest Ever Pancakes

3 eggs
1/3 c. sugar
1 tsp. salt
2 c. flour
2 c. milk
4 tsp. baking powder
4 T. melted butter

Beat eggs and sugar till fluffy. Add salt. Mix in flour and milk alternately. Add baking powder. Do not over beat after adding baking powder. Add melted butter last. Have grill hot so pancakes won't stick. Flip when bubbles appear. Serve with syrup or creamed beef gravy.

Lena King

Potato Pancakes

6 raw potatoes, finely grated
1 tsp. salt
1/4 c. flour

Mix thoroughly. Drop mixture by tablespoons into hot greased skillet. Brown on one side, turn, brown on other side. Can also be deep fried. Delicious when served with creamed beef.

Anna Mae Stoltzfus

All the flowers of all the tomorrows are in the seeds of today.

Tater-Cheese Pancakes

4 lg. potatoes, uncooked
1 sm. onion, chopped
1/3 c. milk
1 egg, beaten
1/2 tsp. salt
3 T. flour
1 1/4 c. cheddar cheese, shredded

Peel and finely shred potatoes. Add remaining ingredients and mix well. Fry in hot butter until brown and crisp. Serve hot with applesauce.

Sarah Esh

Whole Wheat Pancakes

1 c. buttermilk or sour milk or milk
1 egg
2 T. vegetable oil
1/2 c. whole wheat flour
1/2 c. white all purpose flour
1 tsp. baking powder
1/2 tsp. baking soda
1/2 tsp. salt

Mix the first 3 ingredients in a bowl. Add remaining ingredients. Mix just till blended.

Annie Lapp
Sadie Lapp

Fresh Corn Pancakes

1 c. flour
1/2 c. cornmeal
1 T. sugar
1 T. baking powder
1/2 tsp. salt
2 eggs, separated
1 c. milk
1/4 c. butter, melted
1 c. whole kernel corn, cooked
1 sm. onion, chopped
1/2 green pepper, chopped
butter or margarine for frying

In a bowl combine first 5 ingredients. In a small bowl beat the egg yolks, blend in milk and butter. Add to dry ingredients, stir until just mixed. Stir in corn, onion and pepper. Gently fold in beaten egg whites. For each pancake pour about 1/4 cup batter on lightly greased hot griddle. Turn when bubbles appear on tops of cakes. Cook other side until golden brown. Serve with syrup if desired. Makes about 20 pancakes.

Naomi B. Beiler

Oatmeal Griddle Cakes

2/3 c. whole wheat flour
3 tsp. baking powder
1 tsp. sea salt
1 2/3 c. rolled oats
1 egg
1 T. oil
1 tsp. molasses
3/4 c. water
3/4 c. sour milk

Mix all ingredients and beat till smooth. Ladle mixture on hot oiled griddle and brown on both sides.

Anna Mary Smucker

Cream Waffles

2 c. flour
1/2 c. thick sour cream
1 1/2 c. sweet milk
1/2 tsp. salt
1 tsp. sugar
2 tsp. baking powder
2 eggs, separated

Sift dry ingredients together. Beat egg yolks, add milk and cream. Combine with dry ingredients. Fold in stiffly beaten egg whites. Bake in hot waffle iron.

Anna Mae Fisher
Naomi Beiler

Pancake Syrup

1 1/4 c. brown sugar
3/4 c. white sugar
1/3 c. molasses or corn syrup
1 c. water

Bring to a boil, stirring constantly. Simmer on low heat for 5 minutes. Remove from heat and add 1 tsp. vanilla. Maple flavoring may be added.

Lena King
Rebecca Lynn Fisher

Any mother who corrects, knows it is hard work! But any mother who may reap the goodness it brings, knows it's worth all efforts.

Pancake Syrup

4 c. sugar
1/2 c. brown sugar
2 T. light Karo syrup
2 C. water
1 tsp. vanilla
1 tsp. maple flavoring

Bring the first 4 ingredients to a boil, cover and boil gently for 10 minutes. Remove from heat and add vanilla and maple flavoring.

Sylvia Esch

Toasted Cheese Bread

bread
sharp cheese

Toast one side of bread. Turn it and put a slice of cheese on top. Put under broiler till the cheese melts.

Rachel Stoltzfus

Grape Nuts

3 c. graham flour
1/2 c. coconut
1/2 c. cornmeal
1/2 c. oatmeal
1/2 c. molasses
1/2 c. honey
2 c. buttermilk
1 tsp. soda, mixed in the milk

Use amount of molasses according to taste. I use part blackstrap. Mix ingredients together. Bake at 350° for 35-40 minutes.

Anna Mary Smucker

Be bold and courageous; When you look back on your life, you'll regret the things you didn't do more than the ones you did.

Granola Cereal

10 c. oatmeal, scant
2 c. brown sugar
4-5 T. molasses or honey
1 c. butter
2 tsp. vanilla

Melt butter. Add molasses, sugar and vanilla. Add remaining ingredients. Put in cake pans and bake at 200° approx. 1-2 hours, depending how crisp you want it. Stir once while baking. If desired, add nuts, raisins and coconut.

Sylvia Lantz
Amanda Stoltzfus

Granola Cereal Mix

7 c. oatmeal
2 c. coconut
1 tsp. salt
1 1/2 c. brown sugar
1 c. butter or margarine, melted

Mix together well. Spread on cookie sheets and toast in slow oven until brown. Stir often it burns easily.

Sara Ann Lapp

Granola

24 c. oatmeal
3 c. wheat germ
3 c. wheat bran
1 c. salad oil
3/4 c. butter
3 tsp. salt
2 c. honey
2 c. brown sugar
2 tsp. vanilla
cinnamon

Mix the first 3 ingredients. Heat the remaining ingredients and add to the dry mixture, mixing well. Bake at 225° for 45 minutes. Stir every 15 minutes. Then add 4 heaping tsp. peanut butter. Mix well.

Marie Hoover

It is easier to leave angry words unspoken than to mend a heart those words have broken.

Granola Cereal

4 c. oatmeal
2 c. wheat germ
1 c. coconut
1 c. sunflower seeds
3/4 c. brown sugar or 1/2 c. honey
1 c. nuts, optional
1/2 c. oil
1/3 c. water
2 tsp. vanilla
2 tsp. cinnamon

Bake at 325° for 45-50 minutes. Stir every 15 minutes.

Lena Riehl

Highly Nutritious Cereal

1 c. vegetable oil
1 c. honey
1 c. water
5 c. rolled oats
1 c. sesame seeds
1 c. coconut, shredded
1 c. sunflower seeds
1 c. almonds, chopped
1 c. non-instant powdered milk
1 c. soy flour and wheat germ
1 c. pumpkin seeds, if desired

In a separate bowl combine the first 3 ingredients. Combine with dry ingredients. Spread on cookie sheet and bake at 300° for 1 hour or until brown. Serve with cold milk.

Rachel Z. Stoltzfus

Ham and Cheese Muffins

2 c. self rising flour
1/2 tsp. baking soda
1 c. milk
1/2 c. mayonnaise
1/2 c. ham, finely chopped
1/2 c. cheese, shredded

In a large bowl combine the flour and baking soda. Combine remaining ingredients, Stir into the dry ingredients just until moistened. Fill greased or paper lined muffin cups 2/3 full. Bake at 425° for 16-18 minutes to until done. Yields 1 dozen.

Annie King

Six Week Bran Muffins

5 c. flour
3 c. sugar
5 tsp. baking soda
2 tsp. salt
4 eggs
1 c. vegetable oil
1 qt. buttermilk
1 box raisin bran

In large bowl stir together the first 4 ingredients. In another bowl beat the eggs, oil and buttermilk. All at once add to the flour mixture and stir only till moistened. Stir in the raisin bran. Fill greased muffin or cupcake pans 2/3 full. Bake at 400° for 15-20 minutes. Store remaining in refrigerator. This can be kept 6 weeks or more. Dates, raisins or apples may be added. If wanted you may pour 2 cups boiling water over 2 cups of the raisin bran then mix as usual.

Katie Ruth Esch
Amanda Stoltzfus
Linda Stoltzfus

Blueberry Muffins

1 egg
3/4 c. milk
1 c. fresh or 3/4 c. frozen or canned blueberries
1/3 c. vegetable oil
1/4 c. honey
2 c. flour or whole wheat
3 tsp. baking powder
1/2 tsp. salt
1/4 c. brown sugar, packed or 1/2 c. granulated sugar
1/2 tsp. cinnamon
1 tsp. lemon or orange peel, optional

Grease only bottom of 12 muffin cups or line with cupcake papers. Mix dry ingredients, except the brown sugar and cinnamon. Add lemon peel, if desired. Stir in blueberries. Combine milk, oil and eggs, add to the blueberry mixture. Make topping with the brown sugar and cinnamon. Fill muffin cups 2/3 full. Bake at 400° for 20-25 minutes. Cool 1 minute. Serve warm.

Anna Mae Fisher
Sylvia Stoltzfus

Blueberry Muffins

2 T. butter
2/3 c. sugar
1/2 c. milk
1 egg
1/8 tsp. salt
1 1/2 c. flour
1 tsp. baking powder
1 c. blueberries

Cream butter, sugar and egg. Add milk. Add dry ingredients. Fold in blueberries. Sprinkle a bit of sugar on top. Bake at 350° about 30 minutes.

Sadie Lapp

Tongue Twister

Betty Botter bought a bit of butter,
She put it in her batter,
And it made her batter bitter,
So Betty Botter bought a bit of better butter,
She put it in her bitter batter,
And it made her bitter batter better.

Just Smiling

When the weather suits you not
Try Smiling
When your coffee isn't hot
Try Smiling
When your neighbors don't do right,
Or your relatives all fight
Sure, 'tis hard, but then you might
Try Smiling
Doesn't change the things, of course
Just Smiling
Still it seems to help your case
And it sorta rests your face
Brightens up a gloomy place
Just Smiling!

A smile is a tiny sun in each person's face

Vegetables & Casseroles

The Farmer's Love Letter

My dear sweet potato, do you carrot all for me? With your radish hair and turnip nose my heart beets for you! My love for you is as strong as an onion. If we canta-loupe, lettuce marry and we will be a happy pear!

Saucy Summer Vegetables

2 c. cauliflower flowerets
8 sm. new potatoes
8 baby carrots
1 c. peas, fresh or frozen
3 T. sweet cream butter
3 T. all purpose flour
1/2 tsp. salt
1/8 tsp. pepper
2 c. milk
3/4 c. cheddar cheese, shredded

In a 3 quart sauce pan combine cauliflower, potatoes and carrots in enough water to cover. Bring to a boil, continue cooking over medium heat 20 minutes. Add peas, continue cooking until vegetables are crisply tender, 8-10 minutes. Drain; set aside. Meanwhile, in a 2 quart saucepan melt butter. Stir in flour, salt and pepper. cook over medium heat, stirring constantly until smooth and bubbly, 1 minute. Stir in milk. Continue cooking, stirring often until mixture thickens and comes to a boil, 8-12 minute. Boil 1 minute. Remove from heat, stir in cheese until melted. Pour over vegetables. yield: 6 (3/4c.) servings.

Rachel Z. Stoltzfus

Creamed Asparagus

asparagus
2 T. flour
1 c. milk
2 T. butter, melted
6 eggs, hard boiled
bread, toasted

Cook asparagus till tender. Mix flour to milk. Add to asparagus to thicken. Cut toast into pieces and put on a platter. Top with creamed asparagus. Drizzle butter over it and top with eggs that have been grated or chopped.

Sylvia Esch

With a small boy, cleanliness is not next to Godliness. It's also next to impossible.

Asparagus & Bread Dish

bread
4 eggs
2 c. milk
salt & pepper
2 1/2 c. asparagus, cooked
cheese
onion

Layer slices of bread in bottom of a 9"x9" pan. Beat eggs with milk, salt, pepper and onion and pour over bread. Bake at 350° for 25 minutes. Add the asparagus and put sliced cheese on top and bake 10 minutes longer.

Rebecca Speicher

Scalloped Asparagus

1 1/2 lb. asparagus
6 T. butter
6 T. flour
1 tsp. salt
1/2 tsp. pepper
2 c. milk
3/4 c. sharp cheese, diced
2 T. onion, chopped
5 eggs, hard boiled
1/2 c. bread crumbs, buttered

Cook asparagus till tender. Drain. Melt butter; stir in flour and seasonings. Gradually add milk. Cook over low heat. Add half the cheese and stir till smooth. Combine sauce, asparagus and eggs. Top with remaining cheese. Bake at 350° for 30 minutes.

Sylvia Esch

Broccoli Casserole

2 pkg. broccoli, frozen, chopped or 20 oz. fresh, chopped
2 eggs
1 can mushroom soup
1 c. sharp cheese, grated
1/2 c. mayonnaise
1 T. onions, minced
Ritz cracker crumbs

Precook broccoli for 10 minutes. Beat eggs slightly; add soup, mayonnaise, onion and most of cheese. Add drained broccoli. Cover with crumbs and rest of cheese, dot with butter. Bake in a greased casserole at 400° for 40 minutes. You may replace the sharp cheese with your favorite kind.

Sylvia Esch

Broccoli with Sauce

broccoli
2 c. onions, chopped
4 T. flour
1/2 tsp. salt
2 c. milk
1/4 lb. cheese

Cook broccoli in small amount of water. Drain and put half of the broccoli in a buttered casserole. Add onions. Make cheese sauce with flour, salt and milk. Cook sauce till thick; add cheese. Stir till cheese melts. Pour half the sauce on top of broccoli in the casserole. Add remaining broccoli than remainder of cheese sauce. Bake at 375° for about 45 minutes.

Sylvia Esch

Broccoli Puff

20 oz. broccoli, chopped
1 c. Bisquick baking mix
1 c. milk
2 eggs
1/2 tsp. salt
1 c. cheese, any kind

Butter a 1 1/2 quart casserole. Cook broccoli according to package, then drain. Bake at 325° for 45 minutes or until knife inserted in middle comes out clean.

Sylvia Stoltzfus
Susie Blank

Broccoli Puff

1 qt. broccoli, cooked & drained
1 can cream of mushroom soup
1/2 c. cheese, shredded
1/4 c. milk
1/4 c. mayonnaise
1 egg, beaten
1/4 c. Ritz crackers, crumbled
1 T. butter, melted

Place broccoli in casserole. Mix next 5 ingredients until well blended. Pour over broccoli. Combine cracker crumbs and butter. Sprinkle evenly over top. Bake at 350° for 30-40 minutes. This is also good if you use other vegetables such as asparagus, cabbage or carrots instead of broccoli.

Naomi B. Beiler

Cooked Red Beets

3/4 c. sugar
2 tsp. cornstarch
1/3 c. vinegar
1/3 c. water
1 tsp. dry mustard
1 tsp. onion powder
4 c. beets, sliced & cooked
3 T. butter or margarine
1/4 tsp. salt
dash of pepper

In sauce pan combine the sugar and cornstarch. Add vinegar and water; bring to a boil. Add the rest of the ingredients and simmer until heated through.

Katie Ruth Esch

Best Ever Carrots

4 c. carrots, sliced & cooked
1/4 c. butter
1/2 c. onion
1/2 c. celery
1/4 c. flour
2 c. milk
1 tsp. mustard
1 c. cheese, shredded
1 c. cracker crumbs

Sauté the onion and celery in the butter. Add the flour, milk and mustard. In a casserole dish alternate the carrots and the thickened sauce. Top with the cheese and crumb mixture. Bake at 350° for 1/2 hour. Serves 6 or 8.

Sylvia Esch

Marinated Carrots

2 lb. carrots, cut in rounds
2 onions, diced
2 green peppers, sliced
1 can tomato soup
3/4 c. sugar
1/2 c. oil
3/4 c. vinegar
1/2 tsp. salt

Cook carrots in boiling water till almost soft, cool. Put into bowl, add onions and peppers. Heat remaining ingredients. Pour over vegetables and marinate overnight. Keeps well in refrigerator for several days. You can reuse the broth.

Rachel Stoltzfus

Zippy Baked Carrots

5-6 c. carrots, sliced 1/4" thick
6 slices Swiss cheese
1 sm. onion, minced
4 T. butter
3 T. all purpose flour
1 tsp. salt
1 tsp. chili powder
2 c. milk
1 c. soft bread crumbs
2 T. butter, melted
5 bacon strips, cooked & crumbled

Cook carrots until crisp tender. Layer half in a 2 quart shallow baking pan. Cover with half of the cheese, repeat layers. For sauce: sauté onions in 4 T. butter for 2 minutes; blend in flour and seasonings. Cook and stir for 1 minute. Add milk all at once; cook and stir until thickened. Pour over cheese. Combine crumbs and 2 T. butter. Sprinkle over all. Top with bacon. Bake at 350° for 25 minutes.

Katie Mae Stoltzfus
Mattie Beiler

Creamed Corn

2 c. corn
1 T. sugar
1 T. flour
1 c. milk
2 eggs
2 T. butter
1 tsp. salt
dash of pepper

Bake at 350* for an hour.

Elsie Fisher

Baked Corn

3 c. corn
1 1/2 c. milk
3 eggs
2 1/4 T. cornstarch
3 T. sugar
3 T. butter, melted
salt and pepper

Mix well. Bake at 325° for 1 hour or until set.

Marie Hoover

Baked Corn

2 c. creamed corn
2 eggs
1 T. sugar
2 T. butter
1 T. flour
1 c. milk
1 tsp. salt
a little pepper

Bake at 350° for 1 hour.

Mrs. Elmer Stoltzfus
Lena Riehl

Corn Filling

5 c. bread crumbs
1 sm. onion, chopped
2 1/2 c. creamed corn
1 tsp. salt
1/4 tsp. pepper
3 eggs, beaten
1/4 c. water
1/2 c. butter, melted

Beat together the eggs and water. Add to the first 5 ingredients. Pour butter over mixture. Bake at 325° for 30-40 minutes.

Lena King
Anna Mary Smucker
Ada King

Zucchini Squares

3 c. zucchini, sliced
1 c. Bisquick
1/2 c. onion, finely chopped
1/2 c. parmesan or Velveeta cheese, grated
2 T. parsley
3/4 tsp. salt
1/2 tsp. oregano
dash of pepper
dash of garlic salt
1/2 c. vegetable oil
4 eggs, slightly beaten

Bake until golden brown at 350° for 30 minutes. Better if not too thick in pan.

Sylvia Lantz

Cabbage with Mustard Sauce

1 sm. head cabbage
2 T. onions, finely chopped
2 T. margarine or butter
1 T. flour
2/3 c. evaporated milk
1 T. mustard
2 tsp. horseradish
1/4 tsp. salt
dash of pepper
1/2 c. water

Cut cabbage into 4 wedges. Cook in sm. amount of boiling, salted water for 10-12 min.; drain. In a sm. sauce pan cook onion in margarine till tender. Blend in flour, salt and pepper. Add milk and water. Cook and stir till thick and bubbly. Stir in mustard and horseradish. Spoon over cabbage. Top with parsley, if desired. Serves 4.

Katie Ruth

Stuffed Cabbage Rolls

2 lb. hamburger
1 c. rice
2 eggs
salt to taste
pepper to taste
parsley to taste

Mix all together then roll in balls. Steam cabbage leaves then wrap them around the hamburger mixture. Lay them in a casserole and add 2 cans tomato soup; add water as directed on can. Put some tomato sauce on top. Also add sauerkraut, if desired. Bake at 350° for 1-1 1/2 hours.

Ruth Ann Esch

Grandmother's Rice

1 1/2 c. water
1 c. rice
1 tsp. salt
1 tsp. butter
3/4 c. sugar or to taste
1 1/2 qt. milk
1 egg
1 tsp. cornstarch

Cook the first 4 ingredients together slowly until the rice is soft or water all gone. Add the sugar and milk, cook slowly for 1/2 hour. Just before serving add the remaining ingredients. If not thick enough add more cornstarch. Sprinkle cinnamon over rice.

Sylvia Lantz

Creamed Peas and Potatoes

4 med. potatoes, cubed
1 pkg. peas
2 T. butter
2 T. flour
1/2 tsp. salt
pepper
1 1/2 c. milk

Cook potatoes and peas. Melt butter in a sauce pan, add flour, salt and pepper to form a paste. Gradually stir in milk. Bring to a boil. Drain vegetables and lightly stir everything together.

Naomi B. Beiler

Broccoli Cheese Potatoes

6 med. potatoes
1/2 c. sour cream
3 T. butter
1/2 tsp. salt
1/4 tsp. pepper
2 onions
1 1/2 c. broccoli, cooked
1 c. cheddar cheese, shredded
paprika

Bake potatoes at 425° for 45-60 minutes. Cut lengthwise. Slice from the top of the potatoes. Scoop out pulp and place in bowl. Mash potatoes and add sour cream, butter, salt, pepper, onions, broccoli and 3/4 cup cheese. Refill potato shells. Top with cheese and paprika. Bake at 425° for 20-25 minutes.

Barbiann Esch
Rachel Stoltzfus
Linda Ruth Esh

Escalloped Potatoes & Ham

4 c. potatoes, sliced
1 c. ham, cubed
2 1/2 c. milk
1 tsp. salt
1 tsp. flour
pepper to taste

Mix all ingredients in a casserole. Bake 1 to 1 1/2 hours.

Arie King

Scalloped Potatoes

8-9 c. potatoes, shredded
1 tsp. salt
1 can cream of mushroom soup
1 c. cheese, shredded
2 c. milk
1/4 c. margarine
1/2 med. onion

Mix all ingredients in a 9"x13" pan. Sprinkle with pepper. Bake at 350° for 1 1/2 hours.

Anna Zook

Scalloped Potatoes

5 c. boiled potatoes, grated or sliced
1 lg. onion, chopped fine
1 can cream of celery soup
1 soup can of milk
5 T. butter

Boil potatoes in skins. Peel when cold. Either grate or slice the potatoes. Mix with remaining ingredients. Let stand overnight. Bake in oven for 1 1/2 hours at 350°. A handy recipe that you can make the day before.

Linda Stoltzfus

Oven-Crisped Potatoes

4 med. potatoes, peeled & thinly sliced (in wedges)
6 T. butter, melted
2 T. onion, finely chopped
1/4 tsp. pepper

Arrange potatoes in an ungreased baking dish. Combine butter, onion and pepper, pour over potatoes. Bake uncovered at 425° for 1 hour or until potatoes are tender.

Linda Stoltzfus

Mother was wiping Billy's tears, "It's no use" he said, "I'm not finished yet."

Potatoes Supreme

8-10 med. potatoes
1 can cream of chicken soup, undiluted
3 c. shredded cheddar cheese, divided
1 c. sour cream
3 green onions, chopped
salt & pepper to taste

Cook potatoes until almost tender. Drain and cool. Combine soup, 1 1/2 cups cheese, sour cream, onions, salt and pepper; stir in potatoes. Place in a greased 13"x9"x2" baking dish. Sprinkle with remaining cheese. Bake, uncovered, at 350° for 25-30 minutes or until heated through.

Mrs. Elmer Stoltzfus

Potato Casserole

6 med. potatoes
1/2 stick margarine
1 can cream of chicken soup
1/3 c. onion
1/2 pt. sour cream

Cook the potatoes with skins. Let cool, peel than grate or slice. Melt butter in soup over low heat. Add onions and sour cream, mix well. Stir into potatoes. Put in greased casserole. Bake 30 minutes at 350°. Put grated American cheese over top. Return to oven until cheese is melted.

Naomi B. Beiler

Sour Cream & Cheese Potatoes

6 med. potatoes, cook & cool
2 c. cheese (cheddar or Velveeta)
1 1/4 c. sour cream
1/4 c. butter
1/3 c. onion, chopped
1 tsp. salt

Mix cheese, butter and onion in a saucepan. Let it cool and add sour cream. Mix potatoes and sour cream mixture together with paprika. Bake for 25-30 minutes at 350°.

Linda Stoltzfus

Potato Filling

1 c. celery, chopped
1 med. onion, chopped
1/2 c. butter, melted
1 c. water
4 qt. bread cubes
6 eggs, beaten
1 qt. milk
2 tsp. salt
1/2 tsp. pepper
1 qt. mashed potatoes

Bring the first 4 ingredients to a boil and cook for 10 minutes. Mix the remaining ingredients and add to the first mixture, mixing lightly. Pour in greased casserole and bake for 45 minutes at 350°. A delicious way to use up leftover mashed potatoes.

Lena King

Quick Tater Tot Bake

1 lb. ground beef
1 sm. onion, chopped
salt & pepper to taste
1 16 oz. pkg. frozen tater tot potatoes
1 can cream of mushroom soup
1/2 soup can milk or water
1 c. cheddar cheese, shredded

Brown meat and onion, drain the fat. Season with salt and pepper. Place in greased baking pan. Top with potatoes. Combine soup and milk or water. Pour over potatoes. Sprinkle with cheese. Bake at 350° for 30-40 minutes.

Mattie Beiler

Tater-Tot Casserole

2 lb. hamburger
2 tsp. green pepper, chopped
1/2 c. cheese, grated
1/2 c. onion, chopped
2 cans mushroom soup
1 lg. pkg. tater tots
salt & pepper to taste

Add onions and green pepper. Press mixture down in 13"x9" pan. Cover with mushroom soup. Grated Cheese on top. Place tater tots over cheese. Bake 350° for 1 hour. Freezes well.

Susie Blank

Cream Cheese Potatoes

9 lg. potatoes, peeled
6 oz. cream cheese
1 c. sour cream
2 tsp. onion salt
1/4 tsp. pepper
2 T. butter

Salt and cook potatoes till soft, drain. Mash with a little milk till smooth. Add remaining ingredients. Beat until light and fluffy. Place in greased casserole dish. Can be refrigerated for days. Bake at 350° for 45-50 minutes.

Marie Hoover

Sour Cream Mashed Potatoes

5 lb. potatoes
6 oz. cream cheese
1 c. sour cream
2 tsp. onion salt or diced onion
1 tsp. salt
1/4 tsp. pepper
2 T. butter

Cook and mash potatoes and add milk. Add remaining ingredients except butter. Dot top with butter. Bake at 350° for 35 to 40 minutes.

Sadie Fisher

Crunchy Potato Balls

2 c. mashed potatoes (very stiff)
2 c. ham, fully cooked & finely chopped
1 c. cheddar or Swiss cheese, shredded
1/3 c. mayonnaise
1 egg, beaten
1 tsp. prepared mustard
1/4 tsp. pepper
2-4 T. all purpose flour
1 3/4 c. corn flakes, crushed

In a bowl combines the potatoes, ham, cheese. mayonnaise, egg, mustard and pepper; mix well. Add enough of the flour to make a stiff mixture. Chill. Shape into 1" balls and roll in corn flakes. Place on a buttered baking sheet. Bake at 300° for 25-30 minutes. Serve hot.

Mattie Beiler

Potato Balls

4 c. mashed potatoes
4 c. soft bread crumbs
2 eggs, beaten
1/4 c. onion
1/2 c. celery
1/2 c. butter, melted
milk (enough to moisten)
salt & pepper to taste

Mix together all ingredients except milk and butter. Add milk to moisten, form balls. Arrange in flat baking dish. Pour melted butter over all. Bake uncovered for 20 min. at 375°.

Anna Mae Fisher
Sylvia Stoltzfus (Amy)

Golden Parmesan Potatoes

6 lg. potatoes
1/4 c. flour
1/4 c. parmesan cheese
3/4 tsp. salt
1/8 tsp. pepper
1/3 c. butter
parsley

Peel potatoes, cut into quarters. Combine flour, cheese, salt and pepper in a bag. Moisten potatoes with water and shake a few at a time in the bag coating the potatoes well with cheese mixture. Melt butter in a 13"x9" pan. Place potatoes in a layer in the pan. Bake at 375° for about 1 hour turning the potatoes once during baking. When golden brown sprinkle with parsley.

Ruth Esch
Lena King

Ham Stuffed Potatoes

6 lg. baking potatoes
1 c. sour cream
1 c. chipped ham
1 c. American cheese

Bake potatoes in oven till skin is tough and insides tender. Cut in half take the filling out. Mash a little. Mix in the remaining ingredients. Add a little salt & pepper. Put mixture in potatoes skins. Bake them in cupcake pans for 15 minutes.

Ada King

Baked French Fried Potatoes

1 lg. potato
1 T. vegetable oil

Prepare 1 potato for each person. Peel and cut into thin strips. Place in a bowl. Pour 1 T. vegetable oil for each potato over strips, tossing to coat well. Spread out in a single layer on cookie sheet. Broil in a 425° oven for 10 minutes, until lightly browned. Reduce heat to 350° and broil another 20-30 minutes until they are tender. Turn with spatula occasionally. Sprinkle with salt and serve immediately.

Arie Blank

Baked Sweet Potatoes

6 cooked sweet potatoes, canned may be used
1 c. brown sugar, packed
4 T. butter
4 T. water
1/2 tsp. salt

Slice sweet potatoes into baking dish. Make syrup by bringing remaining ingredients to a boil. Pour syrup over potatoes. Bake about 30 minutes at 350°, basting occasionally until syrup thickens and potatoes are glazed.

Lena King

Candied Sweet Potatoes

6 med. sweet potatoes
1 tsp. salt
2 T. butter
3/4 c. water
1 c. light brown sugar
2-3 T. flour

Cook potatoes until almost soft. Remove skins and cut in half length wise. Melt the butter and sugar in a skillet and add the water mixed with flour, bring to a boil and add to sweet potatoes. Bake slowly till liquid is thick and potatoes are brown, about 30 minutes.

Sylvia King (Mervin)
Linda Ruth Esh

Carameled Sweet Potatoes

5 med. sweet potatoes
1 tsp. salt
1 c. brown sugar
2 T. butter
3 T. flour
1 c. thin cream or milk
marshmallows
1/2 c. chopped nuts (optional)

Cook potatoes until tender. Drain and cool. Mash potatoes and mix with salt, sugar, milk and flour. Pour in baking dish and dot with butter. Cover with marshmallows. Bake at 350° for 45-50 minutes.

Amanda Stoltzfus

Sweet Potatoes

5 c. sweet potatoes, mashed
2 eggs
1/3 c. butter, melted
1/2 c. milk
1 tsp. vanilla
1/3 c. butter, melted
1 c. pecans, chopped
1 c. brown sugar
1/4 c. flour

Mix the first 5 ingredients together. Mix the remaining ingredients and put on top of sweet potato mixture. Bake till it bubbles.

Anna Mae Stoltzfus

Sunday Sweet Potatoes

3 c. sweet potatoes, mashed
1 c. sugar
1/2 c. milk
2 eggs
1 tsp. vanilla
1/4 tsp. nutmeg (optional)
1 c. coconut
1 c. pecans
1 c. brown sugar
1/2 c. flour
1/2 c. butter, melted

Mix the first 6 ingredients and put in casserole dish. Blend the remaining ingredients, adding the butter last. Sprinkle over first mixture. Bake at 350° till browned.

Linda Stoltzfus

Creamed Sweet Potato

3 c. cooked sweet potato, mashed or winter squash
3 T. butter
1/3 c. onion, chopped
3 T. flour
1 qt. whole milk
2 chicken bouillon cubes, crushed

Cook onion in butter until clear. Stir in flour. Slowly add milk and cook until mixture thickens slightly. Add bouillon cubes and stir until dissolved. Add mashed sweet potatoes or squash. Heat until hot. You can replace the bouillon cubes with chicken broth and salt, using less milk.

Katie Ruth Esch

Spinach Balls

1 qt. cooked spinach, drained
20 slices bread, cubed
1/2 c. margarine, melted
6 eggs, beaten
1 tsp. salt
2 c. shredded cheese
black pepper
1 tsp. accent
3/4 tsp. garlic powder
1 onion, chopped

Mix together and shape into 2" balls. Bake on a covered cookie sheet. Bake at 350° for 20-30 minutes. Bake only the amount needed and freeze the rest till needed.

Katie Ruth

Baked Corn

2 c. corn, grated
2 eggs, beaten
1 tsp. salt
1/8 tsp. pepper
1 T. sugar
2 T. butter
1 T. flour
1 c. milk

Add salt, sugar, pepper, flour and melted butter to the grated corn. Add eggs and milk. Pour into a greased baking dish and bake at 350° for 35 minutes.

Barbara J. King

Spinach Pie

2 c. seasoned croutons, coarsely crushed
1/4 c. butter, melted
6 T. parmesan cheese, divided
1 oz. spinach, chopped
1 c. small curd cottage cheese
1 c. Monterey jack cheese, shredded
3 eggs, beaten'
2 T. sour cream
1/2 tsp. dried minced onion
1/2 tsp. garlic salt
thin tomato slices

Combine croutons and butter, mix well. Press into the bottom and sides of a 9" pie pan. Combine 1/4 cup parmesan cheese and the remaining ingredients, except the tomato slices. Spoon over crust. Bake at 350° for 40 minutes. Garnish with tomato slices. Sprinkle with remaining parmesan cheese. Let stand 5 minutes before serving.

Mattie Beiler

Homemade Spinach Timbales

2-10 oz. pkg. frozen chopped spinach
4 eggs
1/2 tsp. salt
1 T. lemon juice
1/4 c. sweet cream butter, softened
cheese sauce, if desired

Cook spinach according to package directions; drain. In small mixer bowl beat eggs until foamy. Stir in cooked spinach and remaining ingredients. Divide mixture between 5 greased 6 oz. custard cups. Place custard cups on a rack in 10" skillet. Fill skillet with hot (not boiling) water to 1/2". Cover and cook over medium heat for 18-22 minutes or until knife inserted in center comes out clean. Loosen edge with knife; un-mold.

Rachel Z. Stoltzfus

Barbecued String Beans

1 onion, chopped
5 slices bacon
2 qt. beans
3/4 c. catsup
1/3 c. brown sugar
1 T. mustard
salt & pepper to taste

Fry onion and bacon together. Combine all ingredients and place in casserole. Bake at 350° for 1 hour.

Linda King
Esther Fisher
Sarah Fisher

Barbecued Lima Beans

2 T. butter
2 med. onions, chopped
1 tsp. vinegar
2 T. brown sugar
1 T. flour
1 c. catsup
1 c. or more water
1 qt. lima beans

Fry onions in butter. Add vinegar, brown sugar and flour, mix well. Add catsup and water. Cook limas in salt water until tender, drain. Add sauce and bake 30-35 minutes at 325°. Fry ham with onions, if desired.

Sadie Lapp

Stove Top Beans

3 c. cooked navy beans
1 c. cream
3 T. butter
5 slices Velveeta cheese
1/2 c. brown sugar
1/2 c. ketchup
2 tsp. mustard
1 sm. onion, chopped

Cook on top of stove till well heated and cheese is melted. Add hotdogs.

Elizabeth Kauffman

Serving with pleasure makes duty a delight.

Baked Stuffed Peppers

3-4 peppers
1/2 lb. ground beef
1/4 c. uncooked rice
1/2 tsp. salt
dash of pepper
1/2 tsp. Worcestershire sauce
1 T. onion, chopped
1 egg
1 8 oz can tomato sauce (with cheese optional)

Halve large peppers or cut tops off small ones and remove seeds and membrane. Precook peppers in salted boiling water for about 1 minute and drain. Combine ground beef, rice, salt, pepper, Worcestershire sauce, onion, egg and 1/4 of the tomato sauce. Mix thoroughly. Stuff peppers and place in a small casserole. Pour remaining tomato sauce over stuffed peppers. Cover and bake. Baste peppers with sauce 2-3 times during baking. Bake for 45-50 minutes at 350°

Rebecca Speicher

Stuffed Green Peppers

5-6 med. peppers
3/4 c. uncooked rice
1 lb. ground beef
1 med. onion, chopped
1 8 oz can tomato sauce
1/4 tsp. dried basil
1/4 tsp. dried oregano
1/4 tsp. dried thyme
1/2 tsp. salt
pepper to taste
1/2 tsp. instant beef bouillon

Remove tops and seeds from peppers. In large kettle bring water to a boil, cook peppers for 5 minutes, remove and drain. Cook rice according to directions. Brown beef and onion, drain. Add tomato sauce, herbs, salt and pepper, cook 5 minutes. Stir in rice. Stuff peppers with rice mixture. Place upright in a shallow baking dish. Bake at 375° for 15-20 minutes. Leftover peppers will freeze well to enjoy later.

Mrs. Elmer Stoltzfus

Country Style Stuffed Peppers

1 4.5 oz pkg. Uncle Ben's Country Inn Broccoli Rice Au Gratin
1 3/4 c. water
2 T. butter
1 1/2 c. cooked ham, cubed
2 lg. green peppers

Combine rice, seasoning packets, water and butter in a medium sauce pan, bring to a boil, cover tightly and simmer 20 min. Stir in ham, cover and remove from heat. Let stand 5 min. While rice cooks, cut green peppers in half lengthwise, remove seeds. Boil in salt water for 5 min, drain well. Fill pepper halves with hot rice mixture.

Katie Mae Stoltzfus

Bacon Stuffed Mushrooms

1 lb. fresh mushrooms
2 T. butter
1 c. cheese
2 T. onion, chopped
1 slice bread, shredded
1 c. real bacon crumbs

Remove stems from mushrooms and set aside caps. Cook onions and chopped mushroom stems till tender, add bread. Remove from heat and add bacon and cheese. Mound filling into caps. Place on cookie sheet. Bake at 400° for 15 minutes or until cheese is melted.

Amos and Naomi Beiler

Carrot Drum Sticks

2 c. cooked mashed carrots
2 scant c. cracker crumbs
3 eggs, well beaten
1 onion, chopped
1/2 c. celery, chopped
salt & pepper to taste

Mix well and form into drum sticks. Roll in cracker crumbs. Fry in real hot Crisco or butter. Makes 18. Can also put in a greased casserole and put cracker crumbs on top, dot with butter. Bake at 350° for 30-35 minutes. Sweet potatoes can also be used, instead of carrots.

Sylvia Esch

Pasta Primavera with a Twist

1 can condensed cream of chicken & broccoli soup
1/2 c. milk
1/4 c. parmesan cheese, grated
1/8 tsp. garlic powder
1/8 tsp. pepper
2 c. broccoli flowerets
2 med. carrots, sliced
2 1/2 c. macaroni, cooked
2 5 oz. cans chunk white chicken

In sauce pan mix soup, milk, cheese, garlic powder, pepper, broccoli and carrots. Heat to a boil, cover and cook over low heat 5 minutes or until vegetables are tender crisp, stirring occasionally. Add macaroni and drained chicken. Heat through. Serve 4.

Anna Mae Fisher

Cheese Sauce

2 T. butter, melted
2 T. flour
2 c. milk
1/2 tsp. salt
1/8 tsp. pepper
1 c. cheese, diced

Melt butter in saucepan. Stir in flour, then add half the milk, stir rapidly to remove lumps. Add the remaining milk. Cook for 1 minute; stirring constantly. Add cheese and stir until cheese is melted. Cheese sauce is good with many different vegetables. Pour it over the vegetables just before serving.

Linda Stoltzfus

Mother is the blossom...
Radiant, complete.
The children are the tiny buds...
Delicate and sweet.
Father is the sturdy stem...
That holds them straight and tall.
Love is the root that gives them life
and nourishes them all.

Corn Fritters

1 pt. sweet corn, grated
1 c. flour
1 tsp. baking powder
1/2 tsp. salt
dash of pepper
1 egg, beat separate

Mix together and fry in deep fat.

Naomi King (Jake)
Barbiann Esch

Corn Fritters

2 c. creamed corn
2 eggs
1 c. flour or cracker dust
2 T. sugar
2 tsp. baking powder
1 tsp. salt
1/8 tsp. pepper

Mix together and fry in deep fat until golden brown.

Amanda Stoltzfus
Katie Zook

Corn Fritters

1/2 doz. big ears of corn
2 eggs
1/2 tsp. salt
1 c. flour
1 c. milk
pepper to taste

Cut corn off cob over salad cutter. Mix well and drop by tablespoons into fry pan with melted butter or lard.

Arie King

Corn Puffs

2 c. corn, grated
2 eggs
1/2 c. flour
1/2 c. milk
1 T. sugar
1 tsp. salt
1/8 tsp. pepper
1 tsp. baking powder
1 1/4 c. cracker crumbs

Mix together and fry in deep fat.

Annie Lapp

Onion Patties

3/4 c. flour
2 tsp. baking powder
1 T. sugar
1 tsp. salt
1 T. cornmeal
1 1/2 c. onions, finely chopped
milk

Mix ingredients together using enough milk to make a thick batter. Drop by tablespoons into deep hot fat. Fry to a golden brown on both sides. Flatten patties slightly when turning them.

Katie Ruth

Onion Rings

onions
1/2 c. flour
1/4 tsp. salt
1/2 tsp. baking powder
1 egg, lightly beaten
1/2 c. Mazola oil
1/4 c. milk

Cut onions into rings. Mix remaining ingredients. Dip onion rings into mixture and fry in deep fat.

Esther Fisher

Onion Rings

1 egg, beaten
1/2 c. water
2 tsp. lemon juice
1 T. vegetable oil
1/2 c. corn meal
1/2 c. flour
1/2 tsp. salt
1 1/2 tsp. baking powder

Beat together egg, water, lemon juice and oil. Mix ingredients together. Dip onion rings into mixture and deep fat fry.

Anna Zook

If planning to do a mean thing,
Wait until tomorrow.
If a good thing
Do it today.

Fried Pumpkin or Eggplant

pumpkin
egg
cracker crumbs
vegetable oil

Beat the egg and dip thinly sliced pumpkin into it. Coat the pumpkin slice with cracker crumbs and fry in vegetable oil, about 1/4" of oil on bottom of the pan. Good eaten plain or in a sandwich. Try making zucchini, squash or cucumbers this way.

Katie Ruth Esch

Sweet Potato Patties

2 c. sweet potatoes, cooked and mashed
1/2 c. brown sugar
1 tsp. salt

Form into patties and roll in saltine cracker crumbs. Fry in butter until nice and brown on both sides.

Naomi Lapp

Zucchini Patties

2 c. zucchini, grated
2 T. onion, grated
2 eggs, beaten
1 tsp. salt
1/2 tsp. pepper or season-all
1/4 c. cheese, grated (optional)
1/2 c. cracker crumbs
1 T. vegetable oil

Mix together and fry in butter.

Sylvia Esch

If any lift of mine can ease
The burden of another,
God give me love and care and strength
To help my ailing brother.

Asparagus Casserole

1 1/2 c. asparagus, cooked & drained
1/4 c. butter
1/4 c. flour
1/2 tsp. salt
dash of pepper
2 1/2 c. milk
1 c. cheese, cubed
1 T. brown sugar
3 eggs, hard cooked & sliced

Melt butter, remove from heat and stir in flour, salt and pepper. Gradually stir in milk, bring to a boil stirring constantly. Add cheese and brown sugar. Pour over asparagus and cooked eggs. Top with butter crumbs (optional). Bake at 325° 25-30 minutes.

Annie Lapp
Lena King
Linda King

Carrot Casserole

3 c. carrots, cooked
3 T. butter
3 T. flour
1/4 tsp. pepper
1 c. milk
1 c. Velveeta cheese, diced

Mix flour, pepper, butter and milk in pan. Cook until thick, add cheese. Heat until cheese is melted. Put carrots in greased casserole. Add sauce and top with bread crumbs. Bake at 350° for 15 minutes or until heated.

Ruth Ann Esch

It's the little things we do and say
That mean so much as we go our way,
A kindly deed can lift a load
From weary shoulders on the road.

Carrot Casserole

4 c. carrots, cooked & sliced
salt & pepper to taste
1 1/2 c. buttered bread crumbs
1-2 T. butter
1 T. flour
1 c. milk
1/2 tsp. salt
1/8 tsp. pepper
1/2 c. Velveeta cheese, grated

Combine carrots, salt and pepper in greased casserole. Melt butter. Add flour, salt and pepper, stir until smooth. Slowly add milk stirring constantly, cook until thick and smooth. Add cheese and stir until melted. Pour over carrots and top with buttered crumbs. Bake at 350° for 25-30 min.

Linda Stoltzfus
Lena King

Carrot Casserole

1 qt. carrots
1 can cream of celery soup
Velveeta cheese
bread crumbs
butter

Cook carrots, drain. Mix with soup and put in casserole. Put one layer Velveeta cheese on top and cover with crumbs that have been browned in butter.

Anna Mae Stoltzfus

Cabbage & Beef Casserole

1 lg. head cabbage, shredded
1/4 c. butter
1 med. onion, chopped
1 1/2 c. cooked rice
1 1/2 lb. ground beef
1 1/2 tsp. salt
1/4 tsp. pepper
1/2 c. milk
2 cans cream of mushroom soup
buttered bread crumbs

Boil cabbage a few minutes in salt water. Sauté onion in butter, add to drained cabbage. Brown beef with salt and pepper, add rice. Butter a large casserole dish and place layer of meat on bottom, alternate with cabbage, ending with meat on top. Combine soup with milk and pour over casserole, add bread crumbs. Bake at 350° for 1 hour.

Sylvia Esch

Eggplant Casserole

1 1/2 c. eggplant, cooked and mashed
3/4 c. grated cheese
3 c. bread cubes or 2/3 c. bread crumbs
3 T. butter, melted
1 tsp. salt
dash of pepper
3 eggs
1 c. milk

Mix together. Bake 1 hour at 350°.

Linda Ruth Esh
Elizabeth Kauffman

Golden Mushroom Casserole

5-7 pieces cubed bread
1/4 c. peppers, chopped
1/4 c. margarine or butter
1/2 c. salad dressing
2 eggs
3 c. fresh mushrooms, sliced
1/2 c. celery
1/2 c. onion
1/4 tsp. salt
1/8 tsp. pepper
1/2 c. milk

Combine celery, peppers and butter in a skillet, cook and stir until tender. Add onions and mushrooms, stir till tender. Put in 2 quart casserole. Add bread cubes. Mix eggs, milk, salad dressing, salt and pepper. Beat together. Pour over bread cubes, mix lightly. Cover and refrigerate overnight or for several hours. Bake uncovered at 350° for 3/4 hour or until center is set.

Lena King

When God puts a tear in your eye, it's because He wants to put a rainbow in your heart.

Squash Casserole

3 c. squash
1 c. Bisquick
1 onion, chopped
1/2 c. oil
4 eggs, beaten
1 tsp. salt
1 tsp. garlic
1/2 c. grated cheese

Cook squash, drain and mash. Add remaining ingredients. Pour into a greased casserole. Bake at 350° for 30-45 minutes.

Arie Speicher

Tomato Casserole

tomatoes
pepper rings
onion rings
sugar
salt & pepper
bread crumbs

Slice raw tomatoes into a cake pan. Over those arrange pepper and onion rings. Season with sugar, salt and pepper. Cover with bread crumbs, seasoned with salt, pepper and butter as for filling. Bake at 350° for 1-1 1/2 hours.

Annie King

Potato Cheese Pie

2 1/2 c. leftover mashed potatoes
2 T. flour
1 tsp. baking powder
1 egg
2 T. butter, melted
dash of salt & pepper
2 eggs, beaten
1 c. sour cream
3/4 c. Velveeta cheese, grated

Mix the first 6 ingredients for crust. Press into a pie plate or casserole. Mix remaining ingredients and pour into crust. Bake at 350° for 30 minutes or until it seems baked in center.

Naomi Lapp

Pinwheel Vegetable Casserole

4 slices bread
5 oz. cheese spread, softened
1 T. milk
1 qt. vegetables of your choice
1/2 c. rich milk or cream
2 T. flour
1 tsp. salt
1 T. butter
1 c. ham, cooked and diced

Cut crusts from bread then flatten slightly with palm of hand so it doesn't break when rolling up. Mix milk with cheese spread. Spread on bread. Roll bread up like jelly roll, wrap up and refrigerate. Cook vegetables till almost tender, let 1/2 cup liquid remain with vegetables. Shake milk with flour in shaker until smooth, pour over vegetables stirring to thickened. Add remaining ingredients. Pour into a 2 quart casserole dish. Make the pinwheels by slicing the bread cheese rolls into 1/4"-1/2" thick slices. Arrange over the top of the casserole. Bake at 375° just until bubbly and pinwheels are browned. This is an attractive way to serve vegetables to guests.

Arie Blank

Vegetable Cheese Casserole

4 c. green beans, cooked
2 c. ham, cooked & diced
1 1/2 c. milk
1/2 c. grated cheese
buttered bread crumbs or cubes
2 T. flour
1/2 tsp. salt
2 T. butter

Place green beans and ham into a buttered baking dish. Cover with a white sauce made of milk, butter, flour and salt. Sprinkle with grated cheese and top with buttered bread cubes. Bake at 400° for 15 minutes. Variation: in place of green beans use broccoli, cauliflower or asparagus.

Lena Riehl

Zucchini Casserole

4 c. zucchini, grated
1 c. Bisquick
1/3 c. oil
1/2 c. or more grated cheese
1/2 tsp. garlic powder
1 T. parsley flakes, if desired
4 eggs, beaten
onions

Mix and bake at 350° for about 1 hour.

Sadie Lapp

Zucchini Casserole

3 c. zucchini, grated
1/2-1 onion, chopped
1/2 c. vegetable oil
4 eggs, beaten
1 c. Bisquick or 1 c. flour & 1 tsp. baking powder
1/2 c. Velveeta cheese
1/2 tsp. garlic powder
1 tsp. salt
2 T. parsley (optional)

Bake at 350° for 1 hour.

Linda King

Zucchini Casserole

4 c. zucchini, peeled
1 c. onion, diced
1 can cream of celery or mushroom soup
1 c. grated cheese
1/2 c. butter, melted
3/4 c. soft bread crumbs

Cook zucchini and onion on low heat until tender, drain. Add soup and cheese. Put into casserole. Melt butter, add crumbs and put on top of casserole. Bake at 350° for 20 minutes.

Annie King

Yesterday is a cancelled check. Tomorrow is a promissory note. Today is ready cash. Use it wisely.

Zucchini Casserole

4 c. zucchini, grated
3/4 c. Bisquick
2 tsp. parsley
1 tsp. salt
1/8 tsp. pepper
3 eggs, beaten
1/2 c. onion
1/2 c. oil
1 tsp. oregano
1/2 c. grated cheese
1 c. pizza sauce

Mix everything together except the cheese and sauce. Bake at 350° for 30 minutes. Remove from oven. Spread cheese and sauce on top and put back in oven another 5 minutes.

Ada King

Zucchini Stuffing

5-6 c. zucchini, shredded
1 sm. onion, chopped
1 tsp. parsley flakes
1 tsp. dried basil
2 eggs, beaten
1 tsp. salt
1/8 tsp. pepper
3 T. margarine, melted
12-14 slices bread cubes
1 c. cheese, shredded (optional)

Place zucchini in colander, mix with 1 tsp. salt. Let stand 15 minutes. Using hands, squeeze the excess moisture from the zucchini. Mix all ingredients, add zucchini and mix well. The stuffing will seem dry, but the zucchini will make more liquid when baked. Pour into greased casserole dish. Bake covered at 350° for 1 hour and 20 minutes. Serve with chicken.

Katie Ruth Esch

Baked Beans

2 c. great northern beans, cooked
1/4 lb. bacon
1/4 c. catsup
1 tsp. salt
1/4 tsp. garlic
3 T. brown sugar
1/4 c. molasses
2 T. onion, chopped
1/2 tsp. dry mustard

Mix altogether and bake 1 1/2 hours.

Annie Lapp

Baked Beans

1 lb. dry baby limas
1 lb. bacon
1 c. catsup
1 c. brown sugar
1 c. corn syrup

Cut bacon into small pieces. Combine bacon, dried limas and water in kettle and cook till beans are soft. Do not presoak beans. Add remaining ingredients. Bake 2 hours at 300°.

Amos and Naomi Beiler

Quick Baked Beans

2 16 oz. cans baked beans
1/4 c. brown sugar
1/2 tsp. mustard
1/2 c. ketchup
2 sm. onions, chopped
1 tsp. Worcestershire sauce
bacon, hot dog or sausage slices

Stir all together except the bacon. Put in baking dish, top with bacon slices. Bake at 350° for 1 hour.

Anna Mae Stoltzfus

Bread Pot Fondue

1 round loaf of bread dough
2 c. sharp cheddar cheese, shredded
6 oz. cream cheese, softened
1 1/2 c. sour cream
1 c. cooked ham, diced
1/2 c. onions, chopped
1 4 oz. can green chilies
1 tsp. Worcestershire sauce
2 T. vegetable oil
1 T. butter, melted
peppers & celery, optional

Bake bread dough in a round casserole at 325° for 45 min. Cool, cut off top crust and replace the inside bread with the remaining ingredients. Put the top crust on again and wrap in aluminum foil. Bake at 350° for 70 min. Cube the reserved bread and mix it with 2 T. veg. oil & 1 T. melted butter. Bake at 350° till browned, about 10-15 min. The filling is used as a dip for the cubes, crackers or vegetables.

Elizabeth Kauffman

Sweet and Sour Beans

10 pieces bacon
3 med. onions, chopped
1/2-1 c. brown sugar
1 tsp. mustard
1 tsp. salt
1/4 c. vinegar
3 c. green string beans, cooked
1 lb. 11 oz. can pork and beans
2 1 lb. cans kidney beans

Fry bacon and crumble. Add remaining ingredients except beans, to bacon drippings and simmer 20 minutes. Combine with bacon and beans. Bake at 350° till they are ready to eat.

Anna Mae Fisher

Mexican Stew

1 lb. hamburger
1 can tomatoes
1 can kidney beans
2 bay leaves
2 onions, chopped
2 c. water
3 tsp. chili powder
salt to taste

Combine ingredients. Simmer 1 1/2 hours or till thick.

Arie King

Corny Good Chili

1 lb. ground beef
1 med. onion
1 lg. green pepper
1 15 1/2 oz. can kidney beans, rinsed and drained
2 c. whole kernel corn, fresh or frozen
1 pt. tomato juice
1/4 c. brown sugar
1 T. vinegar
1 T. chili
1 16 oz. can pork and beans

In a Dutch oven brown ground beef, onion and pepper, cook until tender, drain. Add remaining ingredients. Simmer until heated through. Add a little water if necessary. Yields about 6 servings.

Naomi B. Beiler

Wild West Chili

2 bacon strips, diced
1 lb. ground beef or venison
2 tsp. chili powder
1 1/2 tsp. salt
1/4 tsp. garlic salt
1/8 tsp. dried oregano
3-5 drops hot pepper sauce
1-14 1/2 oz. can diced tomatoes
1 c. celery, finely chopped
1 c. onion, finely chopped
1 c. carrots, finely chopped
1/2 c. green pepper, finely chopped
1 16 oz. can chili beans, un-drained

In large saucepan over medium heat, brown bacon and the beef, drain. Add the seasonings. Cook and stir for 5 minutes. Stir in un-drained tomatoes, celery, onion, carrot and green pepper, bring to a boil. Reduce heat. Cover and simmer for 40 minutes. Stir in beans. Cook 30 minutes longer.

Arie King

Chicken Chili

3 T. olive oil
2 onions, diced
1 tsp. oregano
2 1/2 T. chili powder
2 tsp. ground cumin
1/4 tsp. cayenne pepper
1 1/2 c. water
1 1/2 c. chicken broth
1 24 oz. can stewed tomatoes
1 tsp. sugar
1 tsp. salt
1 bay leaf
1 T. cornmeal
2 lb. chicken, cut up
1 bag whole kernel corn, frozen
2 cans string beans

Put olive oil over heat, add onions and cook 5 minutes. Add chili powder, cumin, oregano and cayenne, cook 1-2 minutes. Stir in chicken broth, add tomatoes, water, sugar, salt and bay leaf, bring to a boil and simmer 40 minutes. Remove bay leaf. Slowly sprinkle cornmeal over liquid and add chicken, corn and string beans, bring to a boil and simmer 5 minutes.

Rachel Stoltzfus
Kate Stoltzfus (Steve)

Main Dishes

If We Want To Be Simple Folks

If we want to be simple folks
Let's have simple meals,
And not just cook for honor..
Merely foods that appeal.

To taste-for me must eat
Each day life to sustain,
The simpler that we eat and live
The more we stand to gain.

Christ fed the multitude on fish,
The bread He did not spare.
Simple food for hunger's sake..
To show His love and care.

We thank Him for the lavish meal
And gorge down all the frills,
We pay the price-our sacrifice
In ruined health and all the doctor bills.

Yumzetta

1 pkg. med. size noodles
3 lb. hamburger
1 pt. peas
2 cans mushroom soup
1 can celery soup
1 c. sour cream
buttered bread crumbs

Butter a pan and put in a layer of noodles, a layer of hamburger and a layer of peas. Mix soups and sour cream and pour over top of layers. Top with buttered bread crumbs. Bake 1 hour at 300°.

Lena King

Yumzetta

1 lb. hamburger, browned
1 bag peas, cooked
noodles, cooked
cream of mushroom soup

Brown the hamburger, add salt and pepper. Cook the peas, add salt. Put the first 3 ingredients in a casserole large enough and mix with cream of mushroom soup. Bake at 350° for 25 minutes.

Arie Speicher

Wigglers

3 lb. hamburger
3 onions
3 c. potatoes, diced
3 c. celery, diced
3 c. carrots, diced
1 c. peas
3 c. wigglers or macaroni
2 c. tomato or V-8 juice
2 c. Velveeta cheese, grated
2 cans cream of celery soup
buttered bread cubes, if desired

Fry hamburger and onions until brown. Cook vegetables separately. Cook wigglers. Mix everything together. Top with buttered bread crumbs, if desired. Bake at 350° for 1 hour and 30 minutes.

Linda King

Pizza Casserole

1 lb. hamburger
1/2 c. onion
1 tsp. oregano
1/2 tsp. salt
1 can condensed tomato soup
1/3 c. water
2 c. wide noodles, cooked
1/2 c. cheese

Fry the hamburger with the spices. Add the soup, water and noodles. Top with cheese. Bake at 350° for 1/2 hour.

Marie Hoover

Cheeseburger Bake

1/2 lb. macaroni
10 oz. sharp cheese, grated
2 T. butter
1 c. milk
1 can golden mushroom soup
1 lb. ground beef
2 T. onion, chopped

Cook macaroni in salted water and drain. While macaroni is hot, stir in grated cheese. Set aside. Brown meat and onion in butter. Stir in soup and milk. Grease a 2 1/2 quart casserole. Layer half of the cheese mixture and meat mixture, repeat layers. Bake at 350° for about 25 minutes. Serves 4-6.

Annie Lapp

Hamburger Helper

1 lb. ground beef
3 c. hot water
1 1/2 c. macaroni
1 tsp. salt
a little pepper
1 tsp. chili powder
1/4 tsp. celery seed
Velveeta cheese
onion, chopped (optional)

Brown meat with onions. Add hot water and seasonings. When water boils, stir in macaroni. Simmer until macaroni is soft. Add Velveeta cheese to suit your taste.

Annie Lapp

Hamburg Filling Casserole

1/4 lb. butter
3 pieces celery
1 sm. onion
1 1/2 qt. bread, diced
2 eggs
1/2 c. milk
1 lb. hamburger
1 can cream of mushroom soup

Melt butter and add diced celery and onion. Dice bread and add beaten eggs and milk. Brown hamburger and add salt and pepper. Put 3 layers filling and 2 layers hamburger. Pour mushroom soup on top. Bake 1 hour at 350°.

Katie Ruth Esch

Beef n' Bean Casserole

1 lb. ground beef
1 can cream of mushroom soup
1 med. onion, chopped
1 tsp. garlic salt
1 tsp. onion salt
1 qt. green beans, cooked and drained
cheese

Brown beef and onion. Add cream of mushroom soup, garlic salt and onion salt. Line greased casserole with cheese. Add 1/2 of the green beans and 1/2 of the meat mixture, repeat. Top with cheese. Bake at 350° for 20 minutes serves 6.

Anna Mary Smucker

It's right to be contented with what you have but never with what you are.

Beef and Biscuit Casserole

3/4 lb. ground beef
1/4 c. onion
1/8 c. peppers
1 8 oz. tomato sauce
1 egg, slightly beaten
3/4 c. shredded cheese
1 tsp. chili powder
1 clove garlic
1 can buttermilk biscuits
1/4 c. sour cream

Brown beef, onion and peppers. Stir in tomato sauce, chili powder and garlic. Combine 1/2 of the cheese, sour cream and egg. Mix well into meat mixture. Spread half of the biscuits on the bottom of a deep baking dish. Put remaining biscuits on top. Sprinkle rest of the cheese on top of biscuits. Bake uncovered at 350° for 25-30 minutes or until biscuits are medium brown.

Barbiann Esch

Macaroni Dried Beef Casserole

1 c. macaroni, uncooked
1 can cream of mushroom soup
1 1/2 c. milk
1 1/4 lb. dried beef or ham
1 c. grated cheese
3 T. onion, chopped
1 1/2 c. frozen peas

Mix together. Put into a greased casserole. Let set overnight or for several hours. Bake, uncovered, at 350° for 1 hour.

Lena King

Tuna Noodle Casserole

2 c. noodles
1 tsp. salt
1 7 oz. can tuna fish
1 10 oz. can cream of mushroom soup
1/2 c. milk
1 pkg. frozen peas or 2 c. canned peas
1/4 c. bread crumbs

Cook noodles. Grease casserole dish. Arrange tuna, noodles, peas and soup in layers. Mix in milk. Top with bread crumbs. Bake at 350° for 35 minutes.

Elizabeth Kauffman
Esther Fisher

Tuna Noodle Crispy

1/2 lb. Velveeta cheese, cubed
1 can cream of mushroom soup
1-6 1/2 oz can tuna
1/2 c. saltines, crushed
1/2 c. milk
2 c. noodles, cooked
dash of pepper
2 T. butter, melted

Heat cheese, soup and milk over low heat, stir until smooth. Add tuna, noodles and pepper, mix well. Pour into a 2 quart casserole. Top with saltines tossed with butter. Bake 30 minutes at 325°.

Elsie Fisher

One Dish Meal

1 lb. noodles
2 lb. ground beef
1 c. onions, chopped
1 can cream of celery soup
1 can cream of mushroom soup
1 can tomato juice
1 sm. jar cheese whiz
peas, cook and drain (optional)

Bake 1/2 to 1 hour at 350°.

Anna Mae Stoltzfus

Meal In One

1 round steak
5 med. potatoes
2 sm. onions, sliced
1 can cream of mushroom soup

Place steak in casserole. Slice pared potatoes on top of steak. Slice onions on top of the potatoes. Pour soup over all. Salt and pepper to taste. Add carrots, if desired. Bake at 375° for 2 hours.

Annie King

Walk softly.
Speak tenderly.
Pray Fervently.

Six Layer Supper

potatoes, raw, sliced (thick layer)
1/2 c. rice, uncooked
onions, sliced (thick layer)
carrots, sliced
1 lb. ground beef
1 qt. tomatoes, canned
1 T. brown sugar

Place all ingredients in a casserole in order given. Bake 2 1/2 hours at 350°.

Annie King

Six Layer Casserole

2 c. potatoes, sliced
2 c. carrots, sliced
1 med. onion, chopped
1 lb. ground chuck, fry and drain
Velveeta cheese slices
1 can cream of mushroom soup, undiluted

Layer ingredients in order given in a casserole dish. Bake at 350° for 1 hour and 30 minutes.

Sylvia Stoltzfus (Gid)

Haystack

Ritz crackers, crushed
barbecued hamburger
cooked rice
lettuce
carrots, grated
celery, chopped
bacon, cooked and crumbled
onion, diced
cheese, grated
hot cheese sauce
2 T. butter, melted
2 T. flour
2 c. milk
1/2 tsp. salt
1/8 tsp. pepper
1 c. cheese, diced

Fill separate dishes with the first 10 ingredients. To make the 10th ingredient (hot cheese sauce); Melt butter in saucepan. Stir in flour, add half the milk. Stir rapidly to remove all lumps, add remainder of milk. Cook for 1 minute, stirring constantly. Add 1 cup diced cheese, stir till cheese is melted. Pass the dishes around in order given and each can make their own Haystack. A meal in itself!

Linda Stoltzfus

Haystack Dinner

corn chips, broken
barbecue
rice or potatoes
corn chips, broken
lettuce
tomatoes, chopped
onions, chopped
pickles, chopped
hot cheese sauce

Prepare barbecue and add 2 small cans of baked beans. Cook rice or mashed potatoes. Prepare cheese sauce by making a white sauce with flour and milk and adding cheese. To serve stack the ingredients in layers in order given.

Elizabeth Kauffman

Baked Macaroni and Cheese

1 8 oz. pkg. macaroni
1/2 lb. Velveeta cheese
1 c. dry bread crumbs
3 T. butter
3 T. flour
2 c. milk
1/2 tsp. salt
1/8 tsp. pepper

Cook macaroni in salt water. Make a sauce with the last 5 ingredients. Add 2/3 of cheese to the sauce and stir until melted. Combine cooked macaroni with the sauce and pour into a greased baking dish. Chopped pepper, onion, celery or parsley may be added for variation. Sprinkle crumbs and remaining cheese over the top. Bake in moderate oven 325°-350° for 15-20 minutes.

Arie King

A temper is a valuable possession, don't lose it.

Hearty Cheese and Bacon Pie

1 1/2 c. shredded wheat biscuits, crumbled (4 lg. biscuits)
2 c. natural cheddar or process American cheese, shredded
6 slices bacon, crisply cooked and crumbled
3 T. butter, melted
1 1/2 c. milk
3 eggs
1/8 tsp. pepper
1/8 tsp. paprika

Heat oven to 350°. In medium bowl stir together the crumbled shredded wheat and butter. Press on bottom and sides of a greased and floured 9" pie pan. Sprinkle with bacon and 1 cup cheese. In small mixer bowl combine remaining ingredients except remaining 1 cup cheese and paprika. Beat at low speed, scraping bowl often, until well mixed, 1-2 minutes. Pour into crust. Sprinkle with remaining 1 cup cheese and paprika. Bake for 30-40 minutes or until center is firm to the touch. Let stand 10 minutes before serving. Yield: 6 servings.

Rachel Z. Stoltzfus

Taco Squares

1 c. Bisquick
1/4 c. water
3/4 lb. hamburger
1/4 c. onion
1/4 c. peppers
tomato, chopped
1/3 c. mayonnaise
1/2 c. sour cream
3/4 c. grated cheese

Mix the Bisquick and water together, pat into pan. Brown the hamburger, onion and peppers. Put into pan. Top with chopped tomato. Mix the mayonnaise, sour cream and grated cheese, spread over tomato. Bake at 350° for 25-30 minutes.

Martha Smucker

Impossible Taco Pie

1 lb. ground beef, fried
1/2 c. onion, chopped
1/2 env. taco seasoning mix
1 1/4 c. milk
3/4 c. Bisquick mix
3 eggs
2 c. mozzarella, shredded
1/2 c. cheddar, shredded
2 tomatoes, sliced
2 c. lettuce, shredded
1/2 c. sour cream

Mix the milk, Bisquick mix and eggs. Bake for 25 minutes. Spread sour cream on baked Bisquick then add beef. Cover whole pie with cheese. Bake 8-10 minutes longer. Top with lettuce and tomato.

Anna Mary Smucker

Hearty Ham Pie

1/2 c. fresh broccoli, chopped
1/4 c. green pepper, chopped
1/4 c. fresh mushrooms, chopped
3 T. onions, chopped
1 garlic clove, minced
2 tsp. vegetable oil
2 c. ham, chopped
1 1/2 c. cheese, shredded
1 unbaked pastry shell (9")
4 eggs
1 c. light cream

In a saucepan, sauté the broccoli, green pepper, mushrooms, onion and garlic in oil until tender. Sprinkle half of the ham and cheese into pie crust. Cover with the vegetables and the remaining ham and cheese. Combine eggs and cream, pour over ham and cheese. Bake at 350° for 45-50 minutes or until knife inserted near the center comes out clean.

Amanda Stoltzfus

Today is the tomorrow you worried about yesterday.

Quick Chicken Pie

1 qt. chicken meat	2 c. flour
1 pkg. mixed vegetables	2 tsp. baking powder
3 T. butter	2 T. shortening
3 T. flour	1 tsp. salt
2 c. chicken broth	1 egg
1 c. milk	1 c. milk

Mix the butter, 3 tablespoons flour, chicken broth and 1 cup milk and cook until thick, pour over chicken and vegetables. Mix the remaining ingredients, spread over chicken. Bake at 350° for 30 minutes or until done.

Elizabeth Petersheim

Chicken Pie

3 T. butter	2 c. flour, sifted
3 T. flour	3 tsp. baking powder
1 tsp. salt	1 tsp. salt
1/8 tsp. pepper	1 tsp. paprika
2 c. milk	1/3 c. shortening
2 c. chicken, cook and chopped	2/3 c. milk
1 1/2 pt. frozen vegetables	

Melt butter in saucepan, stir in 3 tablespoons flour, 1 teaspoon salt and pepper. Remove from heat and gradually stir in 2 cups milk. Return to heat and cook until smooth and slightly thick, stirring constantly. Add chicken and vegetables. Pour into baking dish. Mix remaining ingredients and roll out. Cover the chicken and vegetables. Cut in slits to allow steam to escape. Bake at 425° for 20 minutes or until golden brown.

Kate Stoltzfus (Steve)

There's nothing wrong in having nothing to say, unless you insist on saying it.

Chicken Pie with Corn Bread Top

1 lb. chicken meat, cut-up
1/2 c. chicken broth
3 med. carrots, sliced and cook
1/4 c. butter
1 sm. onion, sliced
1 lg. clove garlic, minced
1/4 tsp. black pepper
8 oz. mushroom, sliced
2 T. all purpose flour
1/2 c. heavy cream
1/4 c. fresh parsley, chopped
1/2 c. yellow cornmeal
1/2 c. all purpose flour
1 tsp. baking powder
1/4 tsp. baking soda
1 lg. egg
3/4 c. buttermilk
1 T. butter, melted

Preheat oven to 425°. In skillet, melt 1/4 cup butter over medium-high heat. Add onion, garlic and pepper, cook, stirring frequently for 5 minutes. Add mushrooms. cook, stirring frequently for 5 minutes. Stir in flour, cook for 1 minute. Gradually stir in broth and cream. Bring to a boil, cook, stirring constantly until thickened for 1 minute. Remove from heat, stir in chicken, carrots and parsley. Spoon into baking dish. To prepare topping; Mix together cornmeal, flour, soda and baking powder. Mix together egg, buttermilk and melted butter. Stir into flour mixture just until dry ingredients are moistened. Spoon batter over chicken. Bake pie until topping is golden brown. 30 minutes.

Mattie Beiler

Chicken Rice Casserole

1 c. chicken, cooked
1 c. rice, cooked
1 pt. peas, limas or carrots
onion
butter
1 T. flour
1 tsp. salt
dash of pepper
2 c. milk
buttered bread crumbs

Layer the first 3 ingredients into casserole. Sauté onion in butter. Add flour, salt, pepper and milk. Stir until thickened. Cheese may be added. Pour over casserole. Top with buttered bread crumbs and sprinkle with paprika. Bake at 325° for 1 hour.

Naomi King (Jake)

Chicken Supreme

3 c. chicken, boned and cooked
2 c. macaroni, cooked
1 can cream of celery soup
12 oz. Velveeta cheese, cubed
1 c. chicken broth
1 tsp. onion, diced
2 c. milk

Mix all ingredients together and pour into an oblong baking dish. Bake at 350° for 45 minutes.

Elsie Fisher

Chicken Supreme

4 c. chicken, cooked
4 c. macaroni, uncooked
4 c. milk
2 c. grated cheese
4 cans cream of chicken soup
1/2 med. onion, chopped
1 tsp. salt
1/2 tsp. pepper
6 T. butter

Melt half of the cheese in milk. Combine all ingredients except remaining cheese. Put in greased casserole. Refrigerate overnight. Bake at 350° for 1 hour 30 minutes. Stir occasionally. Top with remaining cheese for last 15 minutes.

Sadie Fisher

Turkey Casserole

1 can cheddar cheese soup
1/2 c. milk
1 c. turkey, cooked and diced
2 c. noodles, cooked
2 T. pimiento, diced
1 T. parsley, finely chopped

In a 1 1/2 quart casserole, stir soup and add milk. Mix in the remaining ingredients. Bake at 350° for 30 minutes.

Arie Speicher

Dried Beef Casserole

1/4 lb. dried beef, chipped
1 - 7 oz pkg. or 1 1/2 c. macaroni, uncooked
1 c. cheddar cheese, grated
1 10 oz. can cream of mushroom soup
2 c. milk or part broth
2 T. green pepper, chopped
3 hard boiled eggs, chopped
1/2 tsp. onion, minced
1 tsp. salt

Combine all ingredients in a 8"x12" baking dish and refrigerate overnight. Can also be mixed in the morning and bake it for the evening meal. Bake at 350° for 1 hour. For chicken casserole use 2 cups diced, cooked chicken instead of dried beef and chicken soup instead of mushroom soup. Makes 8-10 servings.

Arie Blank

If my day seems overcrowded,
More than I'd get done, no doubt
If my husband than comes calling
Wife will you come help me out
Oh that I might leave my doings
And not fret what's yet to do
Pleasantly call back and answer
Sure! What can I do for you?

The smallest act of kindness is worth more than the grandest intention.

So Very Much To Do

The cookie jar was empty,
The bread supply was low.
There were some garments new,
I thought I had to sew.
The mending still was waiting
The kitchen wasn't swept;
There were so many things to do
I very nearly wept.

And then my happy children
Came bursting through the door
From playing in the snow
We had received the night before.
They said, "Oh Mother, are you busy?"
"We wonder if you can
Come out and help us
Make a big snowman?"

My work was soon forgotten
As I joined my children dear,
It seemed the snow and sunshine
Made my worries disappear.
I helped them make a snowman,
And they gave me a sleigh ride.
Then I paused to thank my Maker
Before I went inside.

For blessing me with children,
And so very much to do.
"Oh, thank you, God, my Father,
My blessings are not few."

Meats

Let a pig and a boy have everything they want, and you'll get a good pig and a bad boy.

Ham Loaf

3 lb. ground ham and pork mix
1 c. milk
1 c. bread crumbs
1 or 2 eggs
1 c. brown sugar
1/4 c. vinegar
1/4 c. water
1 tsp. mustard

Combine the meat, milk, bread crumbs and eggs. Add seasonings to taste. Form into loaves for baking. Heat the remaining ingredients. Pour over ham loaves and continue to baste through baking. Bake at 300° for about 2 hours.

Ruth Ann Esch

Ham Loaf

2 lb. ground ham
1 lb. ground pork or beef
1 1/2 c. graham cracker crumbs
3 eggs
1 c. milk
1 tsp. pepper
1/2 tsp. salt
1 c. brown sugar
1 T. prepared mustard
1/2 c. water
1/2 c. vinegar
1 4 oz. can pineapples (optional)

Mix the first 7 ingredients together. Mix the remaining ingredients together and bring to a boil and pour over the unbaked ham loaf. Bake for 1 hour at 350°. Bread crumbs can be substituted for the graham cracker crumbs.

Lena King
Barbiann Esch

The work that's done with thankful hearts,
Not grudgingly and mean,
Will make our home a happier place,
Where God's great love is seen.

Pineapple Ham Loaf

2 eggs
1/2 c. milk
1 c. saltines or graham, finely crushed
1/4 tsp. pepper
2-3 lb. ground ham, fully cooked
1 lb. ground fresh pork
1 c. brown sugar (packed)
1/3 c. vinegar
1 tsp. prepared mustard
1 8 oz. can crushed pineapples

In a large bowl, beat the eggs. Add milk, crackers and pepper. Add the ham and pork. Mix well. Shape into loaf. Bake uncovered 1 hour and 30 minutes at 350°. Combine remaining ingredients. Pour some over loaf. Use the rest of the sauce for basting frequently.

Naomi Esh

Mock Ham Loaf

2 lb. hamburger
1 lb. hot dogs, ground
2 c. cracker crumbs
2 eggs, beaten
1 1/3 c. brown sugar
2 T. vinegar
1 tsp. dry mustard
2 c. water
dash of pepper
1 tsp. salt

Mix the first 4 ingredients. Syrup; Mix the remaining ingredients. Add half of the syrup to meat. Pour rest over top when ready to bake. Bake at 350° for 1 hour or more.

Sara Ann Lapp

Labour not for the meat that perisheth, but for that meat which endureth unto everlasting life, which the son of man shall give unto you. John 6:27

Ham Balls

1 lb. ground pork
1 lb. ground cooked ham
3/4 c. milk
2/3 c. shredded wheat cereal, crushed
2 eggs
1 1/2 c. brown sugar (packed)
2/3 c. water
1/3 c. vinegar
3/4 tsp. ground mustard

Combine first 5 ingredients. Mix well and shape into balls. In a saucepan, combine remaining ingredients. Bring to a boil over medium heat. Reduce heat and simmer 4 minutes. Pour over ham balls. Bake uncovered at 350° for 60 to 70 minutes or until browned.

Sarah Fisher

Iowa Ham Balls

3 1/2 lb. ground ham
1 1/2 lb. ground beef
3 eggs, beaten
2 c. milk
3 c. graham cracker crumbs
2 cans tomato soup
3/4 c. vinegar
2 1/2 c. brown sugar
1 tsp. mustard

In a large bowl, combine first 5 ingredients. Using a 1/2 cup, shape mixture into 2" balls. Place in 2 large shallow roasting pans. Combine all remaining ingredients. Pour over ham balls. Bake at 325° for 1 hour. Turn balls at 1/2 hour. Makes about 32 balls.

Rachel Stoltzfus
Mrs. Elmer Stoltzfus

Anxiety does not empty tomorrow sorrows, but only empties today of strength,

Meatballs to can

12 lb. ground beef
1 c. hot lard or shortening
1/2 lb. salt or scant 1/2 c.
1 c. brown sugar
1/2 T. pepper
1/2 oz. salt petre (scant)

Dissolve the salt petre in hot water. Mix all ingredients together. Shape into small balls. Put in jars. Fill with water and seal. Boil 3 hours.

Anna Mae Stoltzfus
Linda Ruth Esh

Bologna Meat Balls

25 lb. meat, not ground
15 oz. salt
1 1/2 T. pepper
1 T. salt petre
1 T. nutmeg
1 lb. brown sugar
1 c. Wesson oil
1 c. molasses

Mix all the ingredients together except the meat. Pour mixture over the meat and let stand for 5 days. Grind it and shape into balls. Cold pack for 2 1/2-3 hours.

Rachel Stoltzfus

Barbecued Meatballs

1-1 1/2 lb. ground beef
1 sm. onion, grated
2 slices bread, crumbled
1/8 tsp. pepper
1 egg
1 tsp. salt
1/4 c. catsup
3 T. brown sugar
1/2 tsp. dry mustard
1/4 c. catsup

Mix the first 7 ingredients together and form into even sized balls. Place in a shallow baking dish. Mix the remaining ingredients for a topping mixture. Spread over the meatballs. Bake 1 hour at 350°.

Linda King

Meatballs

3 lb. ground beef
1 12 oz. can evaporated milk or plain milk
1 c. oatmeal
1 c. cracker crumbs
2 eggs, beaten
1/2 c. onion, chopped
1/2 tsp. garlic powder
2 tsp. salt
1/2 tsp. pepper
1-2 tsp. chili powder
2 c. catsup
1 c. brown sugar
1/2 tsp. liquid smoke (optional)
1/2 tsp. garlic powder
1/4 c. onion, chopped

Mix all ingredients from ground beef to chili powder (first 10 ingredients) together. The mixture will be soft. Shape into balls. Combine the remaining ingredients (last 5) stir until brown sugar is dissolved. Pour this sauce mixture over the meatballs and bake at 350° for 1 hour. These meatballs can be frozen in a single layer on wax paper lined cookie sheets. Freeze until solid. Store frozen meatballs in freezer bags until ready to cook. Makes 80 meatballs.

Anna Mae Stoltzfus
Sylvia Lantz
Naomi King
Linda Ruth Esh
Lena Riehl
Lena King

Hamburger Balls

1 1/2 lb. ground beef
1 T. salt
1 c. oatmeal
1 c. milk
1 c. ketchup
1/2 c. water
3 T. sugar
3 T. vinegar
3/4 c. onion, chopped
1 T. Worcestershire sauce

Mix the first 4 ingredients and roll into balls and fry until slightly brown all around. Mix the remaining ingredients and pour over meatballs. Bake 1 hour at 350°.

Anna Mary Smucker

Meat Loaf & Glaze

2 lb. ground beef
1 c. Italian bread crumbs
1 c. milk
1 egg
1 1/2 tsp. salt
1 sm. onion, chopped
1/4 tsp. pepper
1/2 c. ketchup
2 T. brown sugar
1 T. mustard
1 tsp. vinegar

Mix the first 7 ingredients (ground beef to pepper). Bake 1 hour at 350°. Mix the remaining ingredients and pour over top the meatloaf. Bake another 1/2 hour longer.

Sylvia Stoltzfus (Gid)

Meatloaf

4 lb. hamburger
1 tsp. salt
2 tsp. hamburger seasoning salt
3 eggs
1/2 tsp. pepper
1 1/2 c. oatmeal
2 c. catsup, homemade preferred
1/2 c. onions, diced

Mix all ingredients and bake at 350° for 1 hour 30 minutes.

Ada King

Meat Loaf

1 1/2 lb. ground beef
1 c. tomato juice
3/4 c. oats, uncooked
1 egg, beaten
2 T. brown sugar
1/4 c. onion, chopped
1 1/2 tsp. salt
1/4 tsp. pepper

Combine all ingredients, mix well. Press firmly into an ungreased loaf pan. Bake in 350° oven for 1 hour. Let stand 5 minutes before slicing. Makes 8 servings.

Esther Fisher
Linda Ruth Esh
Katie Glick

God gives every bird it's food, but He does not throw it into the nest.

Barbecued Meatloaf

1 lb. ground beef
1 egg
1 c. rice krispee cereal
1 tsp. salt
1/4 tsp. pepper
1 T. onion, chopped
3 T. brown sugar
1/4 c. catsup
1 tsp. dry mustard

Combine beef, egg, rice krsipees, salt, pepper and onion. Mix well. Mix together sugar, catsup and dry mustard. Add to meat mixture. Bake at 350° for 45 minutes to 1 hour. It can also be made into meatballs and fried. Delicious!

Annie Lapp

Beef Barbecue to can

10 lb. ground beef
5 c. onions, chopped
1/2 c. salt (scant)
1 1/4 T. pepper
5 c. ketchup
1 c. vinegar
3/4 c. mustard
1 1/2 c. brown sugar
2/3 c. Worcestershire sauce
4 c. beef broth or water

Brown ground beef and onions. Add the rest of the ingredients. Put in jars and cold pack for 2 hours.

Katie Ruth Esch

Barbecued Hamburger

2 lb. hamburger
1 onion
1/2 c. catsup
2 T. brown sugar
2 T. prepared mustard
1 T. Worcestershire sauce
1 tsp. salt

Simmer about 20 minutes. Serve with hamburger buns.

Arie King

To ignore an insult is the true test of moral courage.

Hamburger Cheese Pie

3/4 lb. ground beef
1/2 c. onion, finely chopped
2 c. cheddar cheese, shredded
3/4 c. mayonnaise
3/4 c. milk
4 tsp. cornstarch
3 eggs
1/2 tsp. salt

Cook ground beef and onion in skillet until browned. Arrange meat mixture and cheese in large pie shell. Beat together, mayonnaise, milk, cornstarch, eggs, salt and pepper in bowl until blended, using a rotary beater. Bake at 350° for 35 minutes or until golden brown and puffy.

Lena King

Meat Za Pie

1 lb. ground beef
1 sm. onion
1 egg
1/2 c. bread crumbs
1 T. parsley
1/4 tsp. garlic salt
salt and pepper to taste
1 8 oz. can tomato sauce
1 tsp. parsley
1/2 c. oregano
1/4 tsp. salt
1 1/2 c. grated cheese

Mix beef with onion, egg, bread crumbs, 1 T. parsley, garlic salt, salt and pepper. Pat into a 9" pie plate. Mix the tomato sauce, 1 tsp. parsley, oregano and 1/4 tsp. salt. Pour in beef shell. Top with grated cheese. Bake 350° for 20-30 minutes.

Arie Speicher

Poor Man's Steak

2 lb. hamburger
1 c. cracker crumbs
1 c. milk
1 tsp. salt
1/4 tsp. pepper
1 onion, chopped

Mix together and press on cookie sheet. Chill overnight. Cut into 4" squares. Roll in flour, brown on both sides. Place pieces in roaster. Cover with one can mushroom soup and 1 can water mixed. Bake at 300° for 1 hour 30 minutes.

Ranch Burgers

1 lb. ground meat
1 tsp. salt
1/3 c. milk
3/4 c. cracker crumbs
2 eggs, unbeaten
2 T. onion
2 T. celery
3/4 c. catsup
1/8 tsp. pepper
1/4 tsp. oregano
1/4 c. brown sugar
1 T. lemon juice
1 tsp. mustard
1 1/2 c. water
1 T. Worcestershire sauce
1/2 tsp. garlic salt
1 tsp. salt

Mix the first 5 ingredients together and form an oblong loaf. Chill overnight. Slice and roll in flour. Brown on both sides. Put in casserole. Combine the remaining ingredients and simmer for 10 minutes. Pour over meat. Bake 1 hour.

Elizabeth Stoltzfus

Mince Meat

3 qt. ground beef
1 1/2 qt. apples
1 qt. apple butter
5 c. sugar
1 T. salt
1 tsp. cinnamon
1 1/2 qt. cider
1 tsp. allspice
raisins, if desired

Cook all ingredients together for 2 hours. Use for mince pies.

Arie King

The more you give, the more you get
The more you laugh, the less you fret
The more you do unselfishly
The more you live abundantly
The more of everything you share
The more you'll always have to spare
The more you love, the more you'll find
That life is good and friends are kind
For only what we use, give away
Enriches us from day to day.

Connecticut Beef Supper

2 T. shortening
2 lb. beef, 1" cubes
2 lg. onions, sliced
1 c. water
2 lg. potatoes, pared and thinly sliced
1 can cream of mushroom soup
1 c. dairy sour cream
1 1/4 c. milk
1 tsp. salt
1/4 tsp. pepper
1 c. cheddar cheese, shredded
1 1/4 c. wheaties, crushed

Melt shortening in large skillet. Cook and stir meat and onion in shortening until meat is brown and onion is tender, Add water, heat to boiling, reduce heat, cover and simmer 50 minutes. Heat oven to 350°. Pour meat mixture into ungreased baking dish 13"x9"x2". Arrange potato slices on meat. Stir together soup, sour cream, milk, salt and pepper. Pour over potatoes. Sprinkle with cheese and cereal. Bake uncovered 1 hour and 30 minutes or until potatoes and meat are tender.

Sarah Esh

Creamed Dry Beef

4 T. butter
1/4 lb. dried beef, thinly sliced
1/2 c. water
4 T. flour
2 1/2 c. milk

Brown butter in heavy skillet. Add shredded pieces of dried beef. Brown slightly. Add water and boil until water is evaporated. This helps to make the beef tender. Sprinkle flour over beef and allow to brown slightly. Slowly add milk and cook over low heat, stirring constantly. Cook until smooth and thickened. Serve over baked potatoes or toast.

Rebecca Speicher

Use it up; wear it out. Make it do; or do without.

Beef Tongue

1 fresh beef tongue
2/3 c. salt
1/3 c. brown sugar
pinch of pepper

Mix salt, sugar and pepper. Rub salt mixture into tongue. Place in airtight container in cool place for 3 days, turning daily. On the 4th day remove and rinse well. Cook about 2 hours or until tender. Cool 10 minutes. Peel outer skin from tongue. Cool and slice.

Rebecca Speicher

Liver Patties

1 lb. liver
2 slices bacon
1 sm. onion
1 green pepper
1 tsp. salt
1/8 tsp. pepper
2 T. flour
1 egg

Grind liver. Add other ingredients and fry in butter, fry bacon before adding.

Rebecca Speicher
Sylvia Stoltzfus (Amy)

Hot Turkey Soufflé

6 slices bread
2 c. turkey, cooked and diced
1/2 c. onion, chopped
1/2 c. celery, chopped
1/4 c. pepper, chopped
1/2 c. mayonnaise
3/4 tsp. salt
2 eggs. beaten
1 1/2 c. milk
1 can cream of mushroom soup
1/2 c. cheddar cheese, shredded
dash of pepper

Cube 2 slices of bread, place in bottom of greased baking dish 8"x8". Combine turkey, vegetables, mayonnaise, salt and pepper. Spoon over bread cubes. Arrange remaining bread on top of turkey mixture. Combine eggs and milk, pour over mixture. Cover, chill 1 hour or overnight. Spoon soup on top when ready to bake. Bake at 325° 1 hour or until set. Sprinkle cheese on top last few minutes of baking.

Lena King

Turkey Bake

8 slices white bread, 1" cubes
2 c. turkey, cooked and diced
2 c. Swiss cheese
1/4 c. onion
1 T. butter
3 eggs, lightly beaten
2 c. milk
1/2 tsp. salt
1/4 tsp. pepper

Arrange half the bread cubes in the bottom of a well buttered 9" square baking dish. Spread turkey over the bread and cover with shredded cheese. In a small skillet, sauté the onion in butter, spread over cheese and top with remaining bread cubes. Mix eggs, milk and seasonings. Pour over layers. Bake at 325° for 40 minutes or until crusty and brown.

Sarah Esh

Old Fashioned Pot Roast

1 boneless beef chuck roast
6 T. flour, divided
6 T. butter, divided
3 c. hot water
2 beef bouillon cubes
1 med. onion, sliced
1 tsp. salt
1/4 tsp. pepper
4 carrots, cut in 2" pieces

Sprinkle the roast with 1 T. flour. In Dutch oven brown the roast on all sides in half of the butter. Add the water, bouillon cubes, onion, salt and pepper, bring to a boil, cover and simmer 1 hour. Add carrots, simmer 1 hour longer or until meat is tender. Remove meat and carrots to a serving platter. Keep hot. Strain broth, set aside. In same Dutch oven melt remaining butter, stir in remaining flour. Slowly add 2 cups broth, stir until smooth, cook and stir until thickened. Add additional broth until gravy has desired consistency. Makes very good hot beef sandwiches.

Naomi B. Beiler

Salmon Loaf

2 c. salmon or mackerel fish
2 c. soft bread crumbs or cooked rice
1/2 c. milk
2 eggs, beaten
1 1/2 T. minced parsley
2 T. butter, melted
1/2 tsp. salt, scant

Drain fish, flake the fish and combine with all the other ingredients, including liquid from fish. Place in a greased baking pan or a casserole. Bake at 375° for 40 minutes. Serves 9.

Sylvia Stoltzfus (Amy)

Grilled Bass with Cheese Sauce

6 bass filets
1/2 lb. bacon, fry and crumble
1 stick butter
2 c. heavy cream
1 c. parmesan cheese
black pepper

In saucepan over medium heat melt the butter, add the cream and bring to a boil. Reduce by half, stir in the cheese and pepper. Place fish on a grill with grill screen. Grill over medium heat. Add sauce over each filet. Serve hot.

Dave Esch

Baked Chicken Breast

1 pkg. dry beef
bacon
chicken breast
3/4 c. sour cream
1 can cream of chicken soup

Butter casserole dish. Line bottom with dry beef. Put a slice of cheese inside chicken breast, wrap with piece of bacon around the chicken, insert toothpick to hold together. Mix the sour cream and soup, pour over the chicken. Bake for 2-2 1/2 hours at 350°.

Linda Stoltzfus

Oven Baked Chicken

1 T. butter
2/3 c. Bisquick
1 1/2 tsp. paprika
1 1/4 tsp. salt
1/4 tsp. pepper
2 1/2-3 1/2 lb. chicken pieces

Heat oven to 425°. Melt butter in baking dish. Mix Bisquick, salt and seasonings, coat chicken. Place skin-sides down in dish. Bake 35 minutes, turn chicken. Bake about 15 minutes longer or till done. May take longer for big pieces.

Linda Stoltzfus

Barbecue Chicken

1/2 c. catsup
1 T. lemon juice
3 T. butter, melted
1 T. chili powder
2 T. Worcestershire sauce
4 T. vinegar
3 T. brown sugar
1 T. mustard
1 tsp. salt
1 tsp. paprika
1/2 tsp. pepper

Mix all ingredients. Put chicken in baking dish. Pour sauce over chicken. Bake for 2-2 1/2 hours at 350°.

Anna Zook

Uncle Crist's Chicken Bbq. Sauce

6 c. vinegar
3/4 c. salt
3 c. Mazola corn oil
1 qt. boiling water

Mix the vinegar and salt in a gallon jug, shake well till salt dissolves. Add oil, shake well again. Put water in sprayer, add rest of the ingredients.

Linda Stoltzfus

Shake n Bake

1/2 c. flour
2 tsp. paprika
3 tsp. salt
1 tsp. pepper
1/4 tsp. dry mustard

Mix all ingredients. Shake well.

Lena Riehl
Anna Mary Smucker

Ham or Chicken Rolls

2 c. flour
3 tsp. baking powder
1/2 tsp. salt
1/3 c. margarine
3/4 c. milk
1 1/2 c. ham, cooked and ground
1 T. mustard
2 T. margarine, soft

Sift together the flour, baking powder and salt. Mix in by hand the 1/3 cup margarine until crumbly. Stir in milk until moistened. Press into ball. Roll out in a rectangle 1/3"-1/2" thick. Mix together the ham, mustard and soft margarine. Spread over dough and roll up like a jelly roll. Cut into 1 1/4" thick slices. Place in greased 8" square baking dish. Spoon chicken or ham broth over top. Bake at 375° for 15-20 minutes. Serve plain or with cheese sauce. For chicken rolls use chopped chicken in place of ham and mayonnaise instead of mustard. For the cheese sauce stir until melted, 3 T. margarine, 6 T. flour, 1 tsp. salt, 2 cups milk and 1 1/2 cups grated cheese. Spoon over rolls to serve. Serves 6-8.

Arie Blank

Chicken Divine

4 chicken breast, cooked
2 cans cream of chicken soup
2 10 oz frozen broccoli, cut up
1/2 c. mayonnaise
1 T. lemon juice
salt and pepper
dash of curry
1 c. sharp cheddar cheese, grate

Mix together. Put bread crumbs on top. Bake 350° for 45 minutes.

Amanda Stoltzfus

Chicken Croquettes

2 T. butter
2 1/2 T. flour
1 c. milk
2 c. chicken, cooked and minced
1/2 tsp. salt
1/2 tsp. celery salt
1/4 tsp. onion salt or powder
1/8 tsp. pepper
2 T. parsley

Make a white sauce with the butter, flour and milk. Add the chicken and seasonings. Cool thoroughly. Shape into croquettes. Dip in saltine cracker crumbs, then in 2 beaten eggs and again in cracker crumbs. Fry in deep fat till golden brown. Lard works the best to fry in. Makes about 16.

Sylvia King
Naomi Lapp
Elizabeth Stoltzfus

Barbecued Chicken Wings

20 chicken wings, cut in half
1/2 c. chili sauce
1/2 c. soy sauce
1/2 c. honey
2 T. cooking oil

Mix well, pour over chicken wings in a shallow pan and bake at 350° for approximately 45 minutes or until chicken is brown. Stir occasionally while baking.

Naomi Beiler

Grilled Chicken Breast

3/4 c. soy sauce
2/3 c. oil
1/2 c. lemon juice
1/4 c. Worcestershire sauce
1/4 c. mustard
1/4 tsp. garlic powder

Marinate cooked breast in sauce about 2 hours before grilling. Grill about 3 minutes on each side.

Naomi Beiler

Sweet n Sour Sauce for Chicken

1/2 c. brown sugar, firmly packed
1/4 c. cornstarch
1/2 tsp. ground ginger
1/2 c. frozen orange juice
1/2 c. vinegar
2 T. soy sauce
1 can crushed pineapples, undrained

Cook together. Delicious with chicken nuggets.

Ada King

Pork/Spareribs and Sauerkraut

5-6 lb. country style spareribs or loin of pork
3 1 lb. cans sauerkraut
1 1/2 c. cooking apples, coarsely chopped
3/4 c. onion, coarsely chopped
2-4 T. brown sugar
1/4 tsp. black pepper
1 1/2 c. chicken broth
fresh parsley, chopped

Drain sauerkraut. In a deep Dutch oven; combine the sauerkraut and the remaining ingredients except the parsley. Arrange rib or pork loin, pushing them down into the sauerkraut. Cover and bake for 2 hours at 325°. Make sure liquid does not dry up. If it gets low, add more broth. Sprinkle with parsley.

Katie Ruth Esch

You are welcome here
Be at your ease
Get up when you're ready
Go to bed when you please
Happy to share with you
Such as we've got
The leaks in the roof
The soups in the pot
You don't have to thank us
or laugh at our jokes
Sit down and come often
You're one of the folks

Sweet & Sour Pork

1 20 oz. pineapple chunks
2 T. cornstarch
1/4 c. soy sauce
1 T. honey
1/2 tsp. instant chicken bouillon granules
1 garlic clove, minced
1/8 tsp. pepper
2 T. cooking oil
3/4 lb. pork tenderloin, cut into bite size pieces
1 med. green pepper, sliced thin
hot rice

Drain pineapples, reserving the juice. Set pineapple aside. Add enough water to juice to equal 3/4 cup. Add cornstarch, soy sauce, honey, bouillon, garlic and pepper, set aside. Heat oil in large skillet. Cook and stir pork and green pepper for 6-8 minutes or until pork is no longer pink. Stir pineapple juice mixture into skillet with pineapples. Cook until thickened. Serve over rice.

Naomi Esh

Roasted Pig Stomach

1 pig stomach
2 1/2 lb. ground sausage
1/2 c. celery, diced
1 sm. onion, chopped
1 tsp. salt
1 sm. bag seasoned stuffing
1 c. warm water
1/3 c. butter
1 qt. potatoes, raw & diced

Mix stuffing with warm water and butter. Add the other ingredients and mix well. Wash pig stomach and soak in salt water for 2 hours. Rinse, drain and fill with filling. Secure the openings with picks or sew it. Bake in covered roast pan for 3 hours at 350°.

Elizabeth Kauffman

Kindness can never be given away – it always comes back!

Beef or Deer Jerky

3 lb. meat, cut 3/4" thick
1 tsp. garlic powder
1 tsp. onion powder
1 tsp. black pepper
1 tsp. season salt
3 T. liquid smoked hickory
3/4 c. Chung king sorey sauce

Put in dish and set overnight or 8 hours. Stir to get soaked in. Bake at 150° for 6-8 hours or until desired.

Sara Ann Lapp
Rachel Stoltzfus

Canned Turkey Thighs

turkey thighs, skinless, boneless
1 tsp. salt
1 T. brown sugar
1 T. liquid smoke

Fill can with meat, don't pack. Cold pack 3 hours. This meat is also good soaked in tender quik brine for 24 hours before canning. It tastes like ham. also can be canned with just 1 tsp. salt and it will taste like pork. This is very tender meat.

Elizabeth Petersheim
Sylvia Stoltzfus

Canning Sausage

1 gal. water
1/2 c. salt
1/2 c. sugar
1 tsp. pepper
1 tsp. salt petre

Bring mixture to a boil. Add meat, boil 20 minutes then pack in jars and cover with liquid. Boil 3 hours.

Arie King

You're only cooking up trouble when you stew about tomorrow.

Barbecued Meatballs

3 lb. ground beef
1 12 oz. can evaporated milk
1 c. oatmeal
1 c. cracker crumbs
2 eggs
1/2 c. chopped onions
1/2 tsp. garlic powder
2 tsp. salt
2 tsp. pepper
2 tsp. chili powder

Combine all ingredients, mixture will be soft. Shape into walnut size balls. Place meatballs in a single layer on wax paper lined cookie sheets. Freeze until solid. Store frozen meatballs in freezer bags until ready to bake. For sauce; combine 2 c. ketchup, 1 c. brown sugar, 1/2 tsp. Liquid smoke, 1 tsp. Garlic powder and 1/4 c. chopped onions. Stir until sugar is dissolved. Place frozen meatballs in a 13"x9"x2" pan. Pour on sauce and bake at 350° for 1 hour.

Barbara J. King

Why We Use Recipes

I guessed the pepper, the soup was too hot,

I guessed the water, it dried in the pot,

I guessed the salt – and what do you think?

We did nothing else the whole day but drink!

I guessed the sugar, the sauce was too sweet,

And so by my guessing, I spoiled our treat.

So now I guess nothing, for cooking by guess

Is sure to result, in a terrible mess!

Cakes & Icings

COOKBOOKS ARE EXCITING BECAUSE THEY CONTAIN SO MANY STIRRING EVENTS!

Life's Seasons

Life is like the seasons
Each one its changes bring,
A fertile seed takes root and grows
Thus youth is like Spring.
Maturity comes in Summer
As we work and play and sing,
In the Fall we gather harvest
From the deeds we sowed, and then,
Alas too soon it's Winter
And our eyes have grown quite dim,
Have faith no need to worry
'Tis not the end of everything
For our souls will be returned again
To Heaven, where God is King.

Fudge Icing

1 egg
1/4 tsp. salt
1 tsp. vanilla
2 c. 10x sugar
1/3 c. butter or margarine
2 T. Crisco
5 T. cocoa

Melt the butter, Crisco and cocoa, boil a few seconds. Cool. Mix the egg, salt, vanilla and sugar. Add the butter mixture to the sugar mixture.

Mattie Zook

Brown Sugar Icing

1 c. brown sugar, packed
1 stick margarine
1/4 c. milk
1 tsp. vanilla
2 c. powdered sugar

Cook the first 3 ingredients for 2 minutes then add remaining ingredients.

Mattie Zook

Orange Butter Frosting

1/4 c. butter, softened
3 c. 10x sugar
1/4 c. orange juice
1/2 tsp. orange peel, grated (optional)

Cream butter and sugar. Add orange juice and orange peel. Beat until smooth. Spread over bars.

Mrs. Elmer Stoltzfus

Cream Cheese Icing

1 8 oz. pkg. cream cheese
1 lb. 10x sugar
2 T. butter
1 tsp. vanilla extract

Place all ingredients in a bowl. Beat until fluffy and smooth.

Mrs. Elmer Stoltzfus

Lemon Frosting

1 1/3 c. granulated sugar
1 stick butter or margarine
1 lemon, grated and juiced
3 eggs, beaten
cool whip

Combine the first 3 ingredients into a sauce pan. Add eggs and bring to a slow boil till thick, stirring constantly. Cool. Add cool whip and spread.

Lena King

Angel Food Cake

1 1/2 tsp. cream of tartar
1/4 tsp. salt
1 1/2 c. egg whites
1/2 tsp. almond extract
1 1/2 tsp. vanilla
3/4 c. sugar
1 c. cake flour
3/4 c. sugar or jello

Measure the first 5 ingredients in a large bowl, beat until soft peaks, gradually add 3/4 cup sugar, continue beating until stiff peaks. Sift together the remaining ingredients 3 times and fold in some at a time. Put in an angel food pan. Bake 45 minutes at 375°. Let cool 1 hour upside down before removing from pan.

Katie Ruth Esch

Angel Food Cake Roll

1 angel food cake mix
10 x sugar
ice cream

Take an angel food cake mix. Bake it on 2 regular size cookie sheets with waxed paper on the sheets so it comes off better. Put cake on a tea towel sprinkle with 10x sugar. Roll up like a jelly roll while still warm. When cooled put ice cream on it and roll up again and freeze.

Kate Stoltzfus (Steve)

The best thing to do behind ones back is pat it.

Apple Dapple Cake

2 eggs
2 c. granulated sugar
1 c. Wesson oil
3 c. flour, scant
1/2 tsp. salt
1 tsp. soda
3 c. apples, chopped
2 tsp. vanilla
nuts

Mix the eggs, sugar and oil. Sift the flour, salt and soda. Add to the egg mixture. Add remaining ingredients, mix well, pour into a greased cake pan. Bake 45 min. at 350°.

Elizabeth Kauffman

Banana Cake

1 pkg. yellow cake mix
1/2 tsp. baking soda
1 c. bananas, mashed
2 eggs
pinch of salt
1 tsp. vanilla
3/4 c. cold water
1/3 c. nuts, chopped

Mix together and bake at 350°.

Arie King

Good Banana Cake

1 1/2 c. granulated sugar
2 eggs
1/2 c. vegetable oil
2 c. flour
1/2 tsp. salt
2 tsp. baking soda
2 c. bananas, mashed

Icing:
1/2 c. butter, softened
1.2 c. Crisco
3 T. flour
1 c. sugar
2/3 c. milk
1 tsp. vanilla

Mix the ingredients in the first column (sugar to bananas). Bake. Mix the ingredients in the second column (butter to vanilla) and beat well. Spread on cooled cake.

Sylvia Esch

The journey of a thousand miles begins with one step.

Carrot Cake

2 c. flour
2 c. sugar
1/2 tsp. salt
1 tsp. baking soda
1/2 tsp. cinnamon
1 tsp. vanilla
3 eggs
1 1/2 c. vegetable oil
2 c. carrots, grated
1 c. crushed pineapples, drained
1 c. coconut
1/2 c. nuts, chopped

Mix dry ingredients, add eggs, oil, carrots and vanilla, beat. Stir in pineapples (optional), coconut and nuts. Pour in greased 9"x13" pan. Bake 40-50 minutes.

Marie Hoover
Arie King

Carrot Cake

2 c. brown sugar
4 eggs
1 1/4 c. Wesson oil
2 tsp. soda
2 tsp. cinnamon
1 tsp. salt
2 c. flour
2-3 c. carrots, grated

Icing:
1 8 oz. cream cheese
1/2 c. butter
10x sugar

Mix the first 8 ingredients adding the carrots last. Bake at 350° for about 45 minutes. Cool. Mix the cream cheese, butter and 10x sugar for the icing.

Martha Smucker
Elsie Fisher

Citrus Cake

2 c. sugar
1 1/2 c. vegetable oil
3 eggs
1 1/2 tsp. vanilla
3 c. flour
1 tsp. baking soda
1 tsp. cinnamon
1 tsp. salt
1 18 oz. can crushed pineapples
2 c. nuts, chopped
2 c. bananas, chopped

Bake in layer pans or a 9"x13" pan and a 9" square pan for about 45 minutes at 350°

Katie Ruth Esch

Fruit Cake

1 1/2 c. granulated sugar
2 eggs
1/2 c. salad oil
2 c. flour
1/2 tsp. salt
2 tsp. soda
2 c. applesauce or fruit etc.

Icing:
1/4 lb. butter
3/4 c. granulated sugar
1/2 c. evaporated milk
3/4 c. nuts
1 tsp. vanilla

Mix the first 7 ingredients (sugar to applesauce). Bake at 350° for 40-45 minutes. Mix the butter, sugar and milk, boil hard for 1 minute, remove from heat, add the nuts and vanilla. Pour hot icing over hot cake.

Lena Riehl

Moist Fruit Cake

1 1/2 c. granulated sugar
2 eggs
1/2 c. salad oil
1 c. applesauce, scant
2 c. flour
2 tsp. soda
1/2 tsp. salt
1 1/2 c. fruit cocktail

Icing:
3/4 c. carnation milk
3/4 c. sugar
1/2 c. butter

Mix the first 8 ingredients (sugar to fruit cocktail). Bake at 350° for 40-45 minutes. Mix the remaining ingredients (milk to butter) and boil 2 minutes. Pour on 5 minute cooled cake.

Arie Speicher
Annie Lapp

Apology is often a good way to have the last word.

Zucchini Cake

1 1/2 tsp. cinnamon
1/2 tsp. salt
3 c. sugar
2 tsp. baking powder
4 eggs
3 c. flour
1 tsp. baking soda
1 1/2 c. oil
1 c. nuts, chopped
1 c. coconut
3 c. zucchini, grated
Icing:
1 8 oz. cream cheese
1 stick butter
2 1/2 c. 10x sugar
1 tsp. vanilla

Mix the first 11 ingredients (cinnamon to zucchini) together. Put into a well greased pan, bake for 1 hour at 300°-325°.

Ada King

Strawberry Cake

1 box white cake mix
1 c. 10x sugar
1 8 oz. cool whip
1 8 oz. cream cheese, softened
1 box Danish or pie glaze
1 box strawberries

Bake cake mix as directed. Let cool. Mix sugar, cool whip and cream cheese, spread on top of cake. Mix the glaze and strawberries. Spread on top of cream cheese mixture. Any kind of fruit can be used with this cake. Very good!

Barbiann Esch

Strawberry Shortcake

2 1/2 c. flour
2 tsp. baking powder
1/2 tsp. salt
2 eggs
1 c. sugar
1 c. milk
2 T. butter
1 tsp. vanilla

Sift flour, measure and add baking powder and salt. Beat eggs and add sugar, milk and vanilla. Combine egg mixture with dry ingredients. Add melted butter and beat until thoroughly blended. Pour into 2 greased 8" cake pans. Bake at 375° for 25-30 minutes. Top with fresh strawberries and your favorite whipped topping. Delicious!

Linda Stoltzfus

Pineapple Upside Down Cake

1 20 oz. can sliced pineapples, in juice
2 pkg. instant vanilla pudding, jello brand
10 maraschino cherry halves
1/2 c. light brown sugar
1 pkg. yellow cake mix
4 eggs
1/4 c. oil
1 c. water

Drain pineapples, save juice. Arrange slices in a 13"x9" pan. Put cherry halves in each slice of pineapple. Combine 1 pack instant vanilla pudding mix and the pineapple juice and pour over pineapple slices. Sprinkle with brown sugar. Combine cake mix, eggs, water and oil in large mixing bowl. Blend, then beat at medium speed for 4 minutes. Pour into baking pan. Bake at 350° for 55-60 minutes. Cool cake in pan 5 minutes.

Sylvia King (Mervin)

Hummingbird Cake

3 c. flour
2 c. sugar
1 tsp. baking soda
1 tsp. salt
1 tsp. cinnamon
3 eggs, beaten
1 c. vegetable oil
1 1/2 tsp. vanilla
1 8 oz. crushed pineapples
1 c. pecans, chopped
2 c. bananas, chopped

Combine the first 5 ingredients in a large mixing bowl. Add eggs and oil, stirring until dry ingredients are moistened, do not beat. Stir in vanilla, pineapples, pecans and bananas. Put in 2 small cake pans. Bake at 350° for 40 minutes or until a toothpick inserted in center comes out clean.

Amanda Stoltzfus

Kindness is a special art of living with a loving heart.

Rhubarb Cheese Cake

1 c. flour
1/4 c. sugar
1/2 c. butter
3 c. fresh rhubarb, cut 1/2"
1/2 c. sugar
1 T. flour
12 oz. cream cheese, softened
1/2 c. sugar
2 eggs
1 c. sour cream
2 T. sugar
1 tsp. vanilla

For crust, mix flour, sugar and butter. Pat into a 10" pie plate. Set aside. For rhubarb layer, combine rhubarb, sugar and flour, toss lightly and pour into crust. Bake at 375° for about 15 minutes. Meanwhile, prepare cream layer by beating together cream cheese and sugar until fluffy. Beat in eggs one at a time. Pour over hot rhubarb layer. Bake at 350° for about 30 minutes or until almost set. For topping, combine sour cream, sugar and vanilla. Spread over hot layers.

Ada King

Rhubarb Cake

1 egg, beaten
1/2 c. shortening
1 1/4 c. brown sugar
1 tsp. vanilla
2 c. flour
1 tsp. soda
1/2 tsp. salt
1/2 c. raw sour milk
2 1/2 c. rhubarb
1/3 c. brown sugar
1 tsp. cinnamon

Cream together, egg, shortening, brown sugar and vanilla. Sift the flour, soda and salt. Mix together with milk into first mixture. Add rhubarb last. Mix the brown sugar and cinnamon together. After cake mix is in the pan, sprinkle brown sugar mixture over top. Bake at 375° for 35-40 minutes.

Martha Smucker

Rhubarb Coffee Cake

2 c. flour
1 tsp. baking soda
1/2 tsp. salt
1 1/4 c. brown sugar
1/2 c. shortening
1 egg
1 tsp. vanilla
1/2 c. sour milk
2 1/2 c. rhubarb
1/3 c. brown sugar
2 tsp. cinnamon

Cream shortening, sugar, eggs and vanilla. Add milk. Add dry ingredients. Mix in rhubarb. Sprinkle with brown sugar and cinnamon. Bake at 350° for 35-40 minutes.

Sylvia Esch

Blueberry Buckle

3/4 c. sugar
1/2 c. shortening
1 egg
2 c. unsifted flour
2 1/2 tsp. baking powder
1/4 tsp. salt
1/2 c. milk
2 c. fresh blueberries
1/2 c. sugar
1/2 c. sifted flour
1/2 tsp. cinnamon
2 T. butter or margarine

Mix the first 8 ingredients and put in a cake pan. For crumbs, mix the remaining ingredients and put on top of cake mixture. Bake at 350° for 30 minutes.

Sylvia Esch

Shoo-Fly Cake

4 1/2 c. flour
2 c. brown sugar
3/4 c. butter or margarine
2 c. boiling water
1 c. molasses
2 tsp. baking soda
1 T. blackstrap molasses (optional)

Combine flour, sugar and butter, work in fine crumbs. Reserve 2 1/2 cups crumbs for topping. Mix water, molasses and baking soda, add to remaining crumbs, mix well or till batter is very thin. Pour into a 8"x12" greased and floured pan. Sprinkle crumbs on top. Bake at 350° for 45 minutes.

Katie Ruth

Shoo-Fly Cake

6 c. flour
2 c. brown sugar
1 c. lard or 3/4 c. Wesson oil
2 eggs
2 c. water
2 c. molasses
1 c. brown sugar
1 tsp. cream of tartar
1 tsp. soda

For crumbs, mix the flour, brown sugar and lard. For syrup, mix the remaining ingredients. Put some crumbs on bottom of pan, then syrup and top with rest of the crumbs. Bake at 350° for 1 hour.

Sara Ann Lapp
Sylvia Lantz

Crumb Cake

2 c. brown sugar
1 egg
1/2 c. lard, scant
1 1/2 c. buttermilk
1 tsp. soda
2 1/2 c. flour
1 c. brown sugar
1 T. butter or lard
1 c. flour
cinnamon

Mix the first 6 ingredients, combining the buttermilk with the soda before adding. For crumbs, mix the brown sugar, butter and flour. Sprinkle with cinnamon.

Sylvia Stoltzfus (Amy)
Sylvia Lantz

Crumb Cake

2 c. flour
1 1/2 c. brown sugar
1/2 c. butter
2 tsp. baking powder
2 eggs, beaten
3/4 c. milk
1 tsp. vanilla

Mix the first 4 ingredients with your hands making crumbs. Take out 1 cup and set aside. Put remaining ingredients in the remainder of crumbs. Blend until creamy. Add vanilla. Pour into cake pan. Sprinkle top with crumbs before baking. Bake 1/2 hour at 350°.

Linda Stoltzfus

Coffee Cake

1 box yellow cake
1 3 oz. instant vanilla pudding
1 3 oz. instant butterscotch pudding
4 eggs
1 c. oil
1 c. water
1 c. brown sugar
2 tsp. cinnamon
1 c. nuts, ground (optional)

Mix the first 6 ingredients together as you would a cake. Set aside and mix the remaining ingredients for the topping. Put half of the cake mix into a 9"x13" pan. Sprinkle half of the crumb topping on top. Repeat. Bake at 350° for 40 minutes.

Naomi Lapp

Spice Cake

2 1/2 c. flour
1 c. granulated sugar
1 tsp. baking powder
1 tsp. soda
3/4 tsp. salt
3/4 tsp. cinnamon
3/4 tsp. cloves
1/2 c. shortening
2/3 c. brown sugar
1 1/8 c. sour milk
2 eggs

Mix ingredients together and bake at 350° for 30 minutes.

Lena Riehl

Short Cake

2 tsp. sugar
butter, size of an egg
1 lg. egg
milk, to make soft dough
1/2 tsp. salt
2 tsp. baking powder
2 c. flour

Mix ingredients together and bake at 375° for 25-30 minutes.

Arie King

We can not direct the wind, but we can adjust the sails.

Jimmy Cake

1 box yellow cake mix
1 box vanilla instant pudding
4 eggs
1 c. water
1/2 c. oil
6 oz. chocolate chips
1 sm. container chocolate jimmies

Blend the first 5 ingredients together and add the remaining ingredients. Bake 350° for 30 minutes.

Rachel Stoltzfus

Lazy Daisy Cake

4 eggs
2 c. sugar
2 tsp. vanilla
2 c. all purpose flour
2 tsp. baking powder
1/2 tsp. salt
1 c. milk
1/4 c. butter or margarine

Icing:

1 1/2 c. brown sugar, packed
3/4 c. butter or margarine, melted
1/2 c. half & half
2 c. flaked coconut

In a mixing bowl, beat eggs, sugar and vanilla. Combine flour, baking powder and salt, beat just until combined. Pour into a 13"x9"x2" baking pan. Bake at 350° for 35-40 minutes. For frosting, combine the brown sugar, melted butter, half & half and coconut, spread over warm cake. Broil until lightly browned. About 3-4 minutes.

Sadie Fisher

**Courage is what it takes to stand up and speak;
Courage is also what it takes to sit down and listen.**

Red Velvet Cake

2 1/4 c. all purpose flour
1 tsp. salt
1 1/2 c. sugar
1/2 c. butter
2 eggs
2 oz. red food coloring
2 T. unsweetened cocoa powder
1 c. buttermilk
1 tsp. vanilla
1 T. white vinegar
1 tsp. baking soda

Preheat oven to 350°. Sift flour and salt together. In a large bowl cream sugar and butter, add eggs and beat real well. Stir together food coloring and cocoa, add to creamed mixture. Add buttermilk alternately with flour to creamed mixture. Pour vinegar into a small deep bowl, add soda (it will foam), stir into batter (do not beat). Pour batter into 2 buttered and floured 9" cake pans. Bake 25-30 minutes. Cool cake in pans for 10 minutes. Remove cakes from pans. Cool completely on wire racks.

Mrs. Elmer Stoltzfus

Chocolate Bar Cake

6 egg yolks
1 c. sugar
2/3 c. water
2 tsp. vanilla
1 1/3 c. flour
1/3 c. cocoa
1 tsp. soda
1/2 tsp. salt

In a small bowl beat egg yolks about 3 minutes. Gradually add 1 cup of sugar. Blend in water and vanilla. Combine flour, cocoa, soda and salt. Add to liquid mixture. Beat batter until smooth. Beat egg whites until foamy. Add 1 cup of sugar, beat till stiff peaks form. Fold in chocolate mixture. Pour in paper lined jelly roll pan. Bake at 350° to 375° for 18-20 minutes. Cool cake and cut in half. Spread icing on one half and lay other half on top.

Lena King

Chocolate Sheet Cake

2 sticks margarine
1 c. water
4 T. cocoa
2 c. flour
2 c. sugar
1 tsp. salt
2 eggs
1 tsp. baking soda
1/2 c. milk

Icing:
1 stick margarine, melted
4 T. cocoa
6 T. milk
1 tsp. vanilla
1 box 10x sugar

Bring 2 sticks margarine, water and 4 T. cocoa to a boil. Mix the flour, sugar and salt, add slowly to the first mixture. Beat well the eggs, baking soda and 1/2 cup milk and add to mixture mixing well. Pour onto large cookie sheets. Bake at 350° for 20 minutes. For frosting; Bring to a boil the 1 stick margarine, melted, 4 T. cocoa, and 6 T. milk, remove from heat and add the vanilla and 10x sugar mixing well. Put on the cake while still warm. Cut with cookie cutters.

Sylvia Esch

Zucchini Chocolate Cake

1 1/2 c. sugar
1/4 c. shortening
1/2 c. vegetable oil
1/4 c. margarine
1 egg
1 tsp. vanilla
1/2 c. sour milk
2 1/2 c. flour
4 T. cocoa
2 tsp. baking soda
2 c. zucchini, shredded

Sprinkle 12 oz. chocolate chips on top if desired. Bake at 325° for 45-50 minutes.

Mattie Zook

Chocolate Mayonnaise Cake

1 c. sugar
2 1/2 c. flour
3-4 T. cocoa
2 tsp. baking soda, scant
1 c. mayonnaise
1 c. warm water
1 tsp. vanilla

Bake at 350° for 40 minutes.

Sylvia Esch

Moist Chocolate Cake

1 1/2 c. sugar
1/2 c. oil
2 eggs
2 c. applesauce
2 c. flour
1/2 c. cocoa
1/4 tsp. salt
2 tsp. baking soda

Bake at 350° for 30 minutes.

Sylvia Lantz

Chocolate Chip Cake

1/2 c. butter
1 c. sugar
2 eggs
1 tsp. vanilla
1 c. sour cream
2 c. flour, sifted
1 1/2 tsp. baking powder
1 tsp. baking soda
6 oz. chocolate chips
1/2 c. sugar
1 tsp. cinnamon

Mix the first 8 ingredients together (butter to baking soda). Put half of the batter in a cake pan. Put half of the chocolate chips on top of the batter. Mix the sugar and cinnamon. Put half of the sugar mixture on top of the chocolate chips. Put your remaining batter next and repeat other layers. Bake 350° for 30-40 minutes.

Sylvia Stoltzfus (Gid)

Easy Chocolate Cake

3 eggs
3 c. sugar
3/4 c. shortening
3 T. cocoa
3 tsp. baking soda
3/4 tsp. baking powder
1/2-3/4 tsp. salt
3/4 c. sour milk
3 c. flour
3 tsp. vanilla
1 1/2 c. boiling water

Combine eggs, sugar and shortening, mix well. Add dry ingredients alternately with sour milk, mix well. Add vanilla and boiling water. Bake in hot oven 35-45 minutes.

Lena King
Linda Ruth Esh

Deep Dark Chocolate Cake

2 eggs
2 c. brown sugar
1/2 c. shortening
1 1/2 tsp. baking soda
1 1/2 tsp. baking powder
3/4 c. cocoa
2 c. flour
1 c. water
1 c. milk
1 tsp. vanilla
1/2 tsp. salt

Mix all ingredients. Bake at 350° for 40 minutes or until done. This is a very moist cake.

Anna Zook

Turtle Cake

1 pkg. German chocolate cake mix
14 oz. Kraft caramels
6 oz. nuts
7 oz. condensed milk
6 oz. chocolate chips
1/4 lb. butter

Mix cake according to direction on box. Pour half of the batter into a 9"x13" pan. Bake at 350° for 15 minutes. In top of double boiler melt butter, caramels and milk. Cool slightly and pour over baked cake. Pour rest of the cake batter on top. Sprinkle with chocolate chips and nuts. Bake for 25 minutes or until done.

Rebecca Speicher
Annie King
Katie Mae Stoltzfus

Pistachio Cake

1 white cake mix
1 box instant pistachio pudding
1 box cool whip
1 box instant pistachio pudding

Mix cake mix according to directions adding 1 box pudding mix. Bake at 350° for 30 minutes. For topping; Fold 1 box pudding mix into cool whip. Put on cake when cool.

Linda King

Boston Cream Pie

4 egg yolks
2/3 c. cold water
1 1/2 c. sugar
2 c. flour
3 tsp. baking powder
4 egg whites, stiffly beaten

Filling:
3 c. milk, scalded
1 c. sugar
1/3 c. cornstarch
1/3 c. flour
4 eggs
pinch of salt
2 T. butter
2 tsp. vanilla

Icing:
2 1/4 c. 10x sugar
1/4 c. cocoa
1/8 tsp. salt
1/3 c. butter
5 T. hot milk, (approx.)
1 tsp. vanilla

Mix the egg yolks, cold water and sugar together. Sift together the flour and baking powder, add to first mixture. Fold in the beaten egg whites. Bake at 350° for 20-25 min. Cut apart when cool. For filling; Mix the sugar, cornstarch, flour, eggs and pinch of salt to the scalded milk, bring to a boil, remove from heat, add butter and vanilla. Put filling between layers of the cake. For icing; Mix the 10x sugar, cocoa and salt. Cream in the butter. Blend in hot milk and vanilla. Put on top of cake. Makes 2-9" round pans.

Linda Stoltzfus

Shoo-Fly Cupcakes

2 1/2 c. flour, unsifted
1/2 c. margarine or butter, soft
1 1/2 c. brown sugar
1 tsp. baking powder
1 c. brown sugar
1 1/2 c. boiling water
1 tsp. vanilla
1 tsp. soda

Mix the flour, margarine, brown sugar and baking powder together, save 1/2 cup crumbs for on top. Mix the remaining ingredients together and add to the first mixture, stir until mixed (do not beat). Lumps will disappear. Fill each cupcake paper 3/4 full. Sprinkle 1 tsp. crumbs on top. Bake at 375° for 20-25 minutes. Cinnamon can be sprinkled over top before baking. Makes 18-24 cupcakes.

Rebecca Lynn Fisher

Zucchini Cupcakes

3 eggs
1 1/3 c. sugar
1/2 c. vegetable oil
1/2 c. orange juice
1 tsp. almond extract
2 1/2 c. flour
2 tsp. cinnamon
2 tsp. baking powder
1 tsp. baking soda
1 tsp. salt
1/2 tsp. ground cloves
1 1/2 c. zucchini, shredded

Icing:

1 c. brown sugar, packed
1/2 c. butter or margarine
1/4 c. milk
1 tsp. vanilla
1 1/2 - 2 c. 10x sugar

Beat eggs, add the sugar, oil, orange juice and extract. Combine dry ingredients, add to egg mixture, mix well. Add zucchini, mix well. Fill cupcakes 2/3 full. Bake at 350° for 20-25 minutes or till done. For frosting; Combine brown sugar, butter and milk in a sauce pan. Bring to a boil over medium heat. Cook and stir for 2 minutes. Remove from heat, add vanilla. Cool to lukewarm, add 10x sugar till it reaches spreading consistency. Makes 18-24 cupcakes.

Annie Lapp

Apple Brownies

1 c. margarine
2 c. sugar
2 eggs
2 c. flour
1 tsp. cinnamon
1/4 tsp. nutmeg
1 tsp. baking powder
1 tsp. soda
2 c. apples, diced
2 c. walnuts, chopped
2 tsp. vanilla

Mix ingredients together. Pour into lightly greased and floured cake pan. Bake at 350° for 25 minutes.

Esther Fisher

Cheerfulness is the atmosphere in which all things thrive.

Bars & Cookies

On Taking Big Bites

Once I learned a lesson,
And I'll pass it on to you,
So when you're at a party,
You'll know what not to do.
I was eating chocolate cookies,
And of course was impolite,
But they were so very good,
I took a great big bite.
Just then the hostess asked me,
"Do you want some ice cream, Joe?'
But I could only mumble,
And she thought I said "No."

Congo Squares

2 1/3 c. flour
2/3 c. butter
2 1/4 c. brown sugar
3 eggs
2 1/2 tsp. baking powder
1/2 tsp. salt
1 tsp. vanilla
1 c. English walnuts, chopped
12 oz. chocolate chips

Melt butter and stir in brown sugar. Let cool. Beat in eggs one at a time. Mix flour, baking powder and salt. Add to butter mixture. Fold in nuts, chocolate chips and vanilla. Spread in a greased 9"x13" cake pan. Bake at 350° for 35 – 40 minutes.

Barbara J. King

Rhubarb Bars

2 c. flour
3/4 c. 10x sugar
1 c. butter
4 eggs
2 c. sugar
1/2 c. flour
1/2 tsp. salt
4 c. rhubarb, diced

For crust; Combine flour, 10x sugar and butter. For filling; Mix the remaining ingredients together. Spread filling over crust and bake at 350° for 40-50 minutes. Cool. Cut into bars. Best if kept refrigerated.

Sylvia Lantz

Time is a treasure,
Each moment to use.
For pleasure, for others
Whatever you choose.
Remember that life
Is minute by minute-
Use it with care,
Put quality in it.

Banana Bars

1/2 c. butter, softened
1 c. sugar
1 egg
1 tsp. vanilla
1 1/2 c. bananas, mashed
1 1/2 c. flour
1 tsp. baking powder
1 tsp. baking soda
1/2 tsp. salt
1/4 c. cocoa

Divide the batter in half and add cocoa to half. Spread in a greased 9"x13"x2" pan. Spoon remaining batter on top and swirl with knife. Bake at 350° for 25 minutes.

Katie Ruth Esch

Banana Orange Bars

2 c. bananas, mashed
1 2/3 c. sugar
1 c. vegetable oil
4 eggs
2 c. flour
2 tsp. cinnamon
2 tsp. baking powder
1 tsp. baking soda
1 tsp. salt

Beat bananas, sugar, oil and eggs until well blended. Combine dry ingredients, fold into banana mixture until well mixed. Pour into 15"x10"x1" greased baking pan. Bake at 350° for 25-30 minutes.

Mrs. Elmer Stoltzfus

Christ in the wilderness
Five thousand fed,
With two small fishes
And five loaves of bread.

May the blessing of He
Who made this division
Be upon our provision.

Applesauce Squares

1 1/2 c. applesauce
1/4 c. brown sugar
2 T. flour
1 T. lemon juice
1/2 c. margarine or butter
1/2 c. brown sugar
1/2 c. flour
1/4 tsp. salt
1 c. quick cooking rolled oats
1/2 c. coconut, shredded
1/2 tsp. nutmeg

In saucepan combine first 4 ingredients. Cook and stir till thick and bubbly. Cool. Cream margarine and 1/2 cup brown sugar. Mix in 1/2 flour and salt. Stir in oats. Press half the oat mixture into a 8"x8"x2" pan. Spread cooled filling over crust. Add coconut and nutmeg to remaining oat mixture. Sprinkle over filling. Bake at 375° for 30-35 minutes. Cool. Cut into squares. Serve 8-9.

Katie Ruth
Sylvia Esch

Great Hearts

The greatest heart that ever beat
Was in some patient soul
That found day's common duties sweet
And found God makes life whole.

Pumpkin Bars

4 eggs
2 c. flour
2 c. sugar
2 c. pumpkin
1 c. vegetable oil
1 c. nuts, chopped
2 tsp. baking powder
1 tsp. baking soda
3/4 tsp. salt
1/4 tsp. ground cloves
2 tsp. cinnamon
8 oz. cream cheese
3/4 stick margarine
2 c. 10x sugar
1 T. milk
1 tsp. vanilla

Beat eggs, add sugar and pumpkin. Add dry ingredients. Add oil and beat for 5 minutes. Bake at 350° for 30 minutes in a 18"x12" pan. For frosting; Mix the cream cheese, margarine, 10x sugar, milk and vanilla and spread on bars when cool.

Sylvia Esch

Carrot Raisin Bars

1 1/2 c. brown sugar
1/2 c. margarine
2 eggs
1 tsp. vanilla
1 1/2 c. flour
1/2 tsp. salt
1/2 tsp. baking soda
1/2 tsp. baking powder
1/2 c. raisins
1 1/2 c. carrots, grated
1/2 c. nuts, chopped

Cream sugar, margarine, eggs and vanilla. Add the rest of the ingredients. Bake in a 9"x13" greased pan at 350° for 40 minutes. Allow to cool, then dust with powdered 10x sugar.

Sylvia Esch

Children think not of what is past, nor what is to come, but enjoy the present time. How many of us are like that?

Raisin Crisp Bars

2 1/2 c. raisins
2 T. clear jell
1/4 c. sugar (optional)
2 c. water
2 T. lemon juice
3/4 c. butter or margarine
1 3/4 c. flour
1/2 tsp. soda
1/2 c. brown sugar
1/4 tsp. salt
1 1/2 c. oatmeal

Mix the raisins, clear jell, sugar and water together and boil till thick and clear, remove from heat and add the lemon juice. Mix the remaining ingredients. Put half of the crumbs in a 9"x13" pan. Pour cooled raisins on, then put the rest of the crumbs on top. Bake at 375° for about 25 minutes. Cut into squares.

Anna Mary Smucker

Raisin Bars

1/2 c. margarine
1 c. raisins
1 c. water
1 c. sugar
1 egg
1/2 tsp. cinnamon
2 c. flour
1 tsp. soda
1/2 tsp. salt
1 1/3 c. powder sugar
1/2 tsp. vanilla
2 T. margarine, soft
2 T. milk

Heat the 1/2 cup margarine, raisins and water to boiling, remove from heat. Combine the sugar, egg and cinnamon, add to raisin mixture. Add the flour, soda and salt, mix well. Pour into a 9"x13" greased pan. Bake at 350° for 15-20 minutes. For icing; Beat together the powdered sugar, vanilla, 2 T. soft margarine and milk until smooth. Spread on hot bars 10 minutes after removing from oven.

Arie Blank

Date Bars

1 c. brown sugar
1/2 butter or margarine
1/3 c. shortening
1 3/4 c. flour
1 1/2 c. quick cooking oats
1/2 tsp. salt
1/2 tsp. baking soda
3 c. dates, pitted and cut up
1/4 c. sugar
1 1/2 c. water

Mix the first 7 ingredients (brown sugar-baking soda). Press half of the crumbly mix evenly in bottom of pan. Mix the remaining ingredients (dates-water). Cook till thick. Cool. Spoon date mix evenly over crumbs. Spread remaining crumbly mix over date mix. Bake 25-30 min. at 400°

Sylvia Stoltzfus (Gid)

Chewy Date Torte

2 eggs
1 c. sugar
1/4 c. flour
1 tsp. baking powder
1/4 tsp. salt
2 T. milk
2 T. butter, melted
1 tsp. vanilla
8 oz. pitted dates, chopped
1 c. walnuts, chopped

Beat eggs, gradually add sugar. Combine and add rest of the ingredients. Bake in 9" square pan at 350° for 30 minutes.

Katie Ruth

Granola Bars

1 c. crunchy peanut butter
2 eggs, beaten
4 T. honey
2 1/2 c. oatmeal
1 1/2 c. mixture of sunflower seeds, raisins and chocolate chips

Mix the peanut butter, eggs and honey together in a pan over low heat. When slightly warm add the remaining ingredients. Press into an 8"x8" greased pan and refrigerate. The oatmeal is important, but the other ingredients may be substituted.

Elizabeth Stoltzfus

Sally's Granola Bars

1 1/2 lb. marshmallows
1/4 c. margarine or butter
1/4 c. vegetable oil
1/2 c. honey
1/4 c. peanut butter
9 1/2 c. rice krispies
1 c. graham cracker crumbs
5 c. oatmeal
1 c. crushed peanuts (optional)
1 1/2 c. raisins (optional)
1 c. coconut
1 c. chocolate chips, butterscotch chips or m n' m's

Melt margarine and oil on low heat, add marshmallow and stir till melted. Turn off heat, add honey and peanut butter. In a large bowl mix the remaining ingredients. Make a well in dry ingredients or have someone pour the marshmallow in over the dry ingredients as you stir, because as it runs to the side it gets hard to mix. Spread on greased cookie sheets. Press and cool.

Anna Mary Smucker

Marshmallow Bars

1 1/2 lb. marshmallows
1/4 c. margarine
1/4 c. vegetable oil
1/2 c. honey
1/4 c. peanut butter
9 1/2 c. rice crispys
4 c. oatmeal
1/2 c. coconut
1 c. graham crackers, broken

Melt the margarine, add marshmallows. When melted add the vegetable oil, honey and peanut butter. In another bowl mix rice crispys, oatmeal, coconut and graham cracker pieces. Mix all together. Let set till firm. Coat with chocolate for a good Christmas treat.

Sylvia Esch

Rice Krispie Caramels

1/4 lb. butter
3 c. rice krispies
3 c. marshmallows
40 caramel candy squares
1 can eagle brand milk
1/2 stick butter

Make 1 batch of rice krispies using the first 3 ingredients. Press into a 13"x9" cake pan. In a double boiler melt the caramel candies, milk and butter. Pour this mixture over your rice krispies mixture. Let cool. Make another batch of the rice krispies mixture and place on top of caramel.

Kate Stoltzfus (Steve)

Cream Cheese Bars

1 c. shortening
1 c. granulated sugar
1/2 c. brown sugar
2 eggs
2 tsp. vanilla
2 c. flour
1 1/2 tsp. salt
2 c. chocolate chips
1 tsp. soda
1 c. nuts (optional)
16 oz. cream cheese, soft
3/4 c. sugar
2 eggs
1 tsp. vanilla

Cream sugar, eggs, shortening and vanilla, add flour, salt and soda, add chocolate chips and nuts last. Press half of chocolate chip dough in bottom of a 9"x13" pan. Beat the sugar, eggs, cream cheese and vanilla. Spread on top of chocolate chip dough. Spread the rest of the chocolate chip dough over cream cheese mix. Some cream cheese will show. Bake at 350° for 45 minutes or till edges are slightly brown.

Lena King

Yum Yum Bars

2 c. flour
1/2 c. margarine
1/2 c. sugar
1 1/2 c. brown sugar
1/2 tsp. salt
1 tsp. vanilla
2 T. flour
1/2 c. nuts
1/4 tsp. baking powder
3 eggs, beaten

Mix the flour, margarine and sugar together and press firmly in a 10"x14" pan. Mix the remaining ingredients together and spread over the first mixture. Bake at 350° for 20 minutes or until nicely brown.

Katie Glick

Whole Wheat Chip & Coffee Bars

2 c. all purpose flour
1 c. whole wheat flour
1 tsp. soda
1 tsp. salt
2 eggs
2 c. brown sugar
1 c. oil
2 tsp. vanilla
2 tsp. instant coffee crystals, dissolved in a little water
1 c. chocolate chips
1 c. walnuts, chopped

Mix ingredients together. Bake on a jelly roll pan at 350°.

Sylvia Lantz

Brownies

1 1/2 c. butter
1 c. brown sugar
1 c. granulated sugar
6 egg yolks
2 tsp. vanilla
4 c. flour
2 tsp. baking powder
1/2 tsp. salt
1/4 tsp. soda
6 egg whites
1 c. brown sugar

Mix all ingredients, except the egg white and 1 cup brown sugar. Spread out dough about 1/2" thick. Beat egg whites until frothy, add 1 cup brown sugar. Spread over dough. Sprinkle with chopped nuts, chocolate drops, butterscotch bits or coconut if desired. Bake at 350° for 35 min.

Sylvia Lantz
Lena Rhiel

Toll House Golden Brownies

2 c. flour
1 tsp. salt
1 tsp. baking powder
3/4 c. lard
1 c. chocolate chips
3/4 c. white sugar
3/4 c. brown sugar
1 tsp. vanilla
3 eggs

Mix ingredients together. Spread evenly into a greased cake pan. Bake at 350° for 35 minutes or till done. Best if not over baked.

Annie Lapp

Cookie Dough Brownies

2 c. sugar
1 1/2 c. all purpose flour
1/2 c. baking cocoa
1/2 tsp. salt
1 c. vegetable oil
4 eggs
2 tsp. vanilla extract
1/2 c. walnuts, chop (optional)
1/2 c. butter or margarine, soft
1/2 c. brown sugar, packed
1/4 c. sugar
2 T. milk
1 tsp. vanilla extract
1 c. all purpose flour
1 c. semi-sweet chocolate chips
1 T. shortening
3/4 c. walnuts, chopped

In a mixing bowl combine sugar, flour, cocoa and salt. Add oil, eggs and vanilla, beat. Stir in walnuts if desired. Pour into a greased 13"x9"x2" baking pan. Bake at 350° for 30 minutes or until done. Cool completely. For filling; Cream butter and sugars in a mixing bowl. Add milk and vanilla, beat in flour. Spread over brownies. Chill until firm. For glaze; Melt chocolate chips and shortening in a saucepan, stirring until smooth. Spread over filling. Immediately sprinkle with nuts, pressing down slightly.

Sadie Fisher

Fudge Bars

2 c. brown sugar
1 c. butter
2 eggs
2 tsp. vanilla
1 tsp. salt
1 tsp. baking powder
2 1/2 c. flour
3 c. quick oats
12 oz. chocolate chips
1 can sweetened condensed milk
2 T. butter
2 tsp. vanilla
1 c. nuts, chopped

Cream the brown sugar, butter, eggs and vanilla. Add the salt, baking soda, flour and quick oats and mix well. Spread 2/3 of mixture in a 10"x15" pan. Set the remainder aside. Combine the remaining ingredients (chocolate chips to nuts) in a double boiler and melt. Spread on top of oatmeal mixture. Top with the remaining oatmeal mixture. Bake at 350° for 20 minutes.

Annie King

Triple Chocolate Fudge Bars

1 4 oz pkg. instant chocolate pudding mix
2 c. cold milk
1 box chocolate cake mix
1 c. chocolate chips

Mix pudding with milk, beat till slightly thickened. Add dry cake mix, blend well and pour in chocolate chips. Spread on a greased jelly roll pan. Bake 25-30 minutes at 350°.

Mattie Beiler

Treasure each other, realizing that we don't know how long we shall have each other.

Double Chocolate Mud Bars

1/2 c. butter
1 c. granulated sugar
2 lg. eggs, separated
1 1/2 c. all purpose flour
1 tsp. baking powder
1/2 tsp. salt
1 c. walnuts, chopped
1/2 c. semi-sweet chocolate chips
1 c. mini marshmallows
1 c. brown sugar, firmly packed

Preheat oven to 350°. Grease a 13"x9" baking pan. Beat together the butter and sugar until fluffy. Beat in egg yolks one at a time, until well blended. Mix together the flour, baking powder and salt. Fold flour mixture into butter mixture. Press mixture into prepared pan and pack down firmly. Sprinkle nuts, chocolate chips and marshmallows over mixture in pan. Beat egg whites until stiff peaks form, fold in brown sugar. Spread over mixture in pan. Bake 35 minutes or until crust is formed.

Mattie Beiler

Chocolate Revel Bars

1 c. butter, softened
2 c. brown sugar
2 eggs
2 tsp. vanilla
2 1/2 c. flour
1 tsp. salt
1 tsp. baking soda
3 c. quick cooking oats
6 oz. chocolate chips
14 oz. can sweetened condensed milk
2 T. butter
1/2 tsp. salt
2 tsp. vanilla
1 c. nuts, chopped (optional)

Cream together softened butter and brown sugar in a large mixing bowl. Add eggs, vanilla, flour, salt and baking soda. Stir in oats, mix well. Spread 2/3 of mixture onto a 15"x10"x1" lightly greased jelly roll pan. Melt together chocolate chips, milk, butter and salt, stirring constantly over low heat. Blend in vanilla. Add nuts. Spread over mixture in pan. Dot with remaining dough. Bake at 350° for 30 minutes.

Barbara Stoltzfus

Chocolate Chip Bars

2 c. sugar
4 eggs
1/2 c. butter, melted
1 tsp. vanilla
2 c. flour
2 tsp. baking powder
1 1/2 tsp. salt
2 c. chocolate chips

Mix together. Spread in pan. Bake for 25 minutes at 350°. Do not over bake. Cut into squares when cool.

Linda Stoltzfus

Chocolate Chip Chews

1/2 c. shortening
1 c. brown sugar
3/4 c. granulated sugar
3 eggs, beaten
1 tsp. vanilla
2 1/2 c. flour
1/2 tsp. soda
1/4 tsp. salt
1/2 tsp. baking powder
1 c. chocolate chips

Cream the shortening, brown sugar and add the remaining ingredients except chocolate chips and mix well. Add chocolate chips. Pour on cookie sheet. Bake at 350° for 15-20 minutes. Do not over bake.

Linda Ruth Esh

Choco-Nut Butter Bars

1/2 c. butter, melted
1 c. graham cracker crumbs
1 c. flaked coconut
1 c. semi-sweet chocolate chips
1 c. nuts, chopped
15 oz. can sweetened condensed milk

Preheat oven to 350°. Combine melted butter, crumbs and coconut in bottom of an ungreased 13"x9" pan. Press lightly. Cover with a layer of chocolate chips. Sprinkle with a layer of chopped nuts. Drizzle sweetened condensed milk evenly over surface. Bake for 30 minutes. Cool completely before cutting.

Sarah Esh

Pecan Caramel Bars

2 c. flour
1 c. brown sugar
1/2 c. butter
pecans
1/2 c. sugar
2/3 c. butter

Combine the first 3 ingredients, mix until crumbs are fine and well mixed. Pat firmly into ungreased 9"x13" pan. Sprinkle with pecans. Combine the remaining ingredients, cook over medium heat, stirring constantly. Boil 1 minute. Pour over crust. Bake at 350° until browned, about 15 minutes.

Annie King

Peanut Butter Swirls

2 1/2 c. shortening
5 c. sugar
2 1/2 c. chunky peanut butter
5 eggs
10 T. milk
5 1/4 c. flour
2 1/2 tsp. salt
2 1/2 tsp. baking soda
2 pkg. chocolate chips

Cream shortening and sugar. Beat in peanut butter, eggs and milk. Sift dry ingredients then stir in creamed mixture. Place dough on lightly floured waxed paper. Roll into rectangles 15"x8 1/4". Melt chocolate, then cool and spread over dough. Roll like jelly roll. Chill 30 minutes. Slice. Place on ungreased baking sheet. Bake at 375° for 8-10 minutes.

Anna Mae Stoltzfus

Today will never return, use it well.

Live to learn, and you will learn to live.

If at first you don't succeed, try, try again.

Peanut Butter Fingers

1/2 c. butter
1/2 c. white sugar
1/2 c. brown sugar
1/4 tsp. salt
1/2 tsp. vanilla
1 egg
1/3 c. peanut butter
1/2 tsp. soda
1 c. flour
1 c. oatmeal
6 oz. chocolate chips
1/2 c. 10x sugar
1/4 c. peanut butter
2-4 T. milk

Mix the first 10 ingredients (butter to oatmeal). Spread in a 9"x13" pan. Bake at 350° for 20 minutes. Sprinkle immediately with chocolate chips. Spread when melted. Combine the 10x sugar , 1/4 cup peanut butter and milk. Drizzle over melted chocolate chips.

Kate Stoltzfus (Steve)

Homemade Twix Bars

club crackers
1 stick margarine or butter
1 c. graham cracker crumbs
3/4 c. brown sugar
1/2 c. granulated sugar
1/3 c. milk
1 c. chocolate chips
3/4 c. peanut butter

Line a 13"x9" pan with crackers. Boil butter, cracker crumbs, sugars and milk, cook 5 minutes. Pour over crackers. Add another layer of crackers. Melt chocolate chips and peanut butter. Spread over crackers and cool.

Rebecca Speicher

Most smiles start with another smile.

We can not shine if we have not taken time to fill our lamps.

Gingerbread Torte

1 box gingerbread mix
1 box butterscotch pudding
3/4 c. milk
15 oz. pumpkin, canned
8 oz. cool whip
1/2 tsp. nutmeg
1/2 tsp. cinnamon

Prepare the gingerbread mix as directed. Bake in 2 heavily greased flan pans. Let cool. Mix pudding and milk. Stir in pumpkin. Fold in 3 cups cool whip. Put on top of gingerbread. Decorate with remaining cool whip with a cake decorator. Combine the cinnamon and nutmeg. Sprinkle on top.

Barbiann Esch

Coconut Cookies

1 c. butter
1 c. brown sugar, packed
1/2 tsp. salt
2 3/4 c. flour
1 egg yolk
1 tsp. vanilla
1 egg white
1 T. water
1/2 c. sugar
1 tsp. vanilla
2 c. coconut

Bottom part; Cream the butter and sugar. Blend in egg yolk, salt and vanilla. Add flour and mix well. Top part; Beat egg white with water until soft mound. Slowly beat in sugar and vanilla. Stir in coconut. Put caramel or chocolate bits on top.

Anna Mary Smucker
Elizabeth Stoltzfus

Date Cookies

1 1/2 c. brown sugar
4 eggs
3/4 c. vegetable oil
2 tsp. baking soda
2 T. water
2 T. vanilla
2 lb. dates, chopped
1 lb. nuts, chopped
3 c. flour

Sylvia Esch

Diced Apple Cookies

1/4 c. butter
1/2 c. granulated sugar
1/2 c. brown sugar
1 egg
1 tsp. vanilla
2 c. sifted flour
1 tsp. baking powder
1/2 tsp. baking soda
1/4 tsp. salt
1 tsp. cinnamon
1/4 c. sour cream
1/2 c. raisins
1 c. apples, unpeeled finely diced

Cream butter and sugars, beat in eggs and vanilla. Sift dry ingredients and mix alternately with remaining ingredients. Drop by tsp. onto a greased cookie sheet. Bake at 375° for 12-15 min.

Katie Ruth Esch

Fruit Jumbles

3 eggs
1 1/2 c. granulated sugar
1/2 c. shortening
1 lb. dates, chopped
1/4 c. walnuts
1 tsp. soda, dissolved little water
1 tsp. vanilla
3 c. flour

Combine all ingredients, mixing well. Drop onto cookie sheets and bake at 350°-375° till done. Very moist cookie!

Lena King

Fruit Top Cookies

2 c. brown sugar
1 c. butter
2 eggs
4-5 c. flour
1 tsp. baking soda
4 T. milk
1 tsp. vanilla
any kind of jam

Roll dough into little balls. Place on cookie sheet and make holes with thumb. Fill hole with any kind of jam. A good way to use up leftover jam from church.

Katie Ruth Esch

Honey Carrot Cookies

1/2 c. butter
1/2 c. sugar
1/4 c. honey
1 tsp. vanilla
1/2 tsp. lemon
1 1/4 c. carrots, shredded
2 c. flour
2 tsp. baking powder
1/2 tsp. salt

Mix and bake at 350° till brown.

Katie Ruth Esch

Raisin Filled Cookies

2 c. brown sugar
1/2 c. Crisco
1/2 c. butter
pinch of salt
1 T. vanilla
3 eggs
4 c. flour
1 tsp. soda
1 1/2 c. brown sugar
1 1/2 c. raisins, ground
1 1/2 c. water
3/4 c. flour

Mix the first 8 ingredients (brown sugar to soda). Bake at 400°. For filling; Mix the remaining ingredients. When cookies are cool, put filling in between 2 cookies.

Sadie Lapp

Oatmeal Raisin Cookies

1 c. butter or margarine, soft
1 c. brown sugar, packed
1/2 c. granulated sugar
2 eggs
1 tsp. vanilla
1 1/2 c. flour
1 tsp. baking soda
1 tsp. cinnamon
1/2 tsp. salt
3 c. quick oats
1 c. raisins

Beat butter and sugars until creamy. Add eggs and vanilla, beat well. Combine dry ingredients, except oats and raisins. Add to creamed mixture, mixing well. Add oats and raisins last, mix well. Bake on ungreased cookie sheets until light brown. Bake at 350°.

Anna Mae Stoltzfus

Pumpkin Cookies

1 c. lard
2 c. pumpkin
2 c. brown sugar
4 c. flour
2 tsp. baking powder
2 tsp. baking soda
2 tsp. cinnamon
1 1/2 c. chocolate chips

Mix first 3 ingredients. Stir in the next 4 ingredients, mix well. Then add chocolate chips. Put French vanilla icing on top.

Pumpkin or Banana Cookies

2 c. pumpkin or banana
2 c. sugar
2 eggs
4 c. flour
1 c. Crisco oil
1 tsp. salt
1 tsp. cinnamon
1/2 tsp. nutmeg
1/2 tsp. cloves
2 tsp. baking soda
1 c. raisins, (optional)
1 c. nuts, (optional)

Beat banana pulp or cooked pumpkin, soda, sugar and oil, add flour (may need a little more then the 4 cups), spices, raisins and nuts. Drop on cookies sheets. Bake at 350°.

Rebecca Speicher

Pumpkin Chocolate Chip Cookies

1 c. pumpkin, canned
1 c. sugar
1/2 c. vegetable oil
1 egg, beaten
2 c. flour
2 tsp. baking powder
1 tsp. vanilla
1 tsp. baking soda
1 tsp. cinnamon
1/2 tsp. salt
1 tsp. milk
1/2 c. nuts
1 c. chocolate chips

Mix ingredients together. Bake at 375° for 10-12 minutes.

Ruth Ann Esch

Soft Chocolate Chip Cookies

2 2/3 c. brown sugar
1/2 c. milk
3 eggs
1 c. oil
4 1/2 c. flour
3 tsp. baking powder
2 tsp. soda
1/2 tsp. salt
1 tsp. vanilla
12 oz. chocolate chips

Mix ingredients together. Bake at 375°.

Elizabeth Kauffman

Chocolate Chip Cookies

1 c. Wesson oil
1/2 c. sugar
1 c. brown sugar
1 tsp. vanilla
2 eggs, well beaten
2 1/2 c. flour
1 tsp. soda
1 tsp. salt
1 c. chocolate chips

Cream the oil, sugars and vanilla. Add the eggs and beat until fluffy. Sift the flour, salt and soda. Add to creamed mixture. Add chocolate chips. Bake at 375°.

Annie King

Chocolate Chip Drop Cookies

1 1/2 c. margarine or Crisco
2 c. brown sugar
2 tsp. vanilla
1 tsp. water
4 eggs, beaten
5 c. sifted flour
2 tsp. salt
2 tsp. soda

Combine the margarine, brown sugar, vanilla and water, beat well. Add the eggs, beat well. Add the dry ingredients, mix well.

Naomi King (Jake)

Classic Chocolate Chip Cookies

1 1/2 c. brown sugar
1/2 c. granulated sugar
4 eggs
1 1/2 c. vegetable oil
4 1/2 c. flour
2 tsp. baking soda
2 tsp. vanilla
2 pkg. instant vanilla pudding dry
3 c. chocolate chips

Mix the ingredients together and bake.

Anna Mae Stoltzfus

Chocolate Chip Cookies

3 c. vegetable oil
3 c. sugar
3 c. brown sugar
8 eggs, beaten
4 tsp. baking soda
4 tsp. salt
4 t. vanilla
4 tsp. water
10 c. flour
2 c. chocolate chips
3/4 c. instant vanilla pudding

Mix the vegetable oil and sugars. Add beaten eggs. Add flour, pudding mix, salt and soda. Add water and vanilla. Fold in chocolate chips. Makes approx. 12 dozen cookies. You can also use butterscotch bits instead of chocolate chip for a change of taste. Vanilla pudding keeps them soft and chewy. Do not over bake. Bake 12 minutes or less at 375°.

Ada King

If people learn by their mistakes, many are getting a fantastic education.

Mint Chocolate Crinkle Cookies

6 T. butter, softened
1 c. sugar
1 1/2 tsp. vanilla
2 eggs
1 1/2 c. flour
1 1/2 tsp. baking powder
1/4 tsp. salt
1 1/2 c. mint flavored semi-sweet chocolate morsels
confectioners sugar

Combine the flour, baking powder and salt, set aside. Melt 1 cup morsels, stirring until smooth. In bowl, beat butter and sugar until creamy, add melted morsels and vanilla. Gradually beat in flour mixture and add remaining mint morsels. Wrap in plastic and freeze till firm. Preheat oven to 350°. Shape dough in 1" ball and roll in confectioners sugar. Bake 10-12 minutes, until tops appear cracked. Let stand 5 minutes on cookie sheet.

Sylvia King (Mervin)

Chocolate Marshmallow Cookies

1/2 c. butter or margarine, soft
1 c. sugar
1 egg
1/4 c. milk
1 tsp. vanilla extract
1 3/4 c. flour
1/3 c. baking cocoa
1/2 tsp. baking soda
1/2 tsp. salt
16-18 lg. marshmallows
6 T. butter or margarine
2 T. baking cocoa
1/4 c. milk
1 3/4 c. confectioners sugar
1/2 tsp. vanilla extract
pecan halves

In a mixing bowl cream butter and sugar, add egg, milk and vanilla, mix well. Combine flour, cocoa, baking soda and salt, beat into creamed mixture. Drop by rounded tsp. onto ungreased cookie sheets. Bake at 350° for 8 minutes. Cut marshmallows in half. Press a marshmallow half, cut side down, onto each cookie. Return to oven for 2 minutes. Cool completely on wire rack. For icing; Combine sugar, cocoa and milk in a sauce pan. Bring to a boil, boil for 1 minute, stirring constantly. Cool slightly, put into small mixing bowl, add confectioners sugar and vanilla, beat well. Spread over cooled cookies. Top each with a pecan half.

Katie Ruth Esch

Chocolate Peanut Butter Toppers

- 4 c. flour
- 2 c. butter
- 1 c. sugar
- 2 tsp. vanilla
- 1/2 c. butter
- 2/3 c. brown sugar
- 2/3 c. peanut butter
- 1 c. chocolate chips
- 4 T. milk
- 2/3 c. powdered sugar, sifted

In a large bowl, combine the first 4 ingredients (flour to vanilla) and mix well. Drop on cookie sheets and flatten to 1/4". Bake at 325° for 15-18 minutes. Cream the next 3 ingredients together (butter to peanut butter) until light and fluffy. Spread on warm cookies. Melt the chocolate chips with milk in a sauce pan over low heat, stirring constantly. Remove from heat. Add the powdered sugar, stir till smooth. Drizzle on top of the cookies. Let stand until chocolate glaze is set.

Naomi B. Beiler

Peanut Butter Oatmeal Cookies

- 2 c. lard, scant
- 2 c. brown sugar
- 2 c. white sugar
- 4 eggs
- 6 T. peanut butter
- 2 tsp. vanilla
- 3 c. flour
- 2 tsp. salt
- 2 tsp. soda
- 6 c. oatmeal

Mix in the order given. Drop on cookie sheets and bake at 350° for 10-15 minutes.

Rebecca Lynn Fisher

Peanut Butter Chocolate Chip

- 1 c. butter, softened
- 1 c. peanut butter
- 1 c. granulated sugar
- 1 c. brown sugar
- 2 eggs
- 2 1/2 c. flour
- 1 tsp. baking powder
- 1 1/2 tsp. baking soda
- 1/2 tsp. salt
- 1 c. chocolate chips

Beat the first 5 ingredients well. Add remaining ingredients.

Martha Smucker

Sugar Cookies

4 c. brown sugar
8 eggs
1 c. vegetable oil
2 c. sour cream
2 tsp. baking soda
6 c. flour
2 tsp. baking powder
2 tsp. vanilla
a little salt

Combine the brown sugar and eggs, beat, add oil and beat again. Put the baking soda in the sour cream and add to mixture, beat well again. Add the rest of the ingredients and beat well. Bake at 400° for 6-7 minutes.

Linda Stoltzfus

Sugar Cookies

4 1/2 c. brown sugar
2 c. lard
8 eggs
2 c. milk or evaporated milk
8 c. flour
4 tsp. soda
2 tsp. baking powder

Beat eggs, add sugar, lard and milk. Sift dry ingredients and add to mixture.

Katie Glick

Brer Rabbit Molasses Sugar

3/4 c. shortening
1 c. sugar
1/4 c. Brer rabbit molasses
1 egg
2 tsp. baking soda
2 c. all purpose flour
1/2 tsp. cloves
1/2 tsp. ginger
1 tsp. cinnamon
1/2 tsp. salt

Mix the first 5 ingredients (shortening to baking soda) together. Add remaining ingredients (flour to salt). Chill several hours or overnight. Form into small balls, roll in sugar and bake 8-10 minutes at 375°. Don't over bake.

Anna Mae Stoltzfus

Soft Molasses Cookies

6 c. flour, sifted
1 c. shortening or oil
2 c. brown sugar
1 c. Brer rabbit molasses
2 c. sour milk
1 tsp. vanilla
2 eggs
3 tsp. cinnamon
1 tsp. salt
3 tsp. soda
2 tsp. ginger

Mix ingredients together. Bake. Put icing on top.

Annie Lapp
Naomi Beiler

Lace Cookies

2 c. brown sugar
1 c. butter
2 c. quick Quaker oats
1 egg
1 T. vanilla
1/2 tsp. salt
1/2 c. coconut

Mix ingredients together. Bake at 350°.

Arie Speicher

Love Nut Cookies

1 c. butter or margarine, soft
2 egg yolks
2 c. granulated sugar
1/2 tsp. soda
5 c. flour
1/2 c. milk
1/2 tsp. walnut flavoring

Mix all ingredients, adding milk last. Roll out. Cut into shapes and sprinkle with nuts and decorations. Keep egg whites for top of cookies

Anna Mae Stoltzfus

Snickerdoodle Cookies

1 c. oil
1 1/2 c. sugar
2 eggs
2 3/4 c. king Midas flour
2 tsp. cream of tartar
1 tsp. soda
1/4 tsp. salt
1 tsp. vanilla
2 T. sugar
2 tsp. cinnamon

Mix oil, sugar and eggs. Add remaining ingredients, except the sugar and cinnamon. Mix the sugar and cinnamon together. Roll cookie dough in sugar and cinnamon mixture. Makes 3 1/2 dozen.

Martha Smucker

Sand Tart Cookies

1 c. shortening
2 c. granulated sugar
3 eggs
3 1/2 - 4 c. flour
1 tsp. salt
2 tsp. baking powder
1 tsp. vanilla
1 tsp. lemon, (optional)

Cream shortening and sugar together. Add eggs and flavoring, beat till fluffy. Sift flour, measure, add salt and baking powder. Add dry ingredients to the first mixture, stir until a medium soft dough is formed. Chill dough several hours in refrigerator. Roll very thin and cut in fancy shapes. Brush tops with stiffly beaten egg whites. sprinkle with cinnamon and sugar. Place on greased cookie sheets. Bake at 350° for 8-10 minutes.

Linda Stoltzfus
Mrs. Elmer Stoltzfus

Take time to pray – it is the greatest power on earth.

Christmas Cookies

1/2 c. shortening
1 egg, well beaten
1 c. brown sugar
1/4 tsp. salt
2 c. flour
1/4 tsp. baking powder
1 c. coconut, shredded
1 tsp. vanilla

Roll 1/8" thick and cut out cookies. Bake 8-10 minutes at 375°. These are good with icing on.

Rebecca Speicher

Double Treats

2 c. flour
2 tsp. baking soda
1/2 tsp. salt
1 c. shortening
1 c. granulated sugar
1 c. brown sugar
2 eggs
1 tsp. vanilla
1 c. peanut butter
6 oz. chocolate chips
1 c. peanuts, chopped (optional)

Sift together the dry ingredients. Beat together the next 6 ingredients. Stir in chocolate chips and peanuts. Shape into small balls and smash down a little. Place on ungreased pan.

Lena Riehl

Chocolate Sandwich Cookies

2 pkg. devil's food cake mix
4 eggs, lightly beaten
2/3 c. vegetable oil
8 oz cream cheese, softened
1/2 c. butter or margarine, soft
3-4 c. confectioners sugar
1/2 tsp. vanilla extract

In a mixing bowl, beat cake mixes, eggs and oil. Batter will be stiff. Roll into 1" balls. Place on ungreased baking sheets and flatten slightly. Bake at 350° for 8-10 minutes or until a slight indentation remains when touched lightly. Cool. In another mixing bowl, beat cream cheese and butter. Add sugar and vanilla, mix until smooth. Spread on bottom of half of the cookies. Top with remaining cookies.

Amos and Naomi Beiler

Chocolate Whoopie Pies

4 c. flour
2 c. sugar
2 tsp. soda
1/2 tsp. salt
1 c. oil or lard
1 c. cocoa
2 eggs
2 tsp. vanilla
1 c. thick sour milk
1 c. cold water with 1 tsp. coffee

Mix ingredients and bake.

Sylvia Lantz
Linda King

Molasses Whoopie Pies

2 eggs
2 c. brown sugar
1 c. brer rabbit molasses
1 c. shortening
1 1/2 c. milk
4 tsp. soda, scant
1/2 tsp. ginger
1/2 tsp. cinnamon
1/2 tsp. cloves
5 c. flour or till right texture

Mix well. Drop on cookie sheets. Bake at 400° till done. Use your favorite filling.

Lena King

Pumpkin Whoopie Pies

2 c. brown sugar
1 c. vegetable oil
2 egg yolks
1 tsp. vanilla
3 c. flour
1 tsp. baking soda
1 tsp. baking powder
1 tsp. salt
1 tsp. ginger
1 tsp. cinnamon
1 tsp. cloves
2 c. pumpkin, cooked
2 tsp. vanilla
4 T. flour
2 T. milk
1 1/2 c. vegetable shortening
2 egg whites, unbeaten
1 box confectioner's sugar

Mix the first 12 ingredients (brown sugar to cooked pumpkin). Bake at 375°. For filling; Mix the remaining ingredients. Make approx. 30.

Katie Ruth Esch

Red Velvet Whoopie Pies

1 c. margarine or butter, melted
3 c. sugar
2 tsp. vanilla
4 eggs
2 c. milk
3 T. red food coloring
5 1/2 c. flour
1/2 c. cocoa
3 tsp. baking soda
2 T. vinegar
2 egg whites, beaten
1 1/2 T. vanilla
4 T. milk
4 T. flour
4 c. confectioners sugar
1 1/2 c. Crisco

Combine the first 10 ingredients (margarine to vinegar). Bake at 350° for 10-12 minutes or until done. For filling; Combine and beat the remaining ingredients, except the egg whites. Fold in the egg whites after other ingredients are thoroughly mixed.

Rebecca Lynn Fisher

The Language of a Smile

There's a special language spoken
By everyone on earth
No matter what their country,
No matter what their birth;
It crosses every border,
It transcends all time and space-
It's known alike by old and young
And found in every place.
Those who speak it often
Always find that it's worthwhile
Everybody understands it-
It's the language of a smile!

A Lesson Learned

When we were young and newly-wed,
And we would know some time ahead
Of someone coming for a meal,
The pressure in my head I'd feel.
With rag and soap I'd run about...
The garbage must be thrown out,
The windows must be sparkling bright,
Each lamp must have a glowing light.
No straw or dirt upon the floor...
No smudgy marks on any door.
The floors must glisten with a sheen,
The tablecloth be smiling clean.
The polished cupboard is quite bare-
No toast crumbs lying anywhere.
The bedroom spread is tucked in tight,
Each mat and towel is straightened right.
The cake is made, the icing on,
Potatoes peeled, and bread is done.
Hustling, bustling from morn till night...
Hard on myself, tense and uptight.
I'd follow hubby with a broom,
For fear he'd leave tracks in the room.
By then he was a nervous wreck
Because he dare not leave a speck.
And so he said in kindly tone
That he would feel much more at home
With me, without this spotless look.
I tell you, that was all it took.
To set me straight and think it through
What I had vainly tried to do.
So now I try to make less fuss
For company's sake and for us!

Pies

Sunshine Pie

A lb. of patience, you must fined.
Mixed well with loving words, so kind.
Drop in 2 lb. of helpful deeds,
And thoughts of other people's needs.
A pack of smiles, to make the crust,
Then stir and bake it well you must,
And now, I ask that you may try
The recipe of this sunshine pie......

Apples for Snitz Pies

apples
4 c. brown sugar
2-3 T. cinnamon
1 c. tapioca
white sugar to suit taste

Cut apples in fourths and cut ends off. Put in 12 quart kettle. When half full put the brown sugar and cinnamon in, fill real full with apples. No water. Put over low heat, when hot turn burner as low as possible or put on heater. Do not stir. Don't lift the lid. Let on overnight. Doesn't have to be on more than 6 hours, but longer is okay. Put through tomato press, use juice and all. Add tapioca if too thin. Add white sugar to suit taste.

Naomi King (Jake)

Snitz for Snitz Pies

2 gal. apple butter
4 T. lemon juice
3 gal. applesauce
1 1/2 c. tapioca
3 c. brown sugar
3 c. granulated sugar
4 qt. dried apple snitz
1 tsp. salt
2 T. cinnamon
1 tsp. nutmeg or to taste

Soak the dried apple snitz for a day covered with water. Cook 1 hour till soft. Put through applesauce grinder and mix all ingredients. Use less granulated sugar if ingredients are canned.

Sylvia Esch

Education is a funny thing. At eighteen we knew all the answers – 40 years later even the questions confuse us.

Canned Apple Pie Filling

20 c. water
4 c. brown sugar
5 c. granulated sugar
4 tsp. cinnamon
2 1/2-3 c. therm flow (clear jel)
6 T. lemon juice
2 tsp. salt
apples

Mix the first 4 ingredients and bring to a near boiling point. Mix the therm flow (clear jel) with a little bit of water and add to the water/sugar mixture. Stir until thick and bubbly. Take off heat and add the lemon juice and salt. Add the apples. Put into jars and cold pack for 20 minutes. Makes 11 quart.

Elizabeth Stoltzfus

Apple Pie Filling to can

9 1/2 c. water
4 1/2 c. sugar
1 c. clear jel or cornstarch
1 tsp. salt
2 tsp. cinnamon
3 T. lemon juice, (optional)
7 qt. apple slices
1/4 tsp. nutmeg, optional

Combine the first 5 ingredients (water to cinnamon) in a large sauce pan. Cook until thickened, stirring constantly. Remove from heat, add lemon juice. Slice apples directly into jars, adding layers of syrup as you fill, otherwise there will be too many air pockets. Leave at least 1" head space. If jars are to full, syrup will spew out during processing. Tighten lids and process in boiling water bath for 25 minutes. Makes 7 qt.

Arie Blank

Give your troubles to God; He'll be up all night anyway.

Apple Pie

1/2 c. sugar
1/2 c. brown sugar, packed
3 T. all purpose flour
1 tsp. ground cinnamon
1/4 tsp. ginger
1/4 tsp. nutmeg
7-8 c. apples, peeled and thinly sliced
1 T. lemon juice
pastry for double crust 9" pie
1 T. butter
1 egg white
additional sugar

In a small bowl combine sugars, flour and spices, set aside. In a large bowl toss apples with lemon juice, add sugar mixture, toss well to coat. Line a 9" pie pan with half the pastry. Place apple filling into crust, dot with butter. Top with remaining pastry. Flute the edges and cut slits in top. Beat egg white until foamy, brush over pastry. Sprinkle sugar on top. Bake at 375° for 35 minutes. Increase temperature to 400° and bake 10-15 minutes more or until golden. Yield 8 servings.

Sylvia Esch

Mom's Apple Pie

3 c. apples
2/3 c. brown sugar
1 T. flour
1/2 tsp. cinnamon
2 T. milk
2 T. butter

Mix apples, sugar, flour and spices together until well blended. Place mixture into an unbaked 9" crust. Add milk and dot butter over top of apple mixture. Put pie crust lid on pie. Bake at 350° for 45-60 minutes.

Martha Smucker

No farmer ever plowed a field by turning it over in his mind.

Chocolate Shoofly

2 c. brown sugar
1 c. lard or oil
2 eggs
4 T. cocoa
2 c. molasses
4 c. flour
2 c. hot water
2 T. baking soda
2 T. vanilla
1/2 tsp. cinnamon
1/4 tsp. salt

Bottom Part:
1 qt. water
1 1/4 c. sugar
2 T. cocoa
3 T. clear jel
1 tsp. vanilla
butter size of walnut

Top part; Mix the sugar, oil, eggs and cocoa. Add soda to molasses and hot water. Add to first mixture. Add the flour, cinnamon, salt and vanilla. Bottom part; Cook the water, sugar, cocoa and clear jell. Cool. Add the butter and vanilla. Divide the bottom part into 6-8 (8") unbaked pie shells. Put top part on and bake at 325° for 1 hour. Top with chocolate frosting.

Barbara Stoltzfus

Chocolate Shoofly Pie

1 c. brown sugar
3 T. clear jell
1 T. cocoa
1 qt. water
1 T. butter
1 tsp. vanilla
1/2 tsp. salt
1 egg
1 c. white sugar
1/2 c. shortening
1 T. cocoa
1 tsp. cinnamon
1 c. molasses
1/2 c. thick milk
1/2 c. hot water
1 tsp. soda
1/2 tsp. salt
3 c. flour, scant
4 8" pie crusts

Bring the brown sugar, clear jell, cocoa and water to a boil, stirring constantly. Remove from heat and add the butter, vanilla and salt. Cool before pouring into 4 (8") pie crusts. Beat together the egg, white sugar, shortening, cocoa, cinnamon, molasses, thick milk, hot water, soda, salt and flour. Pour this batter on top. Bake at 350°-375° for 35-45 minutes or until done.

Lena King

Chocolate Cream Pie

- 2/3 c. cocoa
- 2 1/2 c. white sugar
- 2/3 c. cornstarch
- 1/2 tsp. salt
- 6 c. milk
- 6 T. butter
- 3 tsp. vanilla
- 2 baked pie shells

Mix cocoa, sugar, cornstarch and salt. Blend in milk. Cook and stir, boil for 3 minutes. Remove from heat and add the butter and vanilla. Pour into pie shells and cool. Top with whipped cream, if desired.

Anna Zook

Double Peanut Pie

- 2 eggs
- 1/3 c. creamy peanut butter
- 1/3 c. sugar
- 1/3 c. light corn syrup
- 1/3 c. dark corn syrup
- 1/3 c. butter or margarine, melted
- 1 tsp. vanilla extract
- 1 c. salted peanuts
- 1 unbaked 9" pastry shell
- whipped cream or ice cream

In a mixing bowl, beat the eggs, gradually add the peanut butter, sugar, corn syrups, butter and vanilla, mix well. Fold in peanuts. Pour into crust. Bake at 375° for 30-35 minutes or until set. Cool. Serve with whipped cream or ice cream, if desired.

Arie King

Fish Pie

- 3/4 c. flour
- 1/4 c. lard
- 1/2 c. sweet milk
- 1 T. brown sugar
- flour till stiff enough
- 1 c. table syrup
- 1/2 c. brown sugar
- 4 T. flour
- 1 pt. water
- 1 tsp. vanilla

For dough; Mix the first 5 ingredients and roll. For mixture; Boil the remaining ingredients till thick.

Martha Smucker

French Mint Pie

1 1/2 c. chocolate creme-filled cookies, crushed
1/4 c. butter, melted
2/3 c. butter, softened
1 c. sugar
3 eggs
1/3 c. semi-sweet chocolate mint pieces, melted
2 oz. unsweetened chocolate, melted
1 tsp. vanilla

Combine cookie crumbs with butter. Press firmly around sides and bottom of a 9" pie pan. Cool. For filling; In large bowl, cream butter and sugar until light and fluffy. Add eggs one at time, beating well after each addition. Add chocolate and vanilla, beat well. Pour filling into pie shell. Chill 4 hours or overnight. Before serving top with swirls of sweetened whipped cream and chocolate curls, if desired.

Sarah Esh

Lemon Sponge Pie

2 T. flour
1 c. sugar
1 lemon
2 eggs, separated
1 c. milk

Beat egg whites separately and fold into mixture last. Bake at 350° till nice and brown, then bake at 300°. Bake for about 1 hour or until done.

Sara Ann Lapp

Millionaire Pie

1 can crushed pineapples, med. drained
1 carton cool whip
3 T. lemon juice
1 can eagle brand milk
1 c. nuts or pecans, cut up
graham crust

Mix well. Put in 2 graham pie shells. Refrigerate to cool.

Rachel Stoltzfus

Good n' Plenty Pecan Pie

1/2 c. sugar
1 c. light corn syrup
4 T. butter
3 eggs
1 tsp. vanilla
1/2 c. pecans, whole or chopped

Boil sugar, syrup and butter together. Beat eggs and fold into syrup. Add vanilla and pecans. Bake at 350° for 30 minutes. Makes 1 pie.

Annie King
Annie Lapp

Pecan Nut Pie

3 eggs
1 c. dark corn syrup
1/4 c. sugar
1/8 tsp. salt
2 T. butter, melted
1 T. flour
1/4 c. water
3/4 c. pecan nut meats

Combine sugar, flour and salt. Add beaten eggs. Add water to syrup and combine with egg mixture. Add melted butter and chopped nuts. Pour mixture into an unbaked pie shell. Bake at 425° for 10 minutes, then reduce to 350° and bake 35 minutes longer. Makes 1 - 9" pie.

Linda Stoltzfus
Lena Riehl

Pecan Pie

3 eggs
2/3 c. brown sugar
1 c. light corn syrup
1/3 c. butter, melted
1 c. pecans, halves or chopped
dash of salt

Beat eggs thoroughly with sugar, dash of salt, corn syrup and melted butter. Add pecans. Pour into unbaked pastry shell. Bake at 350° for 45 minutes. Make 1 - 9" pie.

Anna Mae Stoltzfus
Sarah Fisher

Peanut Butter Pie

1 1/4 c. chocolate cookie crumbs
1/4 c. sugar
1/4 c. butter or margarine, melted
8 oz. cream cheese, softened
1 c. creamy peanut butter
1 c. sugar
1 T. butter
1 T. vanilla extract
1 c. whipped cream

For crust; Mix the first 3 ingredients together. Bake for 10 minutes. Cool. For filling; In a mixing bowl, beat cream cheese, peanut butter, sugar, butter and vanilla until smooth. Fold in whipped cream. Gently spoon into crust. Garnish with chocolate or cookie crumbs, if desired. Refrigerate. Yield 8-10 servings.

Anna Zook

Peanut Butter Pie

2/3 c. peanut butter
1 1/2 c. 10x sugar
3/4 c. flour, scant
4 c. milk
1 c. granulated sugar
6 egg yolks
1/4 tsp. salt
1/4 c. butter
2 1/2 tsp. vanilla
6 egg whites
3/4 c. sugar
1/2 tsp. cream of tartar
2 tsp. cornstarch

Bake 2 extra thick pie crusts or you can use a graham crust. Mix the peanut butter and 10x sugar until mealy, then sprinkle 2/3 cup in each pie crust. Cook the flour, milk, 1 cup sugar, egg yolks and salt until thick, add the butter and vanilla, put into pie. Beat the egg whites until stiff, add 3/4 cup sugar, cream of tartar and cornstarch. Put in pie. Put the rest of the peanut butter mixture on top. Brown at 400°. If using graham crust, put cool whip on top instead of egg whites.

Sylvia King (Mervin)

Peanut Butter Pie

8 oz. cream cheese, softened
1 c. 10x sugar
1/2 c. peanut butter
1/2 c. milk, heat and cool
8 oz. cool whip

Beat all together, pour into a 9" graham cracker crust. Freeze.

Amanda Stoltzfus
Elizabeth Kauffman
Rebecca Speicher

Peanut Butter Pie

3/4 c. 10x sugar
1/2 c. creamy peanut butter
1 pie pastry 9", baked and cooled
2/3 c. + 3 T. sugar, divided
3 eggs, separated
1/3 c. + 1 T. cornstarch, divided
2 1/2 c. milk
2 T. butter
1 tsp. vanilla
1/2 c. water

Mix 10x sugar and peanut butter until crumbly. Set aside 2 tablespoons for top. Sprinkle remaining crumbs into the pie shell. In a sauce pan combine 2/3 cup sugar, 1/3 cup cornstarch, egg yolks and milk, cook over medium heat until mixture thickens. Remove from heat, add butter and vanilla, stirring until butter melts. Pour into pie shell. In a small sauce pan, combine remaining sugar and cornstarch with water, cook over low heat until mixture thickens, cool slightly. Beat egg whites until stiff, fold in cornstarch mixture. Spread over hot filling, sealing edges. Sprinkle crumbs on top. Bake at 350° for 12-15 minutes until golden brown.

Mrs. Elmer Stoltzfus

Teach a child which way he should go, and walk there yourself.

Pineapple Pie

1/4 lb. margarine
1 1/4 c. 10x sugar
3 egg yolks, well beaten
1 can crushed pineapple, drained
1 T. cornstarch
3 egg whites, beaten

Combine all ingredients, except beaten egg whites, mix well. Add beaten egg whites. Pour into a pie shell and bake at 400° for 10 minutes. Reduce heat to 350° and bake till firm.

Sylvia Esch

Pumpkin Custard Pies

2 c. sugar
2 T. flour
1 tsp. vanilla
1 tsp. cinnamon
2 c. pumpkin
4 c. milk, scalding
6 egg yolks

Beat egg yolks till stiff and add last. Bake at 375° for 10 minutes, then 350° for 35 minutes. Makes 3 large pies.

Elizabeth Petersheim

Pumpkin Pie

1 1/2 c. pumpkin
3/4 c. brown sugar
1 1/2 c. granulated sugar
3 eggs
3 T. flour
3/4 tsp. cinnamon or pumpkin spice
3 c. milk, scalded

Mix ingredients together. Bake 10 minutes.

Lena Reihl
Ada King

It's not how many years we live, but what we do with them.

Pumpkin Pie

3 eggs, separated
2 T. flour
1 tsp. nutmeg
1 tsp. cinnamon
2 c. brown sugar
2 c. pumpkin
3 c. milk, boiling
pinch of salt

Mix egg yolks, flour, nutmeg, cinnamon, brown sugar and pumpkin. Pour milk over mixture. Beat egg whites and add last. Bake at 425° for 10 minutes, then reduce heat to 350° bake for about 30 minutes more. Makes 2 or 3 pies.

Katie Glick

Mother's Pumpkin Pie

6 eggs, separated
1/2 c. sugar
2 1/2 c. sugar
3 T. flour
1 T. nutmeg
3 c. pumpkin
3 c. hot milk

Beat egg whites, add 1/2 cup sugar, beat again, set aside. Beat egg yolks, add 2 1/2 cup sugar, flour, nutmeg, pumpkin and hot milk. Fold in egg whites. Bake in 350° oven till middle is jelled. About 45 minutes.

Linda King

Pumpkin Pie

2 c. pumpkin
1 c. granulated sugar
1 1/4 c. brown sugar
5 lg. T. flour
1 c. molasses
5 c. milk, hot
4 eggs, separated
1 tsp. vanilla
dash of salt
1 lg. T. cinnamon

Beat egg whites and fold in last. Mix other ingredients together. Pour into 5 - 8" pie crusts. Bake 10 minutes at 425°. 30-35 minutes at 350° or until baked.

Lena King

Raisin Pie

1 lb. raisins
1 3/4 qt. water
2 c. sugar
1/2 tsp. salt

Cook raisins, sugar, salt and water for 1 hour. Thicken with clear jell. Good if topped with shoo-fly crumbs. Bake 1 hour at 350°.

Sylvia Lantz

Mother's Rhubarb Pie

2 eggs, beaten
2 c. granulated sugar
2 tsp. vanilla
5 c. rhubarb, diced
4 T. flour
1 1/2 c. flour
1 c. brown sugar
1/2 c. butter

Mix the first 5 ingredients (eggs to 4 T. flour). Put this rhubarb mixture in 3 unbaked pie shells. Mix the remaining ingredients to make crumbs. Cover rhubarb mixture with crumbs. Bake at 400° for 10 minutes, then 350° for 30 minutes or until done.

Linda King

Strawberry-Rhubarb Crumb Pie

1 egg
1 c. sugar
2 T. flour
1 tsp. vanilla
3 c. rhubarb, cut to 1/2" pieces
1 pt. fresh strawberries, sliced
1 unbaked 9" pie shell
3/4 c. flour
1/2 c. brown sugar
1/2 c. oatmeal
1/2 c. butter

In a bowl beat egg, beat in sugar, flour and vanilla. Gently fold in fruit. Pour into pie shell. Mix remaining ingredients for topping and sprinkle over top. Bake at 400° 10 minutes, reduce heat to 350° and bake 35 minutes longer.

Naomi B. Beiler

Fresh Strawberry Pie

1/4 c. instant clear jell
1 c. sugar
2 c. strawberries, blended
2 c. strawberries, sliced
whipped cream

Mix the clear jell and sugar well. Add the blended strawberries. Pour over the sliced strawberries which have been placed in a baked pie shell. Top with whipped cream. Chill and serve.

Marie Hoover

Strawberry Pie

1 c. strawberries, mashed
2/3 c. water
1/8 tsp. salt
1 c. sugar
2 1/2 T. clear jell
1/2 c. cold water
1 T. butter
strawberries
1 baked pie shell
cool whip

Cook the mashed strawberries, water and salt together for 3 minutes. Mix together the sugar, clear jell and water, add to mashed strawberry mixture and boil 1 minute. Add butter. Cool. Mix in ripe strawberries and put in a baked pie shell. Top with cool whip.

Sylvia Lantz

Strawberry Pretzel Cream Pie

1 1/2 c. pretzels, crushed
1/2 c. sugar
1/2 c. margarine, melted
8 oz. cream cheese, softened
1 c. sugar
9 oz. cool whip
6 oz. strawberry jello
2 c. boiling water
2 10 oz. pkg. strawberries, thawed

Mix the first 3 ingredients, pat on bottom and sides of a pie plate. Soften cream cheese with sugar, fold in cool whip. Layer it on the crust. Mix the remaining ingredients, pour on top of filling. Chill. Any flavor jello or dessert may be used.

Katie Ruth Esch

Shoo-Fly Pie

Crumbs:
4 c. flour
1 1/2 c. brown sugar
3/4 c. lard, scant
Syrup:
2 c. molasses
2 c. water
2 tsp. baking soda
3/4 c. brown sugar
3 eggs

Mix crumbs, set aside. Mix the syrup & add 3 c. crumbs. Pour into 4 small pie crusts. Put remaining crumbs on top. Bake at 400° for 15 min. 350° until done.

Lena Riehl

Wet Bottom Shoofly Pies

2 c. molasses
1 c. brown sugar
6 eggs
2 1/2 c. hot water
2 tsp. soda, dissolve in hot water
5 c. flour
1 1/2 c. brown sugar
2/3 c. margarine

For syrup; Mix the first 5 ingredients (molasses to soda). For crumbs; Mix the remaining ingredients. Put half of the crumbs in the syrup. Put in 4 - 9" pie crusts. Put remaining crumbs on top. Bake at 400° for 10 minutes, reduce heat to 350° and bake 30 minutes more.

Elizabeth Petersheim

Vanilla Pies

1 c. sugar
1 egg
1 T. flour
1 c. molasses
2 c. water
1 tsp. vanilla
2 c. flour
1 c. sugar
1/2 c. lard
2 tsp. soda
1 tsp. cream of tartar

Mix the first 6 ingredients (sugar to vanilla). For crumbs; Mix the remaining ingredients (2 cup flour to cream of tartar). Bake at 350° for 35 minutes or more till brown on top.

Arie Speicher

Pie Dough Mix

7 lb. flour
3 lb. shortening
1/2 c. cornstarch
1/2 T. baking powder
1/2 T. salt
1 c. sugar, 10x or brown, sifted

Mix well and store in tight container in cool place. This is handy for making pies. Use 1 cup for 1 pie crust. Wet with water.

Lena King
Elizabeth Petersheim

Mother's Never Fail Pie Dough

1 1/2 c. flour
1/2 c. lard
1/4 c. water, scant
pinch of salt
1/2 tsp. baking powder

Work the flour and lard together. Add water and remaining ingredients. Makes enough for 3 pies.

Linda King

Crumbs for Pie Crust

7 c. flour
1 tsp. baking powder
1 tsp. salt
2 1/2 c. lard
1 c. water

Mix together and refrigerate overnight. Before using get out a couple of hours before you need it. Grab a handful and roll out. You'll have your crust.

Lena Riehl

Three cookies plus two kids equals a fight.

Pie Crust

1 c. shortening
2 1/2 c. flour
1 tsp. salt
1/2 tsp. baking powder
1 egg, beaten
1 tsp. vinegar, with water to make 1/2 c.

Mix the first 4 ingredients together. Add remaining ingredients.

Sylvia Lantz

Pie Dough

12 c. flour
1 c. brown sugar
1 T. salt
4 c. Crisco

Mix the ingredients together.

Anna Mae Stoltzfus

A Recipe to Live By

Blend one cup of *LOVE, and one half cup of KINDNESS,* add alternately in small portions, one cup of *APPRECIATION* and 3 cups of *PLEASANT COMPANIONSHIP* into which has been sifted 3 teaspoons of *DESERVING PRAISE.* Flavor with one teaspoon *CAREFULLY CHOSEN ADVICE.* Lightly fold in one cup of *CHEERFULNESS* to which has been added a pinch of *SORROW.* Pour with *TENDER CARE* in to *SMALL CLEAN HEARTS* and let bake until well *MATURED,* turn out on the surface of society, humbly invoke God's Blessings and it will serve all mankind.

Desserts

Make Life A Little Sweeter

O let me shed a little light
On someone's path I pray;
I'd like to be a messenger
Of happiness today!

It may be just a phone call,
A smile, or a prayer,
Or long neglected letter
Would lift the edge of care.

I want to spread some happiness
In what I say or do,
Make life a little sweeter
For someone else! Don't you?

Frozen Fruit

1 watermelon, cut into balls
2 honey dew. cut in chunks
2 cantaloupes, cut in chunks
3 lb. peaches, cut in chunks
3 lb. green seedless grapes
1 lb. blueberries or sweet cherries
2 c. sugar
2 qt. water
6 oz. frozen orange juice concentrate
1 can frozen lemonade concentrate

Mix the fruit together and drain well. Mix the sugar and water together and boil, add the orange juice and lemonade. Put fruit into freezer boxes and cover with hot syrup and freeze.

Katie Mae S.

Finger Jello

2 pkg. plain gelatin
6 oz. jello, any flavor
2 2/3 c. boiling water

Mix the plain gelatin with the jello. Add boiling water, stir well, 1-2 minutes. Butter the inside of a plastic Easter dip egg. Fill with jello and close. Chill 2 hours. Happy Gacussla!

Martha Smucker

Finger Jello

12 oz jello
2 1/2 c. boiling water

Dissolve and chill.

Katie Glick

He who throws mud gets dirty hands.

Rainbow Dessert

3/4 c. orange Jell-O
3/4 c. red Jell-O
3/4 c. green Jell-O
6 c. hot water
3 c. cold water
2 c. pineapple juice
1/2 c. sugar
3/4 c. lemon Jell-O
1 c. cold water
8 c. cool whip

Use 2 cups hot water and 1 cup cold water for each of the 3 Jell-O's. Pour into separate pans, chill till firm. Heat the sugar and pineapple juice, remove from heat, add lemon Jell-O and water. Chill until syrupy, put cool whip in. Cut the 3 kinds of Jell-O into small cubes, fold into the cool whip mixture. Chill about 6 hours before serving. Makes 4 molds.

Sylvia Lantz

Broken Glass Jell-O

3 oz. pkg. raspberry Jell-O
3 oz. pkg. lime Jell-O
3 oz. pkg. black cherry Jell-O
3 c. hot water
1 1/2 c. cold water
3 oz. strawberry Jell-O
1 c. pineapple juice
1/4 c. sugar
1/2 c. cold water
1 box cool whip

Mix 1 cup hot water and 1/2 cup cold water with the first 3 Jell-O flavors in separate containers. Let set till firm. Heat the pineapple juice and sugar to boiling, dissolve the strawberry Jell-O in the pineapple juice, add 1/2 c. cold water. Chill until syrupy. Add cool whip and Jell-O cubes to the syrupy Jell-O.

Sarah Fisher

All Christians have the same employer. They just have different tasks.

Red Jell-O

6 oz. Jell-O, red
2 c. hot water
2 c. cold water
3 oz. lemon Jell-O
1/2 c. sugar
1 c. hot water
8 oz. cream cheese
1 can evaporated milk

Mix the red Jell-O, 2 cups hot water and 2 cup cold water, let set. Mix lemon Jell-O, sugar and 1 cup hot water until dissolved, add to cream cheese. Pour the milk in and beat real well. Pour on top of red Jell-O.

Kate Stoltzfus (Steve)

Pineapple Dessert

1 can pineapple
2 cans water
2 c. sugar
4 T. tapioca, heaping

Cook together till it boils, then cool. Pour over fresh fruit when ready to eat. Blueberries, bananas, peaches, sweet cherries, etc. Very refreshing on warm summer days!

Linda Ruth Esh
Sylvia Lantz

Fruit Dessert

1 med. size can fruit cocktail, drained
2 1/2 c. cold water
1 c. sugar
4 T. minute tapioca
1 T. your choice Jell-O
1/4 tsp. salt
cool whip

Mix all ingredients, except the fruit and put in a double boiler and boil till tapioca looks clear. 15-20 minutes, stirring occasionally. Cool. Put in fruit and cool whip, mix. To make the above recipe a low sugar dessert, omit sugar and once your done cooking the tapioca add 3 tsp. sweet n' low sugar substitute, then cool. You can use any king of fruit, but then use flavor Jell-O accordingly.

Anna Mary Smucker

Fruit Dessert

1 pkg. orange Kool-Aid
7 c. water
1 c. sugar
3/4 c. clear jel
1 c. water
1/2 c. orange Jell-O

Heat 7 cups water, add Kool-Aid and sugar. Add the clear jel to 1 cup water. Cook till thick and stir in Jell-O. Cool. Add fruit of your choice.

Linda King
Katie Glick

Fruit Cocktail Mix to freeze

4 c. sugar
2 qt. water
6 oz. can frozen orange juice concentrate
6 oz. can frozen lemonade
1 watermelon, balled
2 cantaloupes, cut in chunks
2 crenshaw melons, cut in chunks
3 lb. green grapes
3 lb. peaches, cut in chunks
1 lb. blueberries, fresh or frozen

In a large sauce pan bring sugar and water to a boil, stirring constantly. Stir in frozen orange juice and frozen lemonade. In a large bowl combine the fruit. Put mixed fruit in 12 - 1 pint freezer boxes leaving at least 1" space at the top. Pour hot juice syrup over top. Seal and freeze. Very good to eat while still partially frozen. Makes at least 12 pint.

Linda Stoltzfus

Apricot Nectar Dessert

1 can apricot nectar
1 can water & juice from drained apricots
3/4 c. clear jel
1/2 c. sugar
1 c. orange Jell-O
1 qt. apricots, drained

Bring the apricot nectar and can water/juice to almost a boil and add the clear jel and sugar, cook till clear and slightly thick. Remove from heat and add orange jello and apricots.

Mattie Beiler

Apricot Dessert

1 lg. apricot jello
2 c. hot water
2 c. cold water
1 c. pineapple, drained
2 bananas, sliced
2 c. miniature marshmallows
1 egg
1/2 sugar
2 T. flour
1/2 c. pineapple juice
3 oz. cream cheese
2 T. butter
1 pkg. cool whip

Cook the egg, sugar, flour and pineapple juice until thick, cool, add the cream cheese, butter and cool whip.

Susie Blank

Apricot Dessert

2 4 oz. orange jello
2 c. hot water
1 c. combined apricot & pineapple juice
3/4 c. small marshmallows
1 can apricots
1 can crushed pineapples
1/2 c. sugar
3 T. flour
1 egg, beaten
1 c. combined juice
2 T. butter
4 oz. cream cheese
1 c. whipping cream

Drain and chill fruits, save the juice. Dissolve jello in hot water, add fruit juice. Fold in fruit and marshmallows. Chill until firm and spread on topping. Topping; Combine sugar, flour, egg and juice, cook until thick on low heat. Stir in butter. Add cream cheese. Cool. Fold in whipped cream. Spread on chilled jello.

Lena King

Rhubarb Jello

4 c. rhubarb, diced
1 c. sugar
2 3/4 c. water
1 6 oz. pkg. strawberry jello

Cook rhubarb, sugar and water until rhubarb is tender, only a few minutes. Remove from heat, add jello and stir till dissolved. Pour into serving dish and chill till thickened.

Sylvia Stoltzfus (Amy)

Strawberry Whip

1 lg. box strawberry jello
1 1/2 c. boiling water
1/2 c. sugar
2 c. crushed strawberries
3 egg whites
2 c. ready whipped cream

Add jello to boiling water, dissolve. Add sugar and strawberries. Chill until slightly thickened. Beat the egg whites till stiff, add jello, beat together. Add cream and refrigerate.

Sylvia King (Mervin)

Glazed Peach Cream

3/4 c. peach jello
2 c. boiling water
1 c. cold water
3/4 c. peach jello
2 c. boiling water
1 c. cold water
1 qt. vanilla ice cream
fresh or canned peaches
clear jel or peach jello
cool whip

Mix 3/4 cup peach jello with 2 cups boiling water and 1 cup cold water, let set. Mix another 3/4 cup peach jello in 2 c. boiling water and 1 cup cold water, stir in the vanilla ice cream till melted and smooth. pour over top the first mixture, let set. Arrange the peaches on top of the second jello layer. pour clear jel or peach jello over the peaches, let set. It may be topped with cool whip.

Sylvia Lantz

Even though the tongue weighs practically nothing, it's surprising how few persons are able to hold it.

Pineapple Fluff

3 c. graham cracker crumbs
1/2 c. butter
1/4-1/2 c. brown sugar
3 6 oz. lemon jello
1 c. boiling water
1/2 c. sugar
8 oz. cream cheese
1 can evaporated milk
1 can crushed pineapples

For crust; combine the graham cracker crumbs, butter and brown sugar, keep a few tablespoons to sprinkle on top. Dissolve jello in water, add 1/2 cup sugar. Cook until syrupy. Cool. Beat until fluffy. Beat the cream cheese and milk, add pineapples. Mix jello mixture and cream cheese mixture together. Pour over crust and sprinkle rest of crumbs on top.

Linda Ruth Esh
Lena Rhiel

Rhubarb Cream Delight

1 c. flour
1/4 c. granulated sugar
1/2 c. butter
3 c. rhubarb, diced
1/2 c. granulated sugar
1 T. flour
8 oz. cream cheese, softened
1/2 granulated sugar
2 eggs
8 oz. sour cream
2 T. sugar
1 tsp. vanilla

For crust; Combine the flour, 1/4 cup sugar and butter, pat into a 10" pie plate, set aside. For rhubarb layer; Combine the rhubarb, 1/2 cup sugar and flour, toss lightly, pour on top of crust. Bake at 375° for 15 minutes. For cream layer; Beat the cream cheese and 1/2 cup sugar till fluffy. Beat in eggs one at a time, pour over hot rhubarb layer. Bake at 350° for 30 minutes or until almost set. For topping; Combine the sour cream, 2 T. sugar and vanilla, spread over hot pie. Chill and serve.

Sylvia Lantz
Naomi Beiler

Danish Dessert

1 pkg. kool-aid, any flavor
8 c. water
1 c. sugar
3/4 c. clear jell
1/3 c. jello, same flavor as kool-aid

Combine the kool-aid, 7 cups water and sugar. Heat to boiling. Mix clear jell and 1 cup cold water. Add to hot liquid and cook until thickened. Remove from heat and add jello. Fresh, frozen or canned fruit may be added.

Linda Stoltzfus

Strawberry Glaze

1 gal. water
4 c. sugar
3 pkg. kool-aid
1/2 tsp. salt
1 c. therm flo or clear jel, mix with water
1 c. strawberry jello
butter

Bring the water to a boil, add sugar, kool-aid, salt and therm flo, cook till thickened. Add jello. Add butter for a shiny texture.

Elizabeth Stoltzfus

Jello Tapioca

1 qt. water
1 c. sugar
1/2 c. minute tapioca
1/2 c. orange jello
8 oz. cool whip
fruit, if desired

Bring the water, sugar and tapioca to a boil. Add the jello. Let cool. Add cool whip and fruit.

Naomi Lapp

Time is a short span between two long eternities.

Pearl Tapioca

1 pt. milk
1 egg
1 tsp. vanilla
1/3 c. sugar
pinch of salt
1/4 c. tapioca

Soak tapioca with milk for 1 hour. Heat milk. Beat egg with sugar and add to milk.

Anna Mae Stoltzfus

Pineapple Tapioca

5 cans water
10 T. tapioca
4 c. white sugar
2 cans crushed pineapple

Boil the water and tapioca till clear. Add remaining ingredients. Keep on stove till rolling boil.

Sara Ann Lapp

Rhubarb Dessert

4 1/2 c. water
4 c. rhubarb
2 c. sugar
1/2 c. tapioca
3/4 c. strawberry jello

Boil the water, rhubarb, sugar and tapioca. Add jello.

Sylvia Lantz

You have never tested God's resources until you have attempted the impossible.

Strawberry Tapioca

4 c. water
6 T. lg. ball tapioca
pinch of salt
3 oz. strawberry jello
1/2 c. sugar
1 qt. crushed strawberries
1 pt. whipped cream

Cook the water, tapioca and salt for about 45 minutes. While still hot add the jello and sugar. Cool. Add strawberries and whipped cream.

Esther Fisher

Orange Jello Pudding

5 c. water
2 sm. boxes instant vanilla pudding
2 sm. boxes orange jello
1 can crushed pineapples
1 can oranges
1 box cool whip

Boil water, add pudding and whip a little, add jello. Cool. Add fruit and cool whip.

Anna Mae Stoltzfus

Cornstarch Pudding

8 c. milk
6 egg yolks
1 1/2 c. sugar
1 1/2 T. flour
1 1/2 T. clear jel
2 1/2 T. cornstarch
dash of salt
vanilla

Mix the flour, clear jel and cornstarch with 1 cup milk, beat well. Add to the cold milk, bring to a rolling boil. Beat a couple times during cooling.

Amanda Stoltzfus

It's better to look ahead and prepare than to look back and regret.

Creamy Pudding

4 c. + 1/2 c. milk
1/2 c. brown sugar
1/2 c. granulated sugar
2 T. flour
2 T. cornstarch
2 eggs

Heat 4 cups milk. Beat eggs, sugar and 1/2 cup milk, add flour and cornstarch. Slowly add 1/2 cup milk to heated milk, stirring constantly.

Amy Beilers

Cottage Pudding

1 c. flour
1/2 c. sugar
1/8 tsp. salt
2 tsp. baking powder
1/2 c. milk
1 egg
2 T. butter, melted

Sift together the salt, flour, sugar and baking powder. Add beaten egg, milk and melted butter. 1 cup cherries, floured (optional) I don't add the cherries, but we use this as a shortcake. Bake at 350° to 375°. Eat it warm with raw fruit and milk.

Barbara Stoltzfus

Caramel Pudding

2 T. butter
3/4 c. dark brown sugar
1/2 tsp. salt
4 c. milk
1 T. flour
2 1/2 T. cornstarch
2 eggs, beaten
1 tsp. vanilla

Melt the butter in a pan until brown. Add sugar, salt and a little milk. Cook, stirring well until caramelized. Slowly mix in 3 1/2 cups milk, heat to boiling point. Mix remaining milk, flour and cornstarch to a paste. Add to mixture, stirring constantly. Cook until thickened. Add 1 cup hot mixture to beaten eggs, add to pudding, cook 2 minutes. Remove from heat, add vanilla. Add cool whip when ready to serve.

Sylvia King (Mervin)

Caramel Pudding

6 c. milk
1 c. brown sugar
1/4 c. butter
4 eggs
6 T. flour
2 tsp. vanilla
1/2 tsp. salt

Brown butter and sugar in heavy kettle. Mix other ingredients well. Add to sugar mixture. Cook over medium heat till thick, stirring constantly.

Marie Hoover

Dirt Pudding

1 12 oz pkg. Oreo cookies
8 oz. cream cheese
4 1/2 c. milk
1 8 oz. box whipped topping
3 3 oz. pkg. instant vanilla pudding

Crush cookies. Mix pudding and milk. refrigerate 10 minutes. Mix cream cheese and whipped topping, add pudding. Pour pudding over crumbs. Reserve some crumbs for the top.

Arie King

Oreo Cookie Dessert

Oreo cookies, crushed
6 T. butter, melted
cool whip
1 c. 10x sugar
8 oz. pkg. cream cheese
3 c. milk
instant vanilla or chocolate pudding

1st. layer; Mix well, crushed cookies and melted butter and put in a pan. 2nd layer; Mix well, 1 cup cool whip, 10x sugar and cream cheese. 3rd layer; Mix 1 package vanilla pudding with milk. Top with cool whip and sprinkle with cookies crumbs.

Sadie Fisher

Eclair Cake

1/2 box graham crackers
1 box vanilla pudding
1 1/2 c. milk
1 1/2 c. cool whip
1 1/2 T. cocoa
1 T. oil
1 tsp. cornstarch or flour
1 tsp. vanilla
1 1/2 T. butter
1 1/2 T. milk
3/4 c. 10x sugar

Layer graham crackers on the bottom. Mix the pudding milk and cool whip. Layer on top of graham crackers. Repeat 2 more times. For icing; Mix the remaining ingredients. Put on top of graham crackers. Let set for at least a day before eating.

Arie Speicher

Apple Streusel

2 1/2 c. flour
1 c. shortening
2 T. sugar
pinch of salt
1 egg, beaten with enough milk for 2/3 c.
6 c. apples, sliced
1 c. sugar
2 T. flour
1/2 tsp. cinnamon
raisins (optional)
1 c. 10x sugar

Work the flour, shortening, sugar and pinch of salt together like pie dough. Add the egg and milk mixture to moisten. Roll out half of the dough and place in bottom and up sides of a cookie or cake pan. Place the apples, sugar, flour and cinnamon over dough. Sprinkle raisins also, if desired. Roll out remaining dough and fit over apples. Bake at 350° for 30 minutes or until apples are tender. Let cool a little and glaze with 10 x sugar. I use the canned pie filling for a quick streusel.

Elizabeth Petersheim

Apple Goodie

3/4 c. sugar
1 T. flour
1/8 tsp. salt
1/2 tsp. cinnamon
2 c. apples, sliced
1/2 c. oatmeal
1/2 c. brown sugar
1/2 c. flour
1/4 c. butter
1/8 tsp. soda
1/8 tsp. baking powder

Sift sugar, flour, salt and cinnamon together, combine with sliced apples, mix together well and place in the bottom of a greased casserole. To make topping; Combine oatmeal, brown sugar, flour, soda and baking powder, rub in butter to make crumbs. Put crumbs on top of apple mixture. Bake at 375° for 35-40 minutes. Delicious served warm with rich milk.. Makes 6 servings.

Rebecca Lynn Fisher

Cherry Delight

2 c. graham cracker crumbs
1/4 lb. butter
8 oz. cream cheese, softened
1/2 c. 10x sugar
1/2 tsp. vanilla
2-3 c. whipped topping
1 can cherry pie filling or any pie filling desired

Mix the graham cracker crumbs and butter and make into a crust, refrigerate till hardened. Mix together the remaining ingredients. A little milk can be added to this mixture to make it easier to handle. Spread on crust. Top with pie filling.

Linda Stoltzfus

Cherry Delight

1-21 oz. can cherry pie filling
1-14 oz. can sweetened condensed milk
1-20 oz. can crushed pineapple
1 qt. frozen whipped topping

Mix together. May also be put in cake pan and frozen. Enjoy!

Annie King

Quick Cherry Dessert

1 c. butter or margarine
1 1/2 c. granulated sugar
4 eggs
1 tsp. almond extract
2 c. all purpose flour
2 tsp. baking powder
1-21 oz. can cherry pie filling
powdered sugar (optional)

In a large mixing bowl, cream together the butter and sugar. Add the eggs, beat until light and fluffy. Add the almond extract. Stir in the flour and baking powder, mix until smooth. Butter a 13"x9" cake pan. Put mixture in pan. Spoon the pie filling into the cake in 16 spots, spacing 4 spoonfuls evenly in each direction. Bake at 350° for 45-50 minutes or until done. Place bottom side up on serving plate. Dust with powder sugar, if desired. Blueberry pie filling can be used.

Anna Mae Fisher

Cherry Cobbler

2 c. flour
1 c. milk
4 T. fat
4 T. sugar
3 tsp. baking powder
1 egg
1/4 tsp. salt
1 can cherry pie filling

Put cherry pie filling in a 9"x9" pan. Mix the remaining ingredients and drop by tablespoons over cherry filling. Bake at 350° for 25-30 minutes.

Rachel Stoltzfus

Cherry Crisp

1 can cherry pie filling
1/2 c. flour
1/2 c. oatmeal
1/2 c. brown sugar
1/4 c. butter

Combine the flour, oats and sugar. Cut in butter. Put pie filling in a 9" baking dish. Top with crumb mixture. Bake at 375° for 25 minutes.

Sara Ann Lapp

Colorado Peach Cobbler

1 c. sugar
2 tsp. ground nutmeg
4 c. fresh peaches, peeled & sliced
1 c. sugar
1 c. all purpose flour
1 tsp. baking powder
1 tsp. salt
1/3 c. cold butter or margarine
1 egg, beaten
ice cream (optional)

In a bowl, combine 1 cup sugar, flour and nutmeg. Add peaches, stir to coat. Pour into a greased 11"x7"x2" baking pan. For topping; Combine 1 cup sugar, 1 cup flour, baking powder and salt. Cut in the butter until mixture resembles fine. Stir in egg. Spoon over peaches. Bake at 375° for 35-40 minutes or until filling is bubbly and topping is golden.

Arie King

Raisin Delight

1 c. raisins
2 c. boiling water
1 c. brown sugar
1 T. butter
2 c. flour
1 c. sugar
2 tsp. baking powder
1/4 tsp. salt
1 c. milk

Mix the raisins, boiling water, brown sugar and butter. Pour into a greased casserole. Mix the flour, sugar, baking powder, salt and milk. Pour dough mix on top of the raisin mix. Do not mix together. Bake at 350° for 30-40 minutes. Serve warm or cold with whipped topping.

Lena King

He becometh poor who dealeth with a slack hand; but the hand of the diligent maketh rich (Prov. 10:4).

Caramel Dumplings

2 tsp. butter
2 c. brown sugar
1/2 tsp. salt
3 c. boiling water
3 c. flour
3 tsp. baking powder
1/3 c. white sugar
1/2 tsp. salt
1 1/3 c. milk
1 tsp. vanilla

Mix together the butter, brown sugar, salt and boiling water. This must be boiling before putting the dumplings in. For the dumplings; Mix the flour, baking powder, white sugar, salt, milk and vanilla. Drop the dumplings into the boiling syrup. Keep the lid on for 15 minutes.

Sara Ann Lapp

No Bake Cheese Cake

1-3 oz. box jello, dissolved in hot water
8 oz. cream cheese, softened
1 can evaporated milk, chilled
1 c. sugar
2 pkg. grahams, crushed and mixed with butter

Put the crushed grahams mixed with butter in the bottom of a pan. Beat the milk until fluffy. Add cream cheese, beat a little. Add sugar, then add the jello last.

Elsie Fisher

Cheese Cake

1 c. graham cracker crumbs
3 T. butter
3 T. sugar
2-8 oz. cream cheese, softened
3/4 c. sugar
1/4 c. flour
2 eggs
1 c. light cream
1 tsp. vanilla

Mix first 3 ingredients. Bake at 325° for 10 minutes. Combine cheese, sugar and flour, beating until well blended. Add the eggs, one at a time, beating well after each addition. Blend in the cream and milk. Pour over baked crumbs. Bake at 325° for 35 min. Do not over bake.

Lena King

Cheese Cake Parfait

3 oz. instant vanilla pudding
2 c. sour cream
8 oz, cream cheese, softened
1/4 c. sugar
2 tsp. almond extract
1 tsp. vanilla
fruit topping of your choice

Mix the first 6 ingredients together. Top with the fruit topping.

Anna Mae Fisher

Jello Cream Cheese Dessert

1-6 oz. box strawberry jello
1-3 oz. box lemon jello
1/2 c. sugar
1 c. boiling water
1 can carnation milk
8 oz. cream cheese

Mix the strawberry jello as directed on the box. Put in dish and let it harden. Beat all the remaining ingredients together with an egg beater and pour on top of jello.

Linda Stoltzfus

Cherry Cheese Cake

1 pkg. white cake mix
2-8 oz. pkg. cream cheese, soft
4 c. 10x sugar
1 pt. whipped cream
2 cans cherry pie filling

Prepare cake according to directions on box and bake. In a mixing bowl, beat the cream cheese and sugar until fluffy. Fold in whipped cream. Spread over cake. Top with pie filling. Chill 4 hours or overnight.

Sarah Fisher

All that is necessary for the triumph of evil is that good men do nothing.

Delicious Dessert

2 c. flour
1/2 c. nuts
1/2 c. margarine
8 oz. cream cheese
1 c. whipped topping
1 c. 10x sugar
2-4 oz. butterscotch pudding
3 c. milk
whipped topping

Mix the first 3 ingredients. Bake in a 9"x13" pan at 375° for 15 minutes. 1st layer; Mix the cream cheese, 1 cup whipped topping and 10x sugar. 2nd layer; Mix the pudding and milk. 3rd layer; Cover with whipped topping. Chill.

Ruth Esch

Jimmy Carter Dessert

1 c. flour
1 stick oleo
2/3 c. dry roasted peanuts, chopped
1/3 c. peanut butter
8 oz. cream cheese
1 c. 10x sugar
9 oz. cool whip
1 lg. pkg. instant vanilla pudding
1 lg. pkg. instant chocolate pudding
2 3/4 c. milk

Mix the flour, oleo and chopped peanuts, saving some peanuts for topping. Press into a 13"x9" pan. Bake at 350° for 20 minutes. Mix the peanut butter, cream cheese, 10x sugar and 1 cup cool whip, saving the rest of the 9 oz. cool whip, for the topping. Spread layer of this peanut butter mixture on crust. Mix the puddings and milk. Put a layer of pudding mixture on top of peanut butter layer. Spread the remaining cool whip on top. Sprinkle chopped peanuts on top. Refrigerate.

Ruth Ann Esch

The Lord takes notice, not only of what we give, but of what we have left.

Banana Split Dessert

1/2 c. butter, melted
2 c. graham cracker crumbs
2 c. confectioners sugar
3/4 c. butter, soft
1-20 oz. can crushed pineapples, drained
1/2 c. chopped nuts
2 eggs
1 tsp. vanilla
4 bananas, sliced
9 oz. cool whip
1-4 oz. jar maraschino cherries

Combine melted butter with cracker crumbs. Pat in bottom of a cake pan. Beat eggs 4 minutes. Add powder sugar, softened butter and vanilla, beat. Spread over crumbs. Chill 30 minutes. Spread drained pineapples over cream mix. Arrange bananas next. Cover with cool whip. Sprinkle with nuts and garnish with cherries. Refrigerate 6 hours.

Sadie Lapp

Banana Split Dessert

2-3 bananas
1/2 gal. chocolate, vanilla and strawberry ice cream
1 c. chopped walnuts
1 c. chocolate chips
graham cracker crumbs
1/2 c. butter
2 c. confectioners sugar
1 1/2 c. evaporated milk
1 tsp. vanilla
1 pt. whipping cream

Cover the bottom of a 11"x15" pan with graham cracker crust. Reserve 1 cup crumbs. Slice banana and layer over crust. Slice ice cream in 1/2" slices and place over bananas.

Sprinkle ice cream with walnuts. Freeze until firm. Melt chocolate chips and butter, add powdered sugar and milk. Cook until thick and smooth, stirring constantly. Remove from heat and add vanilla. Cool. Pour over top ice cream and freeze until firm. Whip cream until stiff. Spread over chocolate layer and top with buttered crumbs. Store in freezer.

Elizabeth Kauffman

Banana Split Dessert

3 c. graham cracker crumbs
3/4 c. margarine, melted
2 c. 10x sugar
2 eggs
1 c. margarine
1 1/2 tsp. vanilla
2 c. crushed pineapples, drained
7 bananas, sliced
2 pkg. whipped topping or cool whip
1 c. nuts or 20 maraschino cherries

Mix the melted butter into the cracker crumbs and put in bottom of pan. Beat the 10x sugar, 1 c. margarine, eggs and vanilla and spread on cracker crumbs. Spread well drained pineapples over sugar mixture. Cover with bananas. Spread prepared whipped topping over top and cover with nuts or cherries. Refrigerate overnight. Fills a 9"x13" cake pan. A good way to use up ripe bananas.

Linda Ruth Esh

Yummy Dessert

60 Ritz crackers, crushed
1/4 lb. butter
2 boxes instant pudding
1 1/2 c. milk
2 qt. vanilla ice cream, softened

Mix crumbs and butter together. Line the bottom of a 13"x9"x2" cake pan. Bake 6 minutes at 350°. Mix the pudding and milk together till thick. Add the softened ice cream, mix together. Spread over cold crackers.

Kate Stoltzfus (Steve)

Love, like a spring rain, is pretty hard to be in the middle of without getting some on you.

Peanut Butter Ice Cream Squares

2 c. graham cracker crumbs
1/3 c. margarine, melted
3 T. sugar
1 1/2 c. peanuts, chopped
3/4 c. light corn syrup
1/2 c. chunky peanut butter
1/2 gal. vanilla ice cream

Mix the cracker crumbs, melted margarine and sugar and press into a 9"x13" pan. Place in freezer for 10 minutes to chill. Blend together 3/4 cup of the peanuts, corn syrup and peanut butter. Spoon half of the ice cream over the crumbs. Spread peanut butter mixture over next, then remainder of the ice cream. Sprinkle the remaining 3/4 c. peanuts over next. Freeze until firm. Remove from freezer about 15 minutes before serving to soften.

Arie Blank

Pumpkin Frost

14 oz. ginger snaps, rolled till finely crushed
1/2 stick butter, melted
1 c. canned pumpkin
1/2 c. sugar
4 c. vanilla ice cream, softened
1/2 tsp. salt
1/4 tsp. cinnamon
1/8 tsp. nutmeg
1/2 c. chopped nuts

Add the crumbs to the butter. Press into the bottom of a well greased 9"x13" pan, reserving 1/4 cup for topping. combine remaining ingredients, mix thoroughly. Pour over crumbs. Sprinkle with reserved crumbs. Freeze until firm. Cut into squares and serve.

Katie Ruth

Think of something to give instead of something to get.

Ice Cream Roll

1 angel food cake mix
1 qt. ice cream, any flavor

Mix cake as directed. Line two oblong cake pans with waxed paper. Divide cake pans with waxed paper. Divide dough into pans. Bake at 350° for 20 minutes. Let cool for 5 minutes. Remove from pans and pull off waxed paper, cool again. Spoon ice cream on top of cake. Roll as jelly roll and wrap in aluminum foil. Freeze at least 6 hours.

Linda Ruth Esh

Chocolate Ice Cream Roll

3 eggs
1/4 c. water
1 c. sugar
3/4 c. flour
1/4 c. cocoa
1/4 tsp. salt
2 tsp. baking powder
1 tsp. vanilla
1/2 gal. vanilla ice cream

Beat eggs until thick, add water and sugar, continue to beat. Mix and add dry ingredients, Mix well, add vanilla. Line a sheet cake pan with wax paper. Pour in batter. Bake at 425° for 12-15 minutes. Sprinkle powdered sugar on tea towel. Turn cake onto towel. Cool slightly, roll cake with towel inside. Allow to cool. Unroll and spread with ice cream. Reroll and freeze.

Mrs. Elmer Stoltzfus

Yogurt

1 gal. milk
4 c. powdered milk
2 c. plain yogurt
1/4 c. sugar (optional)

Heat milk to 180° cool down to 120°. Add the remaining ingredients, mix well with wire whisk. Put into jars and set inside your baking oven. Do not turn the baker on. Leave undisturbed for half a day or more. Refrigerate. Try using this recipe instead of cream cheese.

Elizabeth Stoltzfus

Ice Cream

2 1/2 c. sugar
3 T. instant clear jel
6 c. milk
5 eggs, beaten
1 can evaporated milk
1 c. cream
flavoring

Mix well, the sugar and clear jel. Add 2 cups milk, beating well. Add 4 more cups milk. In another bowl, beat the eggs. Add to milk mixture along with evaporated milk , cream, flavoring and enough milk for a 4 quart freezer.

Elizabeth Stoltzfus

Dairy Cream Ice Cream

2 env. Knox blox
1/2 c. cold water
5 c. whole milk
2 c. sugar
2 tsp. vanilla
1 tsp. salt
2 c. cream

Soak the Knox in cold water. Heat the milk until hot, not boiling. Remove from heat. Add the Knox mix, sugar, vanilla and salt. Cool. Add cream. Chill 6 hours before freezing. Makes 1 gallon. Delicious!

Ada King

Chocolate Ice Cream

2 env. unflavored gelatin
1/2 c. cold water
1 c. milk
3/4 c. sugar
2 T. vanilla
1 1/2 c. Hershey's chocolate syrup
2 c. light cream
2 c. heavy cream

Soften gelatin in cold water for 5 minutes. In medium sauce pan, add milk and sugar, cook over medium heat, stirring constantly till gelatin and sugar are dissolved. Remove from heat, add syrup. Cool 10 minutes, add light & heavy creams and vanilla. Freeze in ice cream freezer. Makes 2 quarts.

Sylvia Esch

Ice Cream

6 eggs
2 1/4 c. sugar
1 can evaporated milk
1 can sweetened condensed milk
1 c. instant pudding, any flavor
milk

Mix the pudding with some milk. Mix all ingredients together. Pour into ice cream maker. Fill as full as you can with milk.

Mrs. Elmer Stoltzfus

Ice Cream Sandwich

2 c. brown sugar
1 c. lard
2 eggs
1 tsp. vanilla
1 c. sour cream
4-5 c. flour
2 tsp. baking soda
6 T. cocoa
1 tsp. cinnamon
1/2 tsp. ginger
ice cream

Make dough to handle, chill several hours. Roll to 1/4" thickness. Prick with fork. Bake and cool on sheet, do not over bake. Spread with ice cream.

Katie Ruth Esch

Butterscotch Ice Cream

1 c. light corn syrup
1 c. brown sugar
1 tsp. vanilla
1 tsp. salt
3 tsp. butter
1/2 c. milk

Cook together 5 minutes, stirring constantly. Store in cool place. Tastes like store bought kind.

Anna Zook

There is real strength in gentleness and kindness.

Caramel Topping

1 c. brown sugar
1 c. white karo
1/2 c. milk
pinch of salt

Bring the brown sugar, karo and milk to a boil, stirring constantly. Cook 5 minutes. Remove from heat. Add salt and vanilla.

Lena King

1-2-3 Fudge Sauce

1 lg. can evaporated milk
3 squares unsweetened chocolate
2 c. sugar
1 tsp. vanilla

Bring the milk, chocolate and sugar to a boil over medium heat. Cook 5 minutes, stirring vigorously. Remove from heat. Add vanilla. Beat for 1 minute. Add additional evaporated milk for thinner sauce. Serve hot or cold.

A gentle word, like summer rain, may smooth some heart and banish pain. What joy or sadness often springs from just the simple little things.

Jams & Jellies

Happiness is like jam-you can't spread even a little without getting some on yourself.

Apple Butter

3 gal. cider
2 gal. snitz, apples and pears
sugar, enough to sweeten

This is just a small portion that can be cooked on the stove. Makes 15 to 20 pints.

Arie King

Apple Butter

4 qt. apple sauce, without sugar
1 pt. vinegar
3 lb. sugar
cinnamon, sm. box or to taste
sassafras to taste

Stir all contents together. Put in oven. Bake at 300° for 2 1/2 to 3 hours (or when thick enough). Do not stir anytime during baking. I usually add allspice and cloves to taste also.

Naomi Beiler
Barbiann Esch

Apple Butter

16 c. applesauce
5 c. white sugar
3 c. brown sugar
3 T. cinnamon
3/4 tsp. cloves
pinch of nutmeg

Bake at 325° for 3 1/2 to 4 hours. Jar and cold pack 10 minutes.

Marie Hoover

White American Cheese Spread

3 1/3 qt. milk
5 sticks butter
2 1/2 tsp. salt
10 lb. slices W. A. cheese

Heat milk to almost boiling. Add butter and salt. Remove from burner. Stir in cheese until dissolved.

Linda King

Corn Cob Jelly

12 lg. corn cobs
4 c. water
1 box powdered fruit pectin
4 c. sugar
yellow food coloring

Cut corn kernels from cobs and reserve for another recipe. In a lg. kettle place cobs and water. Bring to a boil. Continue boiling for 10 minutes. Remove and discard cobs; strain liquid. Add water to equal 3 cups, if needed. Return to kettle and stir in pectin. Bring to a full rolling boil. Add sugar and return to a boil. Skim foam, add a few drops food coloring. Pour into hot jars. Cool and refrigerate until ready to use.

Martha Smucker

Peach Jam

12 c. mashed peaches
5 c. sugar
1 1/2 c. orange jello
(jello flavors may vary)

Cook peaches and sugar 15 minutes. Add jello and cook 1 more minute. Jar and seal.

Linda Ruth Esh

Peach Jelly

6 c. chopped peaches
6 c. sugar
1 c. crushed pineapples, drained
2 sm. boxes strawberry jello

Mix peaches, sugar and pineapples together. Cook over low heat until peaches are done. Remove from stove. Mix in jello until dissolved. Put in jars and seal.

Sara Ann Lapp

Don't let what you can not do interfere with what you can do.

Peach Marmalade

5 c. crushed and sliced peaches
1 can crushed pineapples
7 c. sugar
3/4 c. orange or strawberry jello

Cook together 15 minutes. Add jello. Cook until dissolved. Pour into jars and seal.

Lena Riehl
Ada King

Peach and Pineapple Preserves

6 c. peaches, sliced
2 c. crushed pineapples
6 c. sugar
1 lg. pkg. jello, any flavor

Cook the first 3 ingredients for 20 minutes, add whatever flavor jello you wish, stir well. Put in jars and seal. This will thicken after being refrigerated.

Elizabeth Petersheim

Pear and Pineapple Jelly

4 lb. pears, grind
1 qt. crushed pineapples
8 lb. granulated sugar

Boil 20 minutes. Put in jars and seal.

Sylvia King (Mervin)

Pear and Pineapple Jelly

4 lb. pears, peeled
1-1 lb. 4 oz crushed pineapples
8 lb. sugar

Weigh pears before you cook them. Cook pears till soft then mash with potato masher. Add sugar and pineapples. Cook 20 minutes.

Annie Lapp
Sylvia King

Pear Honey

8 lb. pears
8 lb. sugar
2 c. crushed pineapples

Remove peeling and core pears. Grind pears in food chopper. Add crushed pineapples and then add sugar gradually. Bring to a boil and cook until thick, about 30 minutes. Stir frequently.

Sylvia Stoltzfus (Amy)

Pineapple Jam

2 qt. crushed pineapples
2 qt. sugar
2 qt. white karo

Mix together and boil for 20 minutes. Put in jars and seal.

Naomi Esh

Peanut Butter Jelly

5 c. brown sugar
4 c. granulated sugar
1 1/3 c. molasses
4 c. water
5 lb. peanut butter
1 qt. marshmallow creme

Boil the first 4 ingredients for several minutes. When cool add the remaining ingredients.

Elizabeth Stoltzfus

To get out of a jam, the first thing you should do is tell the truth.

Peanut Butter for Church

5 c. brown sugar
2 c. white sugar
1 3/4 c. white karo
3 1/2 c. water
1 tsp. vanilla
5 lb. peanut butter

Bring the first 4 ingredients to a boil, simmer 5 minutes. Add vanilla and cool. Add peanut butter.

Linda King
Sylvia Lantz
Linda Stoltzfus

Red Beet Jelly

6 c. beet juice
1/2 c. lemon juice
2 boxes sure-jell
8 c. sugar
1 pkg. or 3 oz. raspberry jello

Combine beet juice, lemon juice and sure-jell. Bring to a hard boil. Add sugar and jello, boil 6-8 minutes longer. Very Good!

Lena King

Rhubarb Jam

5 c. rhubarb, cut fine
4 c. sugar
1 lg. pkg. strawberry jello

Cook the rhubarb and sugar for 3 minutes, add the jello. Pour into jars and seal.

Esther Fisher

Let the words I speak today be soft and tender, for tomorrow I may have to eat them.

Rhubarb Jam

5 c. rhubarb, chopped
1-3 oz. pkg. strawberry jello
4 c. sugar

Let sugar and rhubarb set overnight. Boil 5 minutes, add jello and boil a few more minutes.

Naomi Lapp

Strawberry Freezer Jam

2 c. strawberries, crushed
4 c. sugar
1 box sure-jell fruit pectin
3/4 c. water

Crush berries, one cup at a time, using a potato masher. Do not puree, jam has bits of fruit. Measure fruit into large bowl. Add sugar, stir into fruit. Set aside for 10 minutes. Stir occasionally. Stir sure-jell fruit pectin and 3/4 cup water in small saucepan. Bring mixture to a boil on high heat, stirring constantly. Boil 1 minute. Remove from heat. Stir pectin mixture into fruit mixture, stir constantly until sugar is completely dissolved and no longer grainy, about 3 minutes. Pour quickly into clean plastic containers to within 1/2" of tops. Wipe off edges, cover with lids. Let stand at room temperature 24 hours to set. Freeze. Will keep 3 weeks in refrigerator. Important: Do not reduce sugar or use substitutes. The exact amounts of all ingredients are necessary for a good set.

Linda Stoltzfus
Kate Stoltzfus (Steve)
Naomi Lapp

A good conscience is to the soul what good health is to the body.

Freezer Jelly with Less Sugar

6 c. strawberries, smashed
6 c. sugar
3 pkg. sure-jell
8 T. instant clear jell
2 1/4 c. water

Mix clear jell with 1 cup sugar. Be sure clear jell is instant. Add berries to 5 cups sugar and let stand 10 minutes. Mix sure-jell into water and boil 1 minute and pour over berries and mix well. Add the clear jell and sugar mixture, mix well for 3 minutes or use an egg beater or it might get lumpy. Pour in jars. Put in freezer.

Katie Glick

Zucchini Jelly

6 c. zucchini
6 c. sugar
16 oz. crushed pineapples
2 T. lemon juice
3 oz. peach jello
3 oz. apricot jello

Peel, seed and grate the zucchini. Cook on low, cover and steam till liquid is formed, then boil 6 minutes, drain some liquid and put back in pan. Add the sugar, pineapples and lemon juice, boil 6 minutes. Add the jello, cool and freeze.

Elsie Fisher

Elderberry Juice for Jelly

3 lb. elderberries
1/4 c. lemon juice
4 1/2 c. sugar
3 c. juice

Crush the elderberries in small amounts, simmer covered for 15 minutes. Extract juice, measure 3 cups juice. Follow jelly preparations as on sure-jel box.

Arie Speicher

Making Ice Cream

**What fun & oh, the merriment
How bright our eyes did gleam
Turning the handle round and round
Making rich ice cream.
The hand-turned bucket filled with ice
And rock salt layered in-between
Squeaked & groaned as the handle went round
Making delicious ice cream.
Each had it's turn at cranking the handle
We worked till our arms were sore
And kept the old handle churning & turning
Till it just wouldn't turn anymore.
Then "Come and get it!" our father would shout
And his eyes held a wonderful gleam
Ours was a close-knit family for sure
When making homemade ice cream.**

Canning & Freezing

We Owe God Thanks

I look upon the scenic land
Bright colors everywhere
The little shrubs and pine trees too
Are dotted here and there.

The cellar's full of jars and jugs
The mow is full of hay
Winters almost here we know
It's coming any day.

We know the Maker of this all
Our Lord and Savior Dear-
He's been so good: He's blessed us with
So many things this year.

Let us fall upon our knees
And thank God while we're here
We owe Him praise, we owe Him thanks
We owe Him words sincere.

Catsup

3 qt. tomato puree
4 T. prepared mustard
3 T. salt
1/2 tsp. pepper
3 drops oil of cloves
5 drops oil of cinnamon
1/2 qt. vinegar
1 1/2 qt. sugar
clear jel

Mix all ingredients, except the clear jel. Cook on low heat for 3 hours. Thicken with clear jel to your consistency. The longer you cook the less clear jel it takes.

Ada King
Annie Lapp

Ketchup

36 qt. tomato juice
2 1/2 c. mustard
1/2 c. salt
4 T. cinnamon
5 qt. vinegar
15 qt. sugar
2 T. pepper
1 T. red pepper

Cook for several hours till it begins to get darker and thicker, then add a paste made from therm-flo and water.

Naomi King

Catsup

4 qt. tomato juice
2 c. sugar
1 T. salt
1 onion
2 c. vinegar
1 tsp. mustard
1/2 tsp. cinnamon
1 tsp. cloves, ground
1 tsp. pepper

Mix all ingredients in a large kettle. Cook till thick or add clear jell to thicken. Jar and seal.

Marie Hoover

If happiness could be bought with money, we would be unhappy about the price.

Ketchup

1 basket tomatoes
2 onions
4 sticks celery
2 peppers
6 c. sugar
2 pt. vinegar
6 T. salt
1 tsp. pepper
1 tsp. cloves
1 tsp. allspice

Cook all the vegetables together until soft. Pour in colanders and let drain a couple of hours. Put pulp through ricer or Foley mill and add remaining ingredients. Cook all ingredients together and boil 10-20 minutes or until thick enough.

Rebecca Speicher

Pizza Sauce

1/2 bu. ripe tomatoes
3 lb. onions
1 hot pepper
1 pt. vegetable oil
2 T. Italian seasoning
1 1/2 c. white sugar
1 tsp. garlic salt
2 T. salt
therm-flo or tomato paste

Cook the tomatoes and put through strainer. Cook the onions and hot pepper in oil for 30 minutes, put through strainer. Add the seasoning, sugar and salts, cook together for 1 hour. Thicken with therm-flo or tomato paste. Put in jars boiling hot and seal.

Elizabeth Petersheim
Barbara Stoltzfus

Tomatoes, like the people who eat them, come in many shapes and sizes. Big round tomatoes are ideal to slice for sandwiches or put in salads. Plum tomatoes taste good in sauces. Cherry tomatoes make convenient snacks. Roma tomatoes are good canning.

Pizza Sauce

1 basket tomatoes
1 stalk celery, celery seed can be substituted
6 onions
4 T. salt
4 tsp. oregano
1 tsp. pepper
4 tsp. Italian seasoning (optional)
3/4 c. parmesan cheese
1 c. vinegar
1 c. sugar
clear jel

Blend vegetables in a large kettle. Add the remaining ingredients, except the clear jel. Cook for 15 minutes, then thicken with clear jel. Put in jars. Cold pack 10 minutes.

Marie Hoover

Pizza Sauce

1 1/2 lb. hamburger
3 c. onions
10 beef bouillon cubes
6 qt. tomato juice
2 c. brown sugar
1/2 c. parmesan cheese
2 tsp. garlic salt
2 tsp. chili powder
2 tsp. oregano
1 1/2 tsp. pepper
2 env. spatini
clear jel

Fry the hamburger, onion and bouillon cubes in oil. Add the remaining ingredients, except the clear jel. Boil 20 minutes. Thicken with clear jel. You can also add chopped peppers and parsley browned in butter. Add this after it is cooked. Boil 20-30 minutes in jars. Makes 14 pints.

Anna Mae Stoltzfus
Kate Stoltzfus

Spaghetti Sauce

10 qt. tomato juice
2 c. sugar
4 T. salt
2 T. oregano
2 T. Italian seasoning
1 T. chili powder
1 T. garlic salt
4 c. onions, chopped
1 T. peppers
1 c. oil

Fry onions and peppers in oil. Add the rest of the ingredients. Boil for 1 hour. Thicken with clear jel. Pour in jars and seal.

Anna Zook

Tomato Sauce

1 gal. tomatoes, chopped
2 c. onion, chopped
2 c. green, yellow and red peppers, chopped
1 c. sugar
3 T. salt
1 T. mustard seed
1 T. celery seed
3 T. mixed pickle spices
2 1/2 c. apple cider vinegar

Measure the vegetables after they are chopped and cook 45 minutes. Add the remaining ingredients, tie the spices in a bag and boil all together until thick or thicken with clear jel. Put in jars. Can be used in chili or meats.

Amanda Stoltzfus

V-8 Juice

1 basket tomatoes
6 green peppers
6 celery sticks and leaves
8 onions
handful parsley
2 qt. or more carrots, shredded
6 tsp. salt
1 c. sugar or honey
1 1/2 tsp. mixed spices & herbs

Cook everything together, except the tomatoes, till almost soft. Other vegetables may be added. Add tomatoes, cook till soft. Put through Victoria strainer. Add the remaining ingredients, cook till thoroughly heated. Pour into jars and seal. This makes delicious tomato soup.

Ada King
Sadie Lapp

Straight Bologna Spread

pickles, suit your taste
6 hard boiled eggs
A little bit onion
1/2 lb. bologna, chopped
enough mayonnaise to spread

Combine all ingredients into a spread. Put on piece of bread. Top with cheese.

Katie Glick

Hot Dog Relish

10 green tomatoes
6 red peppers
12 green peppers
4 c. cabbage, finely shredded
4 c. onion, finely shredded
1/2 c. salt
4 c. vinegar
6 c. sugar
2 c. water
2 T. mustard seed
1 T. celery seed
1 1/2 tsp. turmeric

Grind or finely chop tomatoes and peppers. Mix with cabbage and onions. Sprinkle with salt and let stand 8-10 hours. Drain and rinse. Add the remaining ingredients. Mix well, bring to boiling point. Simmer 5 minutes. Pour into jars and seal. Open jars keep for many weeks in refrigerator. Very good on hot dogs and hamburgers. Mix equal parts with mayonnaise and use as tartar sauce for fish.

Kate Stoltzfus
Sadie Lapp

Pepper Relish

12 red peppers
12 yellow peppers
8 med. onions
4 c. sugar
2 tsp. celery seeds
2 c. vinegar

Grind peppers and onions, pour hot water over them, let stand 5 minutes. Add remaining ingredients. Cook 20 minutes. Put in jars and seal.

Anna Mae Fisher

For fresh tasting canned string beans, cold pack only 1 hour, then turn off heat and let stand in the hot water the remaining 2 hours.

Summertime Picnic Relish

1 c. onion, chopped
1 c. green pepper, chopped
2 T. salad oil
4 firm tomatoes, peel & chop
2 T. vinegar
1 1/2 tsp. salt
1/2 tsp. sugar
1/4 tsp. dry mustard
1/8 tsp. pepper

In a large skillet, cook and stir onion and green pepper in oil over medium heat until onion is tender. Stir in remaining ingredients, heat to boiling. Cool. Cover, refrigerate several days.

Sarah Esh

Cucumber Relish

1 gal. cucumber, sliced thin or grated
8 sm. or 5 med. onions
1/2 c. salt, scant
5 c. granulated sugar
1 1/2 tsp. turmeric, scant
1 tsp. celery seed
2 tsp. mustard seed
2 c. vinegar
3 c. water

Mix the salt into the cucumbers and onions. Let stand 3 hours. Drain, don't save liquid. Combine the remaining ingredients, add with pickles. Heat and put in jars. Yields 7 pints.

Sylvia King

Zucchini Relish

10 c. zucchini squash, peeled & grated
4 c. onions
1 red pepper
1 green pepper
1 T. salt
2 1/2 c. vinegar
1/4 tsp. celery salt
4 1/2 c. sugar
2 T. cornstarch
1 tsp. dry mustard
1 tsp. nutmeg
1 tsp. turmeric

Boil 30 minutes. Put in jars and seal. Delicious on hot dogs!

Linda Ruth Esh
Sylvia Lantz

No Blanch Freezer Corn

15 c. corn, cut off the cob
1/8 c. salt
1/2 c. sugar (optional)
3 1/2 c. ice cubes

Cover with water, stir until ice cubes are melted. Put in boxes or bags to freeze.

Elizabeth Stoltzfus

Creamed Corn for Freezing

8-10 c. corn, cut from cobs
1 lb. butter
1 pt. cream

Combine all ingredients into a roaster. Cook for 1 hour at 350°, stirring every 15 minutes. Ladle in containers and freeze.

Mattie Beiler

Coleslaw for Freezing

1 c. vinegar
1/2 c. vegetable oil
2 tsp. celery seed
2 tsp. sugar
1/2 tsp. salt
3 lb. cabbage, shredded
1 c. onion, finely chopped
1/2 c. green pepper, finely chopped
1/2 c. sweet red pepper, finely chopped
2 c. sugar

Combine the first 5 ingredients (vinegar to salt) in a saucepan, bring to a boil. Cool. Combine, cabbage, onion, peppers and sugar. Let stand until sugar dissolves. Pour cooled dressing over cabbage mixture. Chill. Also keeps well in refrigerator up to 9 days.

Mattie Beiler

To can picked hickory nuts, put in jars with sealing lids. Heat in oven 2 hours at 200° and they'll keep for years.

Frozen Cabbage

1 med. cabbage
1 carrot
1 green pepper
1 tsp. salt
1 celery
2 c. sugar
1 c. vinegar
1/4 c. water

Put cabbage and salt in bowl, let stand 1 hour. Add carrots, peppers and celery, let stand. Boil sugar, vinegar, and water for 1 minute, let stand till cool. Pour over cabbage and freeze.

Mattie Zook

Canned Pepper Cabbage

cabbage
salt
sugar
vinegar
peppers, cut up

Make cole slaw with salt, sugar and vinegar, to your taste, add cut up peppers. Put in cans and add a sweet sour juice of 1 part sugar and 1 part juice (1/2 vinegar & 1/2 water). Cold pack 20 minutes.

Ada King

Canned Red Beets

red beets
2 c. sugar
1 c. vinegar
3/4 c. beet juice

Wash and cook the whole red beets till almost tender. Let cool off a little bit, pull off their skins. Chop into bite size chunks. Pack into jars. Cook the remaining ingredients together, heat thoroughly. Pour, while still very hot, over beets in jars and seal.

Sylvia Esch

Frozen Cantaloupe Balls

4 c. sugar
6 c. water
firm cantaloupe

Heat sugar and water to boiling point. Set aside to cool while preparing balls. Put cantaloupe into freezer boxes. Pour cooled syrup over balls. Do not fill to top because syrup expands when frozen. Balls do not have to be completely covered with syrup. Makes approx. 12 pints. Serve before they are completely thawed.

Rebecca Lynn Fisher

Spiced Cantaloupe to can

6 c. sugar
2 c. vinegar
2 c. water
3 drops oil of cinnamon
3 drops oil of cloves
1/2 tsp. salt
cantaloupe

This is enough brine for 5 qt. cantaloupe in jars.

Rebecca Speicher

Canning Cantaloupe

3/4 - 1 c. white sugar
qt. cantaloupe
pinch of salt
2 T. vinegar

Fill up with water. Cold pack for 30 minutes. Canning Athens Cantaloupes are the best and more solid cantaloupe to use for canning.

Sarah Fisher

To get rid of tiny fruit flies, set a small dish of vinegar and sugar near them.

End of the Garden Pickle

2 c. cucumbers, sliced
2 c. red or green peppers, chopped
2 c. cabbage, chopped
2 c. green tomatoes, chopped
2 c. green string beans
2 c. carrots, diced
1 c. onion, diced
2 T. celery seed
4 T. mustard seed
4 c. vinegar
4 c. sugar
2 T. turmeric
2 c. celery, chopped

Slice cucumbers. Chop cabbage, tomatoes and peppers. Soak overnight in salt water, using 1/2 cup salt to 2 quarts water. In the morning, cut string beans and chop carrots and celery, cook until tender, but not soft.

Rachel Stoltzfus

Thickened Mustard Pickles

2 gal. cucumbers, sliced
1/2 c. salt
2 qt. onion, sliced
2 sweet red peppers
2 tsp. turmeric
2 qt. vinegar
5 lb. sugar
4 tsp. mustard seed
5 T. flour

Slice cucumbers in thin rings, sprinkle with salt, add water. Let stand overnight. Drain. Slice onion and chop peppers. Mix vegetables together, add spices. Cook until slightly thickened. Put in jars. Cold pack 5-10 minutes.

Linda Stoltzfus

Kosher Sweet Dill

1 T. kosher dill mix, in each jar
3 c. sugar
4 c. water
1 pt. vinegar

Cook the sugar, water and vinegar. Pour over pickles. Cook 10 minutes. Makes 4 quarts.

Anna Mae Fisher

Kosher Dill Pickles

5 c. vinegar
11 c. water
2 c. sugar
1/2 pkt. kosher dill mix

Makes 7 quarts. Cold pack 10 minutes.

Annie King

Banana Pickles

Large pickles
1 c. vinegar, can use white
1 c. water
3 c. sugar
1 tsp. salt
1 tsp. celery seed
1 tsp. turmeric
1 tsp. mustard seed

Pare pickles, cut lengthwise in 4 pieces and cut out seeds. Bring the remaining ingredients to a boil. Pack pickles in jars, pour syrup over pickles, fill to rim. Cold pack 5-10 minutes. Makes 3 quarts.

Linda Stoltzfus
Ruth Ann Esch
Naomi Lapp

Sweet Dill Pickles

9 c. sugar
9 c. water
3 c. vinegar
3 T. salt
1/2 tsp. turmeric
1 1/2 T. dill mix
pickles, cut
2 c. lime
2 gal. cold water
1/2 tsp. minced, garlic, for each jar
1 tsp. dill seed, for each jar

Heat the first 6 ingredients (sugar to dill mix) till clear. Cut pickles and soak in lime and cold water overnight. Rinse well, put in jars and put 1/2 tsp. minced garlic and 1 tsp. dill seed on top, fill jar with juice. Cold pack 10 minutes.

Elsie Fisher

Sweet Dill Pickles

3 c. sugar
2 c. vinegar
2 c. water
2 T. salt
garlic cloves
dill sprigs

Fresh garlic and dill is best, but dried dill can be used, 1 tsp. = 1 head dill. Place 1 garlic clove and 1 dill sprig in bottom of quart jar. Fill jar with sliced cucumbers. Place more dill and garlic on top. Mix the sugar, vinegar and water, heat. Fill jars with heated syrup. Place jars in canner of boiling water. Bring to a rolling boil, remove at once. Makes about 3 quarts.

Lena King
Sylvia Lantz
Naomi Beiler

Pickle Rings

1 lg. onion
12 lg. sour pickles
1 T. whole mixed spices
1 c. water
2 c. sugar

Slice the onion in bottom of crock. Slice pickles, add spices. Boil water and sugar, pour hot mixture over pickles. Cool and serve.

Arie King

Garlic & Dill Pickles

4 c. sugar
3 c. water
3 c. vinegar
3 T. salt
2 T. dill seed or dill heads, for each jar
2 garlic cloves, for each jar
2 bay leaves, for each jar

Heat the first 4 ingredients until sugar is dissolved. Fill jars with pickles and put spices on top. Bring to a boil in canner and turn burner off. Leave it set in water for a few minutes. 1 go is about 4 1/2 quarts.

Katie Glick

Chow Chow Syrup

qt. water
qt. vinegar
7 qt. sugar
3 T. mustard seed
3 T. turmeric
1 gal. red kidney beans
1 gal. lima beans
1 gal. corn
1 gal. cauliflower
1 gal. pickles
1 gal. green string beans
1 gal. carrots
1/3 gal. red peppers
1 stalk celery

Boil together the first 5 ingredients for syrup. Vegetables must be soft. Put in jars and fill with syrup. This makes 25 quarts. Cold pack for 10 minutes.

Elizabeth Petersheim

Chow Chow

1 qt. lima beans
1 qt. green & yellow beans
1 qt. kidney beans
1 qt. cauliflower
1 qt. celery
1 qt. peppers
1 qt. carrots
1 qt. corn
1 qt. pickles
1 qt. navy beans
1 qt. onions
1 qt. cabbage
8 c. vinegar
8 c. water
5 lb. sugar
6 T. celery seed
6 T. mustard seed
4 T. turmeric

Cook vegetables separate, only till tender crisp. Gently mix vegetables in large bowl. Boil the remaining ingredients together for syrup. Fill the jars with vegetables and add syrup. Seal and cold pack 10 minutes.

Marie Hoover

Pickled Cauliflower

5 c. vinegar
2 c. sugar
1/2 pkt. kosher dill mix
11 c. water

Cook till thoroughly heated, pour into jars which cauliflower bits have been packed. cold pack 5-8 minutes.

Sylvia Esch

Little Peppers

little peppers
cabbage, shredded
1 c. vinegar
2 c. water
3 c. sugar
1 tsp. salt, scant

Prepare little peppers, cut stems out of top, clean seeds out and wash. Fill and pack with shredded cabbage, put into jars. Mix the remaining ingredients for brine. Fill jars with this brine. Cold pack 15 minutes.

Naomi B. Beiler
Annie King
Sylvia Lantz
Esther Fisher

Canning Fruit

2 qt. fruit or fruit juice
4 qt. water
4 c. sugar
2 1/4 c. therm-flo
water
1 box danish dessert

Bring the fruit, water and sugar to a boil. Add therm-flo, mixed with water, boil 2 minutes. Add danish dessert, boil 1 minute longer. Jar and seal. No need to cold pack if put boiling into jars, but it will keep longer if you do.

Elizabeth Stoltzfus

Canned Strawberries

4 c. strawberries, heaping
1/4 c. water
3/4 c. sugar

Boil 5 minutes. Put in jars and seal. For extra flavor, lay jars out in the sun for half a day.

Arie King

Sweet Potatoes to can

2 c. water
1 c. sugar
sweet potatoes

Mix the water and sugar. Pack potatoes in jars and cover with sugar water juice. Cold pack for 2 hours. Quick and easy to use for casseroles, etc.

Linda Stoltzfus

Baked Beans to can

8 1/2 lb. beans
3 1/2 lb. pork or ham
3 qt. tomato juice
2 lb. brown sugar
1 lb. white sugar
3 T. prepared mustard
2 c. onions, minced
1 qt. ketchup
2 qt. water
1 tsp. pepper
3 T. salt
1/2 c. starch

Soak beans overnight. Cook beans and pork, when nearly done, add salt. Mix the remaining ingredients for the tomato sauce. Fill jars 3/4 full with beans, then fill with tomato sauce. Cold pack 2 hours.

Lena King

A Quicker, Fresher Way to Can Vegetables.

Use lemon juice and pressure can your vegetables and cut your canning time in half. Lemon juice helps preserve the food. Add 1 T. lemon juice per quart, half as much for pints. Process at 10 lb. of pressure for the length of time shown below. Do pints 5 minutes less than quarts.

corn - 30 min. carrots - 15 min. peas - 20 min.
limas - 25 min. green beans - 12 1/2 min.
butter beets 17 1/2 min.

Harvest Time

If ears of corn could really hear
And potato's eyes could see,
What a wacky place in summertime
Our gardens then would be.

If cabbages could use their heads
To think and meditate
How seldom then would they be found
Upon our dinner plate!

The ears of corn would hear complaints
The eyes would shed some tears
The cabbage heads would think it strange
We had so many fears.

Our garden friends don't sit and fret
And shiver in their roots.
When harvest time approaches them
They simply yield their fruits.

Candy

A Favorite Recipe

Take a cup of ***kindness***
Mix it well with ***love***
Add a lot of ***patience***
And ***faith*** in God above
Sprinkle very generously
With ***joy*** and ***thanks*** and ***cheer***
And you'll have lots of angel food
To feast on all year.

Angel Food Candy

1 c. sugar
1 c. dark corn syrup
1 T. vinegar
1 T. baking soda
1 lb. chocolate or almond bark, melted

In a heavy saucepan, combine sugar, corn syrup and vinegar. Cook over medium heat, stirring constantly until sugar dissolves. Cook without stirring until temperature reaches 300°, hard crack stage, on a candy thermometer. Do not over cook. Remove from heat and quickly stir in baking soda. Pour into a buttered 13"x9" baking pan. Do not spread candy, mixture will not fill pan. When cool, break into bite size pieces. Dip into melted chocolate, place on waxed paper till chocolate is firm. Store candy tightly covered.

Mattie Beiler

Caramel Candy

2 1/2 c. sugar
2 c. rich milk or evaporated milk
1/3 c. butter
3/4 c. white corn syrup
1/2 tsp. vanilla
1/8 tsp. salt

Use a 6 quart kettle. Mix together the sugar, 1 cup milk, butter and corn syrup, bring to a boil. Boil constantly for about 15-20 minutes. Slowly add 1 more cup milk. Cook to hard ball stage, till mixture forms a ball. Add vanilla and salt. Pour into a greased 9" square pan. Mark in squares when partly cooled. Wrap individually in wax paper or coat with coating chocolate.

Linda King

Keep your words soft and sweet. You never know when you'll have to eat them.

Caramel Rice Crispy Treats

1/2 stick butter
4 c. marshmallows
4 c. rice crispies
48 milk caramels
1 1/4 - 1 1/2 stick butter
1 can sweetened condensed milk
1/2 stick butter
4 c. marshmallows
4 c. rice crispies

1st layer; Melt 4 cups marshmallows and 1/2 stick butter, do not boil. Add 4 cups rice crispies. Put into a greased 9"x13" cake pan. 2nd layer; Melt caramels and 1 1/4 - 1 1/2 stick butter and milk in saucepan over medium heat, stirring constantly or you could use a double boiler. 3rd layer; Melt 4 cups marshmallows and 1/2 stick butter, do not boil. Add 4 cups rice crispies. Cool between each layer. Cool and cut into squares. Delicious!

Annie King
Esther Fisher

Choco-Covered Mint Cremes

any chocolate whoopie pie recipe
mint flavoring
green food coloring
semi-sweet chocolate, melted

Use any chocolate whoopie pie recipe and make real small cookie. Add mint flavoring and green food coloring to the filling. Form like a whoopie pie and dip into melted chocolate.

Mattie Beiler

Help us, O God, to receive each new day with joy......... a gift from Thee.

Chocolate Chews

1/4 c. butter
1/2 c. dark corn syrup
6 T. baking cocoa
1/2 tsp. vanilla extract
3 1/4 c. 10x sugar
3/4 c. non fat dry milk powder

In a saucepan, melt the butter over medium heat. Stir in corn syrup and cocoa, bring to a boil. Remove from the heat, stir in the vanilla, 2 cups 10x sugar and milk powder, mixture will be stiff. Turn out onto a surface lightly dusted with 10x sugar. Knead in remaining 10x sugar, knead 3-4 minutes longer until stiff. Divide into 4 pieces and roll each into an 18" rope. Cut into 3/4" pieces. Wrap each candy in waxed paper. Store in refrigerator.

Mattie Beiler

Chex Muddy Buddies

9 c. chex cereal, corn rice and/or wheat
1 c. chocolate chips
1/2 c. peanut butter
1/4 c. butter
1 tsp. vanilla
1 1/2 c. powdered sugar

Pour cereals in a large bowl, set aside. In a saucepan, melt chocolate chips, peanut butter and butter until smooth, stirring often. Remove from heat, stir in vanilla. Pour over cereal, stirring until all pieces are evenly coated. Pour cereal mixture into a large ziploc bag with powdered sugar. Shake until all pieces are well coated. Spread on waxed paper to cool.

Mrs. Elmer Stoltzfus

Cream Cheese Eggs

8 oz. cream cheese
1 stick butter
1 c. peanut butter
3 c. 10x sugar
chocolate, melted

Mix together and shape into balls. Dip into chocolate.

Rachel Stoltzfus

Coconut Easter Eggs

1 egg white, whipped
1/2 c. white karo
1/4 tsp. cream of tartar
1 lb. fine coconut, macaroon
chocolate for coating

Whip the egg white, karo and cream of tartar together until stiff. Mix in the coconut. Shape into balls and coat with melted chocolate.

Ruth Ann Esch

Coconut Candy

1 lb. brown sugar
2 T. vinegar
3/4 c. molasses
2 T. butter
pinch of salt
1 fresh coconut, grated (approx. 2 c.)
pinch of cream of tartar

Cook the brown sugar, vinegar, molasses, butter and salt till hard boil. Add coconut and cream of tartar, boil again till point reaches halfway between soft and hard boil. Pour in buttered pan. Cut when almost cold. Roll in 10x sugar or grated coconut. Can also be coated with dipping chocolate.

Lena King

Caramel Candy

1 can condensed milk
1 c. cream
1 1/2 c. red label karo
1 c. light brown sugar
6 oz. butter
2 tsp. vanilla
chocolate to coat

Bring to a soft boil. Add vanilla. Let cool. Cut in squares. Coat with chocolate.

Sylvia Esch

Choice Caramels

2 c. granulated sugar
1 3/4 c. molasses
2 c. cream or evaporated milk
1 c. butter
1 tsp. vanilla
pinch of salt
2 c. rice crispies (optional)

Boil sugar, molasses and half of the cream. Then slowly add the rest of the cream, do not allow to stop boiling. Boil 30 minutes or more till it forms balls in cold water. Add the vanilla and salt. Add rice crispies, if desired. Pour into a buttered pan and cool. Cut into small squares. Can be dipped in coating chocolate or eaten so.

Lena King

Milky Way Meteor Crisps

1/2 c. butter
10 1/2 oz. bag miniature marshmallows
2-15 oz. chocolate covered caramel, nougat candy bars, chopped
6 c. crisp rice cereal
colored sugars, decorator candies, or sprinkles

In a 4 quart saucepan, melt the butter over medium-low heat. Stir in marshmallows until melted. Remove from heat, stir in chopped candy bars, then cereal. With buttered hands, shape mixture into 1" balls. Roll in colored sugar, decorator candies or sprinkles. Place on waxed paper. Store in airtight containers between sheets of waxed paper. For variations; Form into different shapes and sizes.

Mattie Beiler

As the blossom cannot tell what becomes of it's fragrance, so no one can tell what becomes of his influence.

Taffy

4 c. white sugar
1 pt. heavy whipping cream
1/2 piece paraffin
1 pt. white karo
1 pkg. gelatin
1/3 c. cold water

Boil the first 4 ingredients for 5 minutes. Soak gelatin in water, add the gelatin to the first mixture and boil about 10 minutes till it forms a hard ball in cold water. Pour in buttered pie pans. When cool, not cold. Pull taffy till white.

Anna Mae Fisher

Taffy Candy

2 lb. granulated sugar
2 c. karo
paraffin size of a walnut
1 can carnation milk
2 T. gelatin
1/2 c. water

Cook the first 4 ingredients together for 10-15 minutes. Soak the gelatin in water, add to the first mixture and cook another 5 minutes.

Sara Ann Lapp

Peanut Butter Balls

2 lb. 10x sugar
6 c. rice krispies
4 c. peanut butter
pinch of salt
3 sticks butter, melted
chocolate to coat

Mix together and make balls. Chill. Dip into coating chocolate.

Ruth Ann Esch

A house is built by human hands, but a home is built by human hearts.

Peanut Brittle

2 1/2 c. white sugar
1 c. white karo
1/2 c. cold water
3 c. peanuts
2 tsp. soda

Cook the sugar, karo and cold water till it threads from spoon. Put in the peanuts, let boil again till a light brown. Add soda, stir it good. Put in buttered pans to cool.

Katie Zook

Suckers

1 c. white sugar
3/4 c. corn syrup
1/4 c. butter
1/4 tsp. food coloring
1/4 tsp. peppermint flavoring
1 egg white
1 c. powdered sugar

In a heavy pan, bring sugar, syrup and butter to a boil, stirring, add food coloring, stir to blend, continue cooking to 265°, stirring occasionally. Remove from heat. Stir in flavoring. Place sticks on cookie sheets. Drop by tablespoons on stick. Mix the egg whites and powdered sugar. When suckers are hard, decorate with powdered sugar mixture.

Anna Zook

Cereal Fudge

1/2 c. white corn syrup
1/4 c. brown sugar, packed
dash of salt
1 c. chocolate chips
2 tsp. peanut butter
1 tsp. vanilla
2 c. rice crispies or cheerios

Bring corn syrup, brown sugar and salt to a boil and cook about 2 minutes till sugar is dissolved. Take off from heat, add the the chocolate chips, peanut butter and vanilla. Coat all cereal and pour into buttered pan. Cool. Cut into bars.

Sylvia Esch

Fudge

4 c. 10x sugar
1 stick butter, melted
1/2 c. peanut butter
1/2 c. cocoa
2 T. milk
2 T. vanilla

Combine all ingredients into one large bowl. Mix all ingredients together and pour in a small pan. Refrigerate 2 hours and cut into small pieces.

Sarah Esh

Yummy Fudge

2 sticks butter, melted
2 c. cream or milk
6 c. granulated sugar
8 c. miniature marshmallows
4 c. chocolate chips
1 tsp. salt
4 tsp. vanilla
2 c. nuts

Boil the butter, cream and sugar together about 5 minutes on medium heat. Add remaining ingredients. Pour onto a cookie sheet.

Linda King

Peanut Butter Fudge

1 c. packed brown sugar
1 c. sugar
1/2 c. milk
5 large marshmallows
1-12 oz. jar creamy peanut butter

In a heavy 2 quart saucepan, combine the sugars, milk and marshmallows. Bring to a boil over medium heat, stirring until sugar dissolves and marshmallows melt. Remove from heat. Stir in peanut butter. Pour into a buttered 8" square baking pan. Cool. When firm, cut into pieces.

Mattie Beiler

Chocolate Pixies

1/4 c. sweet cream butter
1 oz. unsweetened chocolate
2 c. all purpose flour
2 c. sugar
4 eggs
2 tsp. baking powder
1/2 tsp. salt
1/2 c. walnuts or pecans, chopped
powdered sugar

In a 1 quart saucepan, melt the butter and chocolate over low heat, 8-10 minutes. Cool. In a large mixer bowl combine, melted chocolate and remaining ingredients, except, 1 cup flour, nuts and powdered sugar. Beat at medium speed, scraping bowl often, until well mixed, 2-3 minutes. Stir in remaining 1 cup flour and nuts. Cover, refrigerate until firm, 2 hours or overnight. Heat oven to 300°. Shape rounded teaspoonfuls of dough into 1" balls. Roll in powdered sugar. Place 2" apart on greased cookie sheet. Bake for 12-15 minutes or until firm to the touch.

Rachel Stoltzfus

Clark Bar Taste Alikes

1 c. margarine
1 lb. crunchy peanut butter
2 1/2 c. powdered sugar
3 tsp. vanilla
1 lb. graham crackers, crushed
chocolate to dip

Mix first 5 ingredients. Roll into bonbon size balls and dip in chocolate.

Katie Zook

S-More's

1/3 c. light corn syrup
1 T. butter or margarine
1-5.75 oz. pkg. milk chocolate chips
1/2 tsp. vanilla
4 c. golden grahams cereal
1 1/2 c. miniature marshmallows

Boil syrup and butter. Remove from heat, add chips, marshmallows and vanilla. Stir until chips are melted. Fold in cereal. Press into a 9"x9"x2" pan.

Anna Zook

Snickers

1/2 c. white sugar
1 c. brown sugar
1 c. shortening
2 eggs
2 3/4 c. flour
1 tsp. soda
2 tsp. cream of tartar
1/4 tsp. salt
1/2 c. brown sugar
1 tsp. cinnamon

Mix well, the first 8 ingredients (white sugar to salt). Chill dough overnight. Form into balls. Mix the 1/2 cup brown sugar and cinnamon. Roll balls into the brown sugar and cinnamon mixture. Bake.

Arie King

Caramel Marshmallow Delights

1-14 oz. can sweetened condensed milk
1/2 c. butter
14 oz. Kraft caramels
16 oz. large marshmallows
Cereal (rice krispies)

In top of a double boiler, combine the milk, butter and caramels. With a fork dip the marshmallow quickly into the hot caramel mixture, then roll in cereal. Place on cookie sheet. Store in airtight container in the refrigerator.

Susie Blank

When angry, count to ten before you speak; when very angry, count a hundred.-Thomas Jefferson

Notes

Miscellaneous

A Recipe For Better Understanding

One cupful of listening when a person speaks; measure words carefully. Add a heaping teaspoonful of sympathetic consideration. Sift together to get a smooth batter for a consistent reply. Use generous amounts of long suffering and forbearing, tempered with mercy. Cook on front burners, keep temperature low and do not boil. Add a pinch of warm personality and clear unhurried speech. Season to taste, using possibly a dash of humor to bring out a good flavor. Serve in individual molds.

Love Herb Mix

2 c. celery leaves, dried
2 c. parsley, dried
2 c. basil, dried
1/2 c. thyme, dried
1/2 c. oregano, dried
1/2 c. tarragon, dried

If you don't have the exact amounts, just put in what you have. Be sure to use parsley, celery leaves and basil in the largest amount. Use in all cooked dishes or casseroles to eliminate salt. Excellent sprinkled on home fries, while frying.

Martha Smucker

Play Dough

2 c. flour
2 c. water
1/2 c. cornstarch
1 c. salt
1 T. powdered alum
1 T. salad oil
food coloring, your choice

Place all ingredients in a saucepan. Stir constantly over low heat until mixture thickens into dough consistency. Remove from heat and let stand until cool enough to handle. Place on foil, waxed paper or Formica top and knead until smooth. Store in an airtight container. It will keep for months. Hint; have children wash hands before using.

Katie Glick

Play Dough

1 c. flour
2 T. cream of tartar
1 c. water
1 T. vegetable oil
1/4 c. salt
1 env. unsweetened kool-aid

Mix together the flour, cream of tartar, and kool-aid. Add oil, water and salt. Cook, stirring, less than 3 minutes. Knead 1 minute on floured surface. Does not get sticky and smells good. Keeps for a long time if kept clean and in a tight container. Children love it!

Anna Mary Smucker

Gunk Playdough

2 c. elmer's glue
1 1/2 c. water
couple drops food coloring
2 tsp. 20 mule team borax
1 c. warm water

Mix well, the glue, 1 1/2 cup water and food coloring. Mix the borax and warm water. Slowly add and stir this mixture into glue mixture. You may have to use your hands to mix thoroughly. Store in refrigerator.

Martha Smucker

Soap Bubbles For Children

2/3 c. water
1/3 c. dish detergent, Palmolive
3/4 tsp. glycerin
food coloring (optional)

Mix ingredients together. Palmolive works best. Glycerin can be bought at drug stores.

Katie Ruth Esch

Decoration Cinnamon Hearts

1 c. cinnamon
3/4 c. applesauce
2 T. elmers glue
1 T. cloves
1 T. nutmeg

Mix together in a bowl. If too wet, add cinnamon. If to dry, add applesauce. Shape into balls, then into hearts. Poke a hole through the top to put ribbon when dry. Let dry 4 or 5 days. Makes 12 - 3" hearts. Have plenty of soap, water and paper towels ready for when you're done! For decorations only.

Matterstown School

Crystal Garden

3-4 sm. pieces of coal
1 c. water
4 tsp. bluing
6 T. salt

Lay pieces of freshly washed coal in a bowl. Pour the water, salt and bluing over the coal. Set bowl in sunlight and in a few hours your garden will begin to grow. For a more colorful garden, add a few drops of food coloring. I enjoyed watching this garden grow when I was a child.

Linda Ruth Esh

Windex

3/4 pt. alcohol
1 T. ammonia
1/2 tsp. dish soap
few drops bluing

Put in a quart can and fill with water. Have sparkling clean windows.

Anna Mary Smucker

Baby Wipes

2 c. boiling water
3 T. baby bath
1 T. baby oil
2 T. baby lotion (optional)
1 roll bounty paper towels

Cut roll of bounty towels in half. Remove center cardboard. Place upright in an airtight container and pour above solution over it. Cover tightly and it's ready to use in one hour. The wipes can be pulled out from center like store bought ones and torn off at any length.

Linda Ruth Esh
Esther Fisher

Laundry Spot Remover

1/3 dawn dishwashing soap
1/3 white vinegar
1/3 water

When your dawn soap bottle is at 1/3 amount left, add remaining ingredients. Excellent for stains on clothing. Squirt on and rub a bit.

Martha Smucker

Fertilizer for House Plants

1 tsp. salt petre
1 tsp. Epsom salt
1 tsp. ammonia
1 tsp. baking powder

Add above ingredients to 1 gallon water. Use once a month to water flowers.

Marie Hoover

Spray for Blight

1 cake ivory hand soap
1 qt. water
4 oz. salt petre
4 oz. borax
3 qt. rain water
1 pt. ammonia

Dissolve ivory in 1 quart water. When dissolved remove from heat. Add remaining ingredients. Mix well. Can be stored in a glass jar for more than a year. To use, mix 1 T. in 1 quart water to spray plants. If blight is bad, don't give up with 1 or 2 times. Keep it up and apply at least once or twice a week. Can be used on tomatoes, cabbage, cauliflower, celery and possibly more plants.

Sylvia Lantz

A new broom sweeps clean, but an old broom knows the corners.

Suet for Birds

1 c. peanut butter
1 c. lard
1/2 c. raisins
1 c. oatmeal
1 c. flour
4 c. corn meal

Mix together and shape in a square and freeze. Keep frozen until ready to put in suet holder.

Barbiann Esch

Peanut Butter for Birds

1 c. peanut butter
1 c. shortening or leftover bacon drippings
1 c. white flour
4 c. corn meal

Mix together and put outside on the bird feeder or fence post. Birds love it!

Linda Ruth Esh

Bird Feed

4 c. cornmeal
1 c. regular flour
1 c. peanut butter
1 c. grease or lard

Mix all ingredients.

Amy Beilers

Bug Spray

3 oz. skin so soft
1 oz. citronella oil
12 oz. white vinegar
12 oz. water

Mix together and rub on skin of humans and animals.

Dave Esch

White Wash

5 lb. hydrated lime
1 gal. water
1 1/2 lb. salt
1/2 gal. water

Mix well, the hydrated lime and 1 gallon water. Let stand overnight. Dissolve salt in 1/2 gallon water. Add salt mix to lime mix, mix thoroughly. Let stand 12-24 hours. Stir well.

Dave Esch

To Get Rid of Ants

1 c. laundry borax
1 c. sugar mix

Sprinkle mixture lightly on counter top. Also good for garden paths, shrubs and trees.

Sylvia Lantz

Roach Bait

1/4 c. shortening or bacon drippings
1/8 c. sugar
8 oz. powdered boric acid
1/2 c. flour
1/2 sm. onion, chop (optional)
water

KEEP OUT OF REACH OF CHILDREN AND PETS. First cream together the shortening and sugar in a bowl. In another bowl, mix the boric acid, flour, and chopped onion. Add this to the shortening mixture and blend. Add just enough water to form a soft dough. Shape the dough into small balls and place several in small plastic bags. Place around the house or areas where you have the most problems. Leave the bags closed so dough won't dry out so quickly. As it gets hard, replace with a new batch.

Cooking Tips

Before measuring honey or other syrup, measure the oil first.

For fluffier omelets, add a pinch of cornstarch before beating.

Spray furniture polish on your sad iron so it irons smoothly.

Substitute thick applesauce in equal amounts to the shortening called for in a recipe for a fat free cake.

Dry celery leaves until crumbly. Grind in a meat grinder. Use to flavor soups and fillings, etc.

Grind green celery stalks and freeze in ice cube trays. When a recipe calls for celery just use a cube or 2.

Substitute cornstarch for eggs. Use 1 heaping teaspoon of cornstarch for each egg when baking or cooking. Can use when out of eggs.

Milk will not sour so quickly if you put a speck of salt in when you get it.

To take away unpleasant onion taste, lick some peanut butter.

To prevent a messy stove when baking a casserole, set it into a larger pie plate.

When opening a can of applesauce, store it in a glass dish rather then Tupperware, it keeps much longer.

Mashed potatoes improve in texture and taste when a beaten egg white is added. The potatoes will also whip up lighter if the milk is hot when you add it.

Cooking Tips

When boiling potatoes, add milk to the water. About 1/4 cup to every 2 quarts of water. To improve the flavor and keep the potatoes white.

Salt turns the trick. When beating egg whites for angel food cakes, the egg white will beat faster if you add a speck of salt. Things will cool faster if salt is added to the pan of cold water in which you set the dish. Parsley will chop easier and finer if a little salt is added when chopping.

To make perfect poached eggs, add 1 tablespoon of white vinegar to the water. Swirl the water in a whirlpool-like pattern before dropping in eggs.

Add a pinch of salt to egg yolks to enhance yellow color of cake.

Eggs will beat up lighter if warmed to room temperature.

Dishwashing soap works great to wash hands that are greasy from meat.

For tender, juicy meatloaf. First mix all ingredients, except beef, then add meat and mix lightly. When shaping loaf, handle only as much as necessary.

It's easier to cut rhubarb into pieces with the kitchen shears than with a knife.

A potato helps to bind soup seasonings together.

To make whole wheat bread rise higher and feel lighter, add 1 tablespoon lemon juice to the dough as you're mixing it. The juice will add lightness, but won't influence the taste.

Substitute 2-3 T. minced fresh herbs for 1/2 tsp. of dried.

Helpful Hints

Squirt a bit of hair spray on your fingers and apply to the end of a thread. The thread will stiffen just enough to ease it into the needle.

Spray recipe cards with hair spray to help keep them clean.

To get rid of plant lice on African Violets, use hair spray and a plastic bag big enough to hold the potted violets. Spray hair spray into the plastic bag. Never spray hair spray on the plant. Put plant into the bag. Twist or tie it shut and let the plant stay in the bag for a day.

Use baby oil to get chewing gum out of hair. Soak in baby oil and it will easily comb out.

When watering African Violets, pour hot water on the tray and let the roots absorb to. Never let the leaves get wet.

Ferns and other houseplants like leftover coffee or coffee grinds.

To increase the life of your flashlight batteries, Take some sand paper and sand the ends of the batteries after they are dim and they will brighten up.

Remove stubborn smells from hands with toothpaste. It even works on fishy smells.

Use toothpaste to remove spots and stains on polyester clothing, ink spots from cloth and spots from dress shoes.

Use lemon juice to remove ink spots on cloth.

To remove gum, press ice cubes against it until it becomes brittle and breaks off.

Helpful Hints

To renew the finish on furniture, use equal parts of boiled linseed oil, turpentine and white vinegar. Applied with a bit of woolen rag and polished with a silk cloth , will renew the finish and also help to conceal some of the smaller blemishes.

For water stains on hardwood floors, rub the spots with a cloth dampened in turpentine, using a circular motion while rubbing, dry with a clean cloth.

To remove black scuff marks from a tile floor, make a paste of baking soda and water. Rub it into the marks and let dry. Vacuum, then wet mop.

Buttons sewed on with dental floss will stay on and on.

Water marks on furniture can be removed from furniture by applying lard on the spot and leave it on half a day or longer. Wash off the lard and the spot should be gone.

Restore old aluminum furniture by rubbing it with steel wool dipped in kerosene. Brush with clear lacquer or car paste wax to protect the restored finish.

For clean, crisp curtains, wash as usual, then fill the sink with cool water and add 1 cup Epsom salt. Swish the water around till Epsom salt is completely dissolved. Now add the curtains, soak a few minutes and hang out to dry.

To get rid of bathroom odors. Holding a lighted match for a second to two in the bathroom will get rid of odors faster than any deodorant.

Yellowed bathtubs and sinks will return to their original whiteness if washed in turpentine and salt.

Helpful Hints

To remove mildew from fabrics, soak in a solution of 1/2 cup vinegar, 1/2 cup bleach and 2 quarts water for 1-2 hours or overnight.

To prevent damp cellars or milk rooms, place a peck of fresh lime in an open box and set on the floor.

Equal amounts of turpentine and ammonia will remove paint from clothing even if the paint has hardened.

To remove old paint, mix 2 lb. sal-soda, 1/2 lb. lime and 1 gal. hot water. Apply to the old paint while still warm.

To remove tar, rub butter or lard on the tar spots then let stand awhile before washing with soap and water.

For black marks on linoleum apply lighter fluid and wipe clean. It will not harm linoleum.

For homemade flypaper, simmer equal amounts of sugar, corn syrup and water till granules dissolve. Brush onto narrow strips cut from brown paper bags.

To get socks white, add a slice of lemon to a pot of boiling water. Add socks and soak about an hour.

For blood stains, cover stain with meat tenderizer. Apply cool water to make a paste. Wait up to half an hour and sponge off with cool water.

For perspiration stains, soak the garment in warm vinegar water.

To remove mildew, dry clothes in the sun after covering with lemon juice and salt. Then wash with detergent.

Helpful Hints

To shine stainless steel or chrome like the faucets in the sink, use a soft, dry cloth sprayed with WD-40 (the lubricant).

A little salt in the oil reservoir of the lamp will give better light.

Rubbing alcohol will remove ink marks

Baking soda will remove grime on glass or smooth surfaces.

Make a paste of water and cream of tartar to remove rust.

Use peroxide and cream of tartar to clean tubs.

To soften hard paint brushes, heat vinegar to the boiling point and soak hardened paint brushes for 25 minutes, then boil the brushes in strong soap suds for a few minutes. The bristles should be soft.

To keep diapers soft, spotless and white, wash out the soiled diapers with cold water, then rub a bar of ivory soap over all stains. Wash out diaper again. All dirty diapers should be put in a diaper pail that is half filled with water and Lysol, or another cleaner. Dreft soap with borax in it is good to wash diapers with. Rinse diapers twice. Use a fabric softener or vinegar in the last rinse. When the temperature is freezing, a softener isn't needed. A few flurries of snow or a sprinkle of rain makes them soft. On hot summer days, bring diapers in as soon as they are dry.

To remove crayon from carpet or cloth, cover with a brown paper bag and iron with a warm iron, shifting the bag until no wax appears.

Gardening Tips

To keep worms away, powder the cabbage with sand

To keep bugs away from roots of cucumbers, water once a week with a mixture of 1 tsp. salt petre and 8 quart water.

Put egg shells around egg plants. Scatter broken egg shells over the garden for fertilizer.

To keep potatoes from sprouting, put apples on top in the bin of potatoes.

To ward off bugs and worms from melon and cucumber plants, put seeds into kerosene, fish out immediately, then plant.

Store carrots in sawdust over winter.

For raspberry plants, mix 2 parts of lime to 1 part of sulfur. Throw a handful at roots 3 or 4 times a year.

Tasteless melons may be from disease or lack of magnesium or iron in the soil. Such soil can be corrected by giving them a mixture of 6 1/2 T. Epsom salt and 3 1/2 T. borax in 5 gallon spray water. Apply when vines start to run and again when fruit is approx. 2" in diameter.

For watermelon and cantaloupe plants. Put a T. red pepper and a T. Epsom salt in a large sprinkling can of water. Water plants once a week with the solution. May also apply sulfur to each hill.

To choose melons, tap for hollow sound in watermelon, compare several. Check for soft end and good sweet aroma with cantaloupes. Shake honeydew and crenshaw melons, when ripe seed rattle.

Gardening Tips

Baking soda for grapes. Grape fungi, especially black root, live on acid in the developing skin of the fruit. For the fungi, prepare a solution of 4 tsp. baking soda dissolved in 1 gallon of water. Spray the mixture evenly over the grapes and vines. Apply once the fruit starts to appear and weekly thereafter for about 2 months. Also reapply after each rain.

Leftover Pickle juice can be used to attract flies and other insects. In the spring fill bottles 1/3 -1/4 full of juice and hang them in fruit trees. Leave them hanging till fall.

Eggshell fertilizer; Take your eggshells and crush them up. Put about a cup of crushed eggshells in a large jar. Fill jar with either distilled water or rain water. (do not use chlorinated water!) Put the jar in a cool and dark place for a minimum of 10 days. Use 1 tsp. of this eggshell water in a quart of distilled or rain water to fertilize your house plants. It doesn't smell nice, so take the plants outside to feed them. It makes the plant leaves much greener and they seem to love it. This eggshell fertilizer is also great to keep the slugs and snails off your marigolds or cabbage that you have planted in your gardens.

Tomatoes; To improve growth and flavor, interplant parsley, calendula, borage and bee balm in with your tomatoes.

Hair, either animal or human, worked into the soil or the compost pile, provides many nutrients including oil, magnesia and sulfur.

Fish, any and all fish parts, buried or composted were made famous by the Indians at the first Thanksgiving. Fish remains are excellent fertilizer.

Home Remedies

If you burn your tongue from hot food or drinks, put sugar on your tongue.

For sore throat, take equal parts of honey and vinegar, gargle often.

For sprains, beat one egg white till stiff. Add 1 or 2 T. powdered alum, beat again. Put this plaster on a cloth and wrap around the sprain. Place the leg or arm in a plastic bag or wrap for the night to keep from soiling the bed. Alum is also good for wounds, even for livestock.

Cough medicine. Mix equal amounts of lemon juice, castor oil and honey. Take as necessary.

Cough Remedy. 1 tsp. cinnamon, 1 tsp. cloves, 1 tsp. nutmeg, 1/2 tsp. ginger, 1 tsp. allspice, 1/2 tsp. mustard, enough lard to make a paste. Make a poultice and apply on chest or throat.

For a cold. Mix 3 T. whole flax seed, juice of 1 lemon, 2-3 T. honey, 2 cups water and 1 tsp. boneset herb. Simmer the flax seed and boneset in water for 25 minutes, strain. Add lemon juice and honey. Take often, by tablespoonful. Boneset will keep inflammation out of the lungs.

For fever, take an egg white, beat with a spoon till a little foamy, add a little sugar and a little hot water. Drink it and you will be surprised how soon the fever will be gone. A valuable remedy!

For fever, put the fried onions in an old stocking and put on the feet for overnight.

For fever, soak feet in a bucket of warm water with 1/2-1 cup vinegar.

Home Remedies

To clear congestion of the lungs and bronchial colds, chop an onion and fry slightly in a T. of unsalted lard. Fry only till soft and clear looking. Drain fat and apply the onions to the chest and back. Cover with a warm flannel cloth or put onions on the cloth and apply as a poultice.

A dandelion recipe, good for colds. Use 1 gallon dandelion flowers and 1 gallon hot water, boil for 5 minutes, let stand for 3 days, it is best kept in a crock jug, strain. Use 2 lemon peelings and 1 orange peeling, boil with the dandelion water for 15 minutes, let stand until lukewarm. Slice in the 2 lemons and 1 orange. Add 2 tsp. yeast and 3 lb. or less sugar. Let stand 6 days. Bottle. 1 T. should be taken at bedtime, or as needed.

Pumpkin seed tea, to rid of worms. Pour a small amount of boiling water over 8 pumpkin seed and let stand awhile. This can be put in milk or juice a few times a day. Use 3 days then wait 3 days, then use the tea 3 days in succession again, to get rid of worms.

Pumpkin seeds eaten raw, peeled, or made in a tea by cutting the seed pieces and simmered for a few hour in water is very good for retention and also for dropsy.

For external infections, put an egg skin (the thin layer right inside the hard shell) on to pull it out.

Raw red beets, grated make a good drawing poultice.

For sore throat, gargle with peroxide. Do not swallow.

To cure athlete's feet, soak in a bucket of hot water and wood ashes. This is also good to use when someone has stepped in a nail or fork.

Home Remedies

Bleeding of severe cuts may often be stopped by applying a mixture of salt and flour, spread on thickly.

For sinus trouble relief, add 1/2 tsp. salt and Listerine to 1 cup warm water. Clean out nasal passages with this and gargle.

Mouth ulcers. Wet ulcers with water, then dust with powdered alum.

For hay fever, don't drink raw milk. Heat milk to boiling point, then cool before using.

Diarrhea remedy for babies. Boil carrots and grind them, or use strained carrots for younger babies. If they don't like carrots, cook them in beef broth. Only a few bites every 15-30 minutes will bring good results.

Liniment recipe; 1/2 cup eggs, 1/2 cup vinegar, 1/2 cup turpentine.

An arthritis tonic; 6 lemons, squeeze and cut up, 1 pint alfalfa honey, 1 small can cream of tartar and 1 tsp. Epsom salt. Pour 1 quart boiling water over the above ingredients. Let stand overnight. Strain and keep liquid in a glass jar in the refrigerator. Take 1 T. in the morning and at bedtime.

For chapped hands, mix equal amounts of ammonia and glycerin in a bottle. Shake well. Apply mixture to your hands before going to bed.

If children have trouble taking pills or capsules because they stick to the tongue, just coat the pills with oleo or butter.

For appendicitis, take 1 T. flax seed in some water.

Home Remedies

For diabetes, eat raw cabbage to keep sugar count down.

To cure poison ivy, bathe the infected area with the first milk from a cow that has just given birth.

For burns and scalds, use a poultice of tea leaves. The Aloe Vera plant is also good to use. Just break open a leaf and rub on burned area.

When very sick, drink Gatorade to keep from dehydrating.

For upset stomachs in babies, homemade pedialyte. Boil 1 quart of water, add 1 T. sugar and 1/4 tsp. salt. This works most times even when they can't keep nothing else down. Good to prevent dehydration.

For whooping cough, rub chest with olive oil first, then rub oregano oil on top of olive oil. Do not use oregano oil without putting olive oil on first as it will burn.

Bread and milk remedy, to draw out splinters and infection; Heat a little milk. Dip a piece of bread in the milk and put on the sore, bandage it to keep it in place. Do this overnight, as often as it is needed. This also works for blood poisoning.

To loosen a hard chest cold, slice an onion and boil till soft. Put the onion inside your stockings at your feet this will loosen a hard chest cold.

For soaking wounds, pour boiling water over wood ashes and soak wound in water as hot as you can stand. Leave ashes in water while you are soaking.

When your knees knock-kneel on them.

Livestock Remedies

Clover blossom salve; Mix 1 lb. clover blossoms and 1 lb. Vaseline (petroleum gel). Heat in a very slow oven or in the hot sun for an hour. Strain through a cloth and store in jars. Good for cows' chapped teats. Also good for chapped hands.

Boil clover blossoms in water for 10-15 minutes. Good to bathes sores. Use as warm as possible.

When feeding cats milk, mix some hot water with the milk for a healthy coat.

When washing horses, mix 4 oz. absorbine liniment with 24 oz. water and 8 oz. vinegar. Sponge it on them. It makes them feel good!

For sick calves, mix 1 cup (double strength) coffee and 2 raw eggs. Give it to them.

Cobwebs work to stop bleeding of severe cuts.

Heave cure for horses; 2 oz. salt petre, 2 oz. cream of tartar, 4 oz. alum and 2 oz. ginger. Mix and feed 1 tsp. twice a day. Recipe from 1917.

For healthy, shiny coat on horses, drop one raw egg on top of their grain per day.

For bloated cows, Give in a pop bottle, 2-4 oz. each of pure turpentine and aromatic spirits of ammonia well diluted with milk or 1 quart raw linseed oil or 1 quart mineral oil. 1-2 oz. of raw turpentine may be added to any of these. Linseed and mineral oils may also be mixed 1/2 of each. This dose may be repeated if necessary. Use same dose for prevention if cow gets into feed box and over eats.

Pre-School Activities

Toys strewn all over? Give your child a kitchen tong and ice cream bucket and it will be fun picking up toys!

Play handicap for 30 minutes. Wrap a leg or arm in blankets, put a blind fold on and remind your child to thank God every day for a healthy body.

Using a cloth basket or bucket, let your child use it as a target to throw a soft ball in. Give points and small rewards if you wish.

Homemade blizzards; Mix 3 cups vanilla ice cream and 1 cup whipped topping with 1/2 cup M & M's or your favorite candy for a snack.

Play eraser tag in the house. The child who is "it" must have the eraser on his head to tag another person. No running!

Make a work chart. Give stars when jobs are done without reminding them. Give stickers or other small rewards for a certain amount of stars.

Keep everyday plates and glasses in a lower drawer or shelf where your children can reach them by themselves to set the table and put dishes away.

Make picture recipe cards for the little "cooks" at your house. It is fun when they are allowed to use their own recipe cards and little play tables are great to let them make their creation at their own level.

An easy way to keep children entertained is to let them string Cheerios. Give them some string on a big needle (rounded tip works best for small fingers).

Food Index

Food Index Continued

Food Index Continued

Food Index Continued

Food Index Continued

Food Index Continued

Food Index Continued

Food Index Continued

Food Index Continued

Food Index Continued

Food Index Continued

Food Index Continued

Food Index Continued

Food Index Continued